The School Library Media Center

LIBRARY SCIENCE TEXT SERIES

An Introduction to Classification and Number Building in Dewey. By Marty Bloomberg and Hans Weber.

Introduction to Public Services for Library Technicians. 2nd ed. By Marty Bloomberg.

Introduction to Technical Services for Library Technicians. 3rd ed. By Marty Bloomberg and G. Edward Evans.

A Guide to the Library of Congress Classification. By John Phillip Immroth.

Science and Engineering Literature: A Guide to Reference Sources. 2nd ed. By H. Robert Malinowsky, Richard A. Gray, and Dorothy A. Gray.

The Vertical File and Its Satellites: A Handbook of Acquisition, Processing and Organization. By Shirley Miller.

Introduction to United States Public Documents. By Joe Morehead.

The Humanities: A Selective Guide to Information Sources. By A. Robert Rogers.

The School Library and Educational Change. By Martin Rossoff.

Introduction to Library Science: Basic Elements of Library Service. By Jesse H. Shera.

Library Management. By Robert D. Stueart and John Taylor Eastlick.

The School Librarian as Educator. By Lillian Biermann Wehmeyer.

Introduction to Cataloging and Classification. 5th ed. By Bohdan S. Wynar, with the assistance of John Phillip Immroth.

The School Library Media Center

Second edition

Emanuel T. Prostano
and
Joyce S. Prostano

1977

LIBRARIES UNLIMITED, INC.
Littleton, Colorado

LIBRARIES UNLIMITED, INC.
P.O. Box 263
Littleton, Colorado 80160

Library of Congress Cataloging in Publication Data

Prostano, Emanuel T
   The school library media center.

   (Library science text series)
   Includes bibliographies and index.
   1. School libraries. 2. Instructional materials
centers. I. Prostano, Joyce S., joint author. II. Title.
Z675.S3P758 1977   027.8   76-30402
ISBN 0-87287-137-1

TABLE OF CONTENTS

LIST OF ILLUSTRATIONS

For Steve and Lori

PREFACE

This text deals with the library media center program as a unified media system or network of interrelated elements. The LMC is the nerve center of the media system. Since the media system exists within and for the educational program of a school, a secondary focus of the text is to relate elements of the media system to the school program.

This second edition has been restructured to provide substantial direction for users. The basic premises used in developing the text are as follows:

1. The textbook should provide a system of guidelines for teaching and learning. It is a starting point for discovery.
2. Fundamental to the use of this text is the need for substantial investigation of the literature of the field and the need for field investigation to gain a first-hand view of conditions as they exist.

Each chapter of the text begins with a statement of learner objectives. After reading the text and the supplementary readings, then performing field investigation and other activities, the learner will be able to perform the stated objectives. At the end of each chapter are brief lists of literature and of related field investigations. Although it would be desirable and beneficial for the learner to carry out each suggested activity, this ordinarily is not possible. It is recommended, however, that selected activities be pursued.

Appreciation is expressed to Gary Corrigan for his graphics work and Elaine S. Mazeika for her assistance in typing the manuscript.

E.T.P.
J.S.P.

1

THE LIBRARY MEDIA CENTER PROGRAM

OBJECTIVES

Identify and describe various standards and guidelines that affect the development of the library media center (LMC) program.

Describe the external and internal forces that influence educational developments in a school and/or school district.

State the philosophy and describe the elements of a unified media system (program).

Identify and describe media system elements, beyond the individual school, that can enhance and supplement the school LMC program.

The years 1960 to 1975 represent a period of unprecedented growth for school libraries in the United States. While it is obvious that a multitude of factors in society influenced this growth, there were three related factors that precipitated directly the change. The first was the publication of national standards and guidelines in 1960, 1969, and 1975, which set the stage for the development of the modern library media center.[1] The second was the funding by the Knapp Foundation of two national projects—one demonstrated effective school library service, the second was directed to improving the effectiveness of personnel.[2] The third was the Elementary and Secondary Education Act of 1965, which provided funds for library and audiovisual resources, personnel, facilities, and equipment. Each of these factors caused related activity at state and local levels to bring about significant change.

During this period, one recurring problem associated with change and improvement was a proliferation of new terminology. For example, the terms "Learning Center," "Resource Center," "Instructional Resource Center," "Instructional Media Center" and "Media Center" have been cited as appropriate names for a modern facility. Although the national guidelines have suggested terminology to be used, the confusion continues. The elements of the modern library media center program are drawn from the fields of instructional technology and library science, where the general goals and functions are similar and in some cases overlapping. Both fields are concerned with the management of an organization and the personnel within the organization. Both fields focus on similar functions, though extended definitions of these functions differ somewhat. For example, both are concerned with research and evaluation. Both are concerned with the process of acquiring, organizing, and disseminating media, though the terms used are different (instructional technology uses "support/supply"; library science uses "technical services"). Both are concerned with the relationship of professionals and media to users, though again the terms used are different (instructional technology uses "utilization"; library science uses a variety of terms, including "instruction," "in-service," "guidance" and "consultation"). Finally, both fields are concerned with design and production functions, though the definitions of these are considerably broader in instructional technology than in library science.

The library media center (LMC) program described in this book is a unified media system designed for the improvement of teaching and learning. "Unified" implies the joining of traditional library and audiovisual components into a single administrative configuration. "Media" implies that the program will accommodate existing printed and audiovisual forms and that program personnel will participate in the development of new media forms that may hold future benefits for learning. The term "system" used in this context means a multi-faceted operation having, throughout the school, diverse elements that share a common purpose.

IN THE CONTEXT OF EDUCATION

The library media center (LMC) remains, in a very real sense, the new frontier in education. Despite years of continuous operation of library and audiovisual programs in the schools, the unified media approach offered today provides an opportunity to create a new educational perspective.

The library media specialist should enter this profession with the intention of operating the best program in the district, region, and state. In order to function effectively, one must know how the schools are organized and what forces shape the educational enterprise and thereby influence development of the LMC. This knowledge may come in part from a textbook, but what is needed is a personal analysis and evaluation of the total school operation. Each school and school district has unique conditions.

On the following pages a checklist of external and internal organizational factors is provided. The term "external" refers to factors outside the individual school that have a bearing on how each school's educational program is carried on; "internal" refers to factors within the school which act in concert with or independent of factors outside of the school.

The library media specialist must be aware of these factors if he is to cope successfully with the individual school situation and broaden his leadership role throughout the district. Once aware of the power structure and how innovative ideas have been implemented, he will be in a better position to develop a successful management strategy. Studying these factors requires several approaches. Sometimes the study results in information that is simply to be stored, such as grade organization. At other times, however, a complex, continuing activity is required, as in the study of an individual's personality.

External Factors: The School District

◆ Composition of the community

Socioeconomic and ethnic composition.

Political structure and community power structure.

School board organization: members elected or appointed, positions taken on vital issues, relations with central administrative staff, involvement of the community in the board's operation.

◆ Organization of the school district

Town, city, county, regional district

Organizational pattern of the school district: central headquarters and individual schools, a district divided into distinct regions for day-to-day operations, other patterns.

The graded structure of schools: recent changes in graded structure or anticipated changes, school attendance boundaries fixed or changing to accommodate overcrowded conditions or to integrate schools.

◆ A "community" school focus employing extensive programs to foster community interaction.

Special federal and state funded programs influencing organizational structure.

Regional or state cooperative educational services providing direct or indirect benefits to the district.

A clearly articulated philosophy governing educational planning and programing for the district.

◆ The administrative hierarchy

The administrative structure used to conduct the business of the district: a strong central administrative organization, authority decentralized on a regional or individual school level, action people in the administrative hierarchy.

Curriculum development: responsibility vested in one individual or dispersed, projects currently underway or planned, selection of participants.

Development of federal and state funded projects: planners and participants.

District budget: average percent of increase, participants in budget-making process, administration of budgets at what level, distribution of funds allocated to various programs.

History of library media service in the district: district-wide administration, system media center functions, school coordinating components.

* Teacher organizations

Teacher power structure in the district: success in representing professional viewpoint, leadership of organization, support of educational improvement as function.

* Priorities and constraints

Programs receiving priority for development, factors influencing priorities, constraints imposed by priorities, constraints on library media center development for other reasons.

Internal Factors: The Individual School

* Physical plant

Organization of space: adequate space to house existing program and students.

Design traditional or flexible to accommodate innovative programing.

Library media center design: adequate for programing potential.

* Curriculum design

Grade organization and class size: fixed or flexible design, scheduling traditional or modular.

Curricular structure: subject matter constant, methodology employed by teachers, teacher guides available, student learning guides employed.

Changes or modifications of curriculum planned: areas for change, participants.

* Administrative structure

Experience, educational background, interests of administrators.

Leadership role in the school: stimulate innovative instructional practices, assist teachers and students in their work.

Commitments to district-wide and community-oriented activities: budget planning, project writing and implementation, policy making, community action programs.

+ Professional staff

    Experience, educational background, departmental structure.

    Teacher power structure: leadership responsibility, advisory council to principal and his administrative staff.

    Teaching methodology employed by individuals and groups: traditional, innovative.

    Elements of departmental and individual cooperation and team action.

+ Special programs

    School validated to receive federal and state funds for the disadvantaged: projects initiated, participants, media requirements.

    Innovative programs: gifted child, subject areas, individualization, other types, media requirements.

    Organization of special projects: participants in development, evaluation program, media requirements.

+ In-service education

    Organization at school or district level: continuing pattern for professionals, release time from teaching provided.

    Teacher participation in planning and implementation: school level, district level.

    School and district-wide in-service training related to media utilization.

+ Priorities and constraints

    Administrative, community, teacher priorities relating to curriculum and student needs: how determined, leadership exercised.

    Constraints on media service development: existing school priorities, instructional methodology, attitudes.

+ Students

    Age, grade levels.

    Experiential, socioeconomic, ethnic background.

    Interests, potential, ability.

    Social, emotional, psychological, physical development.

    Involvement in educational programing, social and political action.

To do an effective job in the library media field, one must continually analyze external and internal factors. The checklist only outlines the information needed for constructing a management strategy that can implement a comprehensive LMC. If media budgets, space, personnel, and resources are inadequate, one must know the "why" of it before a remedy can be found.

While it may be satisfying to the individual to go through the mental gymnastics of organizing and administering the ideal LMC using the 1975 guidelines[3] as a model for requirements, one must remember that those who developed the standards envisioned a model educational program. One must examine the educational philosophy and program of the individual school, and must work for comprehensive changes in a structure that imposes constraints on LMC development. Knowing how to organize and administer an LMC technically is only one facet of the professional's job. The restructuring of education is by far a greater challenge. The LMC must be considered a vehicle for constructive educational change in the school.

DEVELOPING THE MEDIA PROGRAM

Someone who is familiar with school curriculum can readily evaluate educational philosophy and teaching through a period of observation in an LMC. This idea was expressed by Donald Emory[4] some time ago in an article entitled "Show Me a Poor Library—I'll Show You a Poor Educator." It was Emory's contention that the school library developed for the educational program of the school tells more about a superintendent's philosophy than does any other department or area of the school. Small libraries, meager collections, modest budgets, and minimal staffing reflect a philosophy of education suited to the days of the kerosene lamp. They are not compatible with today's focus on the individual in teaching and learning.

A community and school philosophy that exalts the individual and makes grand pronouncements about individualization, inquiry, and independent study can implement this philosophy only by providing a comprehensive LMC. Unfortunately, many schools pay lip service to the grand philosophy without having even a reasonable facsimile of an LMC. Other schools observe the grand philosophy and have a reasonable LMC facility, but they make no effort to translate the philosophy to teaching, so that the center does not become a viable educational force.

While the LMC program usually reflects the philosophy and instructional program of the school, it should be recognized that the LMC has a unique educational philosophy of its own. More than any other aspect of the school program, it is geared to the individual and his needs—both educational and personal.

Programing the Individual School

National guidelines for 1975 offer some assistance in program development. While some accept these guidelines as today's reality, others refer to them as projective guidelines, which merely tend to establish goals, or direction, for future development. In any case, the guidelines provide assistance for those who would apply them in the field. They provide the following definition of media program:

" . . . patterns of interfacings among program components, e.g., people, materials, machines, facilities, and environments, managed by media professionals who establish and maintain relationships between or among the components."[5]

In this book the LMC program is defined as a media system, designed for the improvement of teaching and learning. Beyond this definition, what is the program and how do we arrive at the concrete components required? There are several ways of making this determination. An analysis of the literature in the field provides some indication of the types of service required in the schools.

One method would be to consider, as Ralph Ellsworth did, what students and teachers do in libraries and to base a program on their observable behavior. In answer to the question "What do students do in school libraries?," Ellsworth stated:

— Find answers to specific questions that arise either from the teaching process or from ordinary curiosity.

— Go alone or as a member of a committee sent to get information.

— Carry out study hall assignments: that is, spend a specific amount of time studying in the library.

— Find material for projects such as a written report, a book review, a debate brief, or a research paper.

— Learn how to use the keys of a library—card catalog, bibliographies, reference books, periodical indexes, etc.

— Look at motion picture films, filmstrips or other audiovisual materials. Study with a teaching machine, listen to phonograph records or tapes, listen and record voice for language study.

— Locate quotations, excerpts, or data for speeches or projects.

— Read just for the fun of reading—one book or a hundred.

— Browse through current magazines and newspapers or look at the new book shelf.

— Talk with other students.

The second part of the same question is: What do teachers do in school libraries? Activities similar to those mentioned for students, but they also

— Confer with the library staff on relevant materials to use for class work: those appropriate for general presentation in the classroom, those most suitable for students working in small groups, and those appropriate for use on an individualized basis.

— Preview films and filmstrips; confer on the purchase or rental of audiovisual materials, and on local production of same.

— Consult with librarians on book purchases, on the handling of special materials (pamphlets, sample magazines, government documents, etc.), on classification and cataloging problems, and on reader's problems and difficulties that the students may be having.[6]

Another method for determining what the elements of the LMC program should be is to refer to the national guidelines:

— Finding needed information on an appropriate level and in an acceptable format.

— Selecting and using appropriate means for retrieval of information in all media formats.

— Obtaining resources from the media center, district center, local agencies, and networks.

— Communicating in many modes, demonstrating an understanding of the structure and language of each mode.

— Utilizing instructional sequences of tested effectiveness to reach personal and program objectives.

— Designing and producing materials to achieve specific objectives, as well as using materials designed and produced for them by the media staff.

— Employing a variety of media to find, evaluate, use, and generate information.

— Enjoying the communication arts and gaining inspiration from them.

— Receiving assistance, both formally and informally, in the use and production of learning resources.

— Functioning in learning environments that reflect their developmental level as well as the tasks at hand.

— Locating space in which to accomplish a variety of activities responding to curricular and personal needs.

— Participating in the formulation and implementation of both general and specific media program policies.[7]

A recent survey of the tasks performed by library media personnel in LMC's provides additional insight into the media program. Those schools selected to participate in the study had to meet certain minimal standards, referred to as the "Criteria of Excellence," which defined the essential program elements to be found in superior LMC's at the school building level:

    1. At the district level, a school library supervisor who gives direction and leadership in the development of a total district-wide school library program.

    2. At the building level, at least two trained librarians (and/or audiovisual personnel), with additional paid supporting staff.

    3. A unified program which reflects a depth and variety in the selection of all types of media, with the necessary equipment available for use in the support of the instructional program.

    4. Effective design in physical arrangement of facilities to accommodate use by teachers and students, individually and in small or large groups.

    5. Efficient organization and easy accessibility to all services, materials, and equipment for teachers' and students' use before, during, and after the school day.

    6. Provision for, and assistance to, teachers and students in the production of new materials for instructional uses.

    7. Participation of library personnel with teachers in the planning and implementation of the curriculum as a means of integrating library services with the instructional program of the school.

    8. Planned and coordinated inservice programs for teachers to provide training in the production and use of instructional media.

    9. Purposeful instruction for students, as individuals or in small or large groups, in library and research skills evolving from the needs of the instructional program.

    10. Consultative and special services to teachers to provide support in the performance of their educational roles.

    11. Availability of a wide variety of learning opportunities for the individual which offer the challenge and motivation necessary to aid a student in his intellectual, social, and emotional development.

    12. Continuous evaluation of the library program in support of the educational philosophy and purposes of the school and the needs and interests of the teachers and students served.[8]

Ellsworth and the national guidelines attempted to place the program in perspective through an analytical process of determining what specific activities are engaged in by students and teachers in the LMC. A basic problem of this approach is simply that the boundaries of activity are already drawn by the existing program structure. The program elements cited in the "Criteria of Excellence" were based on a judgmental or consensus approach to program development. The authors determined what the responsibilities and program elements should be through an investigation of the literature, observation, and the individual and collective experience and knowledge of the authors.

Fundamental to the consideration of an LMC program is the realization that it must fit the individual school. The program must be built on the needs assessed by the media staff and others having a vital interest in improving education. Although this evaluation requires a great deal of time and effort on the part of staff, it is one essential factor that cannot be overlooked. Without this information, no rational program can be structured for an individual school.

Practically speaking, an analysis of the philosophy and the external and internal organization of the school and school district is required. Beyond this, student and teacher needs relative to the existing and projected curriculum structure must be evaluated. This will require an analysis of content, methods employed in teaching and learning, activities programed for learning, and the variety and depth of media required. A teacher-dominated, textbook-oriented instructional approach in a school provides quite a different concept of immediate media needs than does an individualized, student-directed approach to learning that calls for extensive use of media.

An additional assessment must be made of the personal needs of students and teachers. A service program must take into account the age, grade, sex, interests, and intellectual capacities of students. The personal needs of teachers, as discussed here, relate only to the improvement of the professional in his work. One other important consideration is simply that student and teacher needs are not necessarily articulated or even known to them. The knowledgeable and experienced administrator and/or library media professional will both anticipate and create needs in the school. Working through the limitless potential of a comprehensive LMC program, he can provide needed inputs in anticipation of demand.

Student Needs

Student needs for an LMC program are of two kinds: those related to the curriculum of the school, and those related to individual personal needs. No attempt will be made here to catalog all of the needs of students. However, some are fairly obvious and are illustrative of the types anticipated in the school. Each need brings into focus interrelated aspects of a unified program. The checklist below provides an overview of student needs generated both by personal interest and by the curriculum; it is used to structure requirements for program inputs such as media, personnel, facilities, budget, and so on.

Checklist of Student Needs

A need to **read** from a variety of printed media, such as books, periodicals and pamphlets. Location of the activity may vary from the classroom, to the library media center, to any situation within or outside the school building. The student may require assistance in selecting and using media.

A need to **view** audiovisual media, such as filmstrips, 8mm and 16mm films, television, transparencies, pictures, and so on.

A need to **listen** to audiovisual media, such as records and tapes.

A need to **write** using media as the source of ideas.

A need to **use various combinations** of media, such as filmstrip and record, tape and slides, or simply to use many media forms to glean information and ideas.

A need to **practice skills** related to various types of machine use, such as typewriters, adding machines, and calculators. Location of the activity is ordinarily confined to specialized areas in the library media center. The student may require assistance in this activity.

A need to **create** media, such as tapes, slides, transparencies, filmstrips, 8mm films, and videotapes. Location of this activity is ordinarily confined to specialized areas in the library media center. Media created may become a part of the collection.

A need for **instruction** in the efficient use of the library media center and of the various service elements available in the program. Some basic instructional needs include orientation to the program, care and use of media and equipment, use of the "keys," selecting media for use, producing media, and investigative and study methods. This may be accomplished in a variety of ways. Location of the activity is partially confined to the library media center.

A need for **guidance** in selecting media for reading, viewing, listening, and writing; using "keys" and equipment; investigating, organizing and presenting ideas; and producing media. This may be a continuing requirement for many students.

A need for **information** about media relating to the various areas of the curriculum or areas of personal interest, to academic and vocational programs, and to school and community activities and services. The kinds of information required by students appear to have no limits.

A need to **interact** with peers, with teachers, with media personnel, or with other adult specialists on an individual or small group basis in relation to media. Location of activity is ordinarily confined to specialized areas in the library media center.

A need for **opportunity** to function as an individual who may be totally dependent initially as a student, partially independent as he begins to function in a library media center, and ultimately an independent learner who can function fully and competently in the library media center.

The following conditions generally apply to student use of the LMC:

1. Student use will be as individuals, in small groups, or in traditional class-size groups.

2. Access to the facility by individuals and small groups will be assured at any time. Class groups will ordinarily use the facility during a time period scheduled jointly by the teacher and the media staff for a specific purpose.

3. In their use of the facility, students may interact with media alone, with their peers, with adults, or with any combination of these.

4. Student use may be curriculum-oriented or related to personal needs and interests.

5. Student use may be independent, partially dependent, or dependent. The individual's needs and previous experience in using the facility will be the governing factors.

    Independent use implies that a student knows what he needs, knows how to locate media and equipment, and knows how to use the information found.

    Partially independent use implies that a student may have some idea of what he needs, some idea of how to locate media and equipment, and some idea of how to use the information found. His dependence may be the result of only one factor or a combination of factors. Some assistance is required.

    Dependent use implies that the student is not equipped to handle a particular situation and must rely on professional assistance.

Teacher Needs

Teacher need for an LMC program is perhaps greater than student need. In the past, when the pattern of media service in the schools was divided between separate school library and audiovisual departments, libraries focused primarily on student needs, whereas audiovisual departments directed their attention exclusively to teacher requirements. Today's unified media approach should allow library media specialists to correct any imbalances of the past.

A comprehensive focus on teacher needs is required for two basic reasons. In the first place, reaching the teacher guarantees that student needs will be clarified and adequately provided for. Secondly, analyzing what the educational program is supposed to accomplish highlights the need for expert assistance if the program is to be successful. As a director of student learning experiences, the teacher is expected to diagnose individual student needs on a continuing basis and to prescribe the experiences required for the student to perform to his maximum capability. This is no easy task. Without an efficiently organized LMC, the job probably cannot be done.

Teachers will rely on the LMC for two kinds of service: that related to the curriculum and their students' needs, and that related to their own professional needs. But they will rely on the LMC only if the center has demonstrated the capacity to meet their needs. Like those of students, not all of the needs of teachers are articulated or even recognized by the teaching staff.

The checklist that follows provides an overview of teacher needs; it is used to structure requirements for program inputs, such as media personnel, facilities, budget, and so on.

Checklist of Teacher Needs

A need for **curriculum development assistance** in structuring innovative educational experiences for students. Teachers require the assistance of media specialists in content selection, methodology, activities and media utilization.

A need for instructional **planning assistance** on a continuing basis. Teachers require the assistance of the media professional on a day-to-day basis in determining methods, activities, and media to employ in specific teaching-learning situations.

A need for **cooperating teacher specialists**. Team teaching may be structured to include the media specialist, or the media professional may have to contribute expertise in research or independent study methods.

A need to **create and modify media** related to the improvement of instruction. This means the creation of original media forms such as tapes, slides, filmstrips, transparencies, 8mm films, videotapes, and various graphic representations needed in teaching and learning. Also, it is necessary to modify existing media forms for individual and small group use if teachers actually are to individualize instruction; an example is the development of a simple worksheet to accompany a filmstrip. Creation and modification may be accomplished by teachers individually or in groups, with or without assistance from the media staff.

A need for **production services**, specifically in the reproduction and duplication of media.

A need to **improve knowledge and skills** in order to operate effectively in an extensive media approach to learning. Teachers need to learn more about the organization and potential of media and services. Ordinarily, this requires considerable assistance from a competent media staff.

A need for **information** about media, service, utilization, students. Also included here is the need for information about educational opportunities and newer concepts and approaches in education.

A need for **assistance in the selection of media** to be used in teaching and learning. The previewing, evaluation, and selection of media related to instruction are particularly critical areas of need in the school situation.

A need for **interaction** with media, students, associates, and library media specialists on a continuing basis.

A need for **assurance** that their expectations for students are being met. Teachers expect students to learn to use the library media center efficiently, to receive whatever guidance is necessary to learn to work independently, and to locate and use media suited to their abilities and interests.

A need for **opportunity** to be creative and effective in their work. This opportunity is found in a comprehensive library media center.

This listing of student and teacher needs, while not comprehensive in nature, indicates the type of analysis that an individual school should undertake when developing an LMC program. Not considered in this analysis are what might be called the unarticulated needs of students and teachers.

The LMC program is predicated on these and other needs of the school. Each need calls into play various related elements in the program.

MEDIA SYSTEM

Using the term "system" in connection with the library media center program requires an explanation of the term as it applies to libraries in general. For example, Chapman[9] defined six basic library systems: acquisitions, cataloging, circulation, reference, serials, and administration and planning, which together comprise a total library system. Each of these six systems is composed of subsystems. For example, the acquisitions subsystem is composed of: order, preorder search, accounting and reporting, and receiving and checking.

We do not intend to use the term "system" in this manner. We prefer the flexibility offered by Webster's definition: "A complex unity formed of many often diverse parts subject to a common purpose."[10] This definition commonly applies to a school system, public library system, or a regional system or network.

The media system for the individual school is made up of three basic components, which we call foundation, support, and primary elements. The elements are mutually dependent. The proper "mix" can be determined only by an analysis of student and teacher needs in the individual school. (See Fig. 1-1).

Fig. 1-1. The Media System

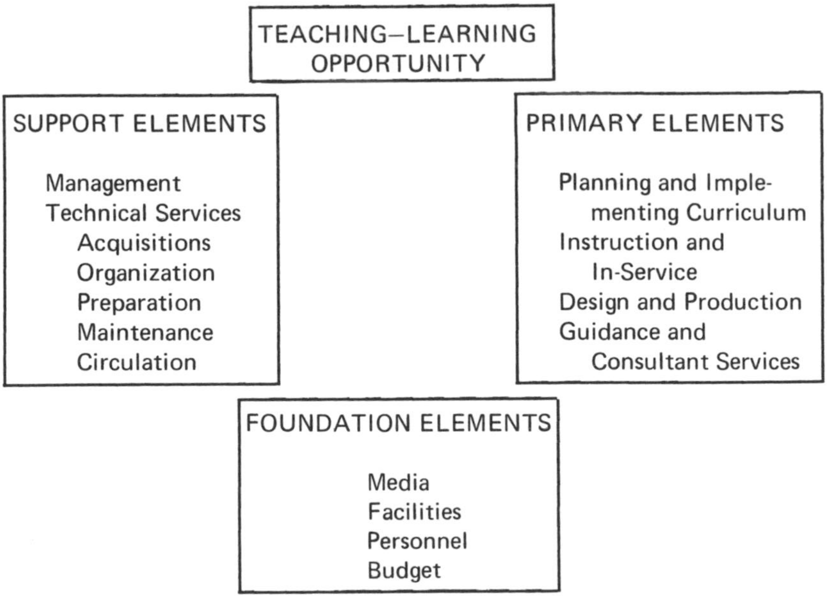

TEACHING–LEARNING OPPORTUNITY

SUPPORT ELEMENTS

Management
Technical Services
Acquisitions
Organization
Preparation
Maintenance
Circulation

PRIMARY ELEMENTS

Planning and Implementing Curriculum
Instruction and In-Service
Design and Production
Guidance and Consultant Services

FOUNDATION ELEMENTS

Media
Facilities
Personnel
Budget

Foundation Elements

A comprehensive media service system is made up of these elements: 1) media, 2) facilities, 3) personnel, and 4) budget. These represent the foundation of the media system. Without these basic elements, no service program can be initiated.

1. The media component implies a comprehensive and unified collection with accompanying technology for audiovisual forms. The elements needed are quality media in sufficient quantity at varying levels of interest and understanding for an extensive learning approach.

2. Facilities for the media service system provide varied spaces with furniture and equipment suited to the needs of students and teachers.

3. Media personnel—professionals, technicians, and aides—are required to structure the support and primary elements of the system and to assist students and teachers in the educational process.

4. The media system requires adequate financial support. The budget places the philosophy of the school in perspective and provides the wherewithall to plan effectively for instructional improvement.

These basic inputs are the foundation of the media system and the educational program of the school. To be effective, the elements must be balanced. Balance in this situation means creating responsible relationships between the basic elements. The national guidelines[11] provided a reasonable example of the balance required by establishing quantitative specifications for media, facilities, personnel, and funding.

Support Elements

Support elements imply a structuring of the services required to support any type of media system. The specific elements needed are 1) management and 2) technical services, such as acquisitions, preparation and organization of media and equipment, maintenance of media and equipment, and circulation of media and equipment.

1. Management refers to the overall responsibility for the media system. In essence, management means creating and implementing policies and procedures for efficient and effective service to students and teachers. The success of the system depends on the outcome of the management process.

2. Technical services are essential, time consuming, and probably the least noticed aspect of the system. Since the logical and efficient organization of media is one of the principal advantages of the media system

over the piecemeal distribution of media to classrooms in the school, time and effort must go into this operation.

— The acquisitions service is concerned directly with obtaining media and equipment required for use in the school.

— Organization and preparation refer to the logical organization and physical preparation of media and equipment for use.

— Media and equipment must be maintained in good condition for use at all times or the entire system will break down.

— The circulation or distribution of media and equipment follows technical services in a logical progression and rounds out the mechanics of acquiring, organizing and preparing, and maintaining media in condition for use.

The prime management function in relation to supportive elements is simply to structure the performance of these services as efficiently and unobtrusively as possible. They are the means to an end—the implementation of primary elements that relate directly to student and teacher needs.

Primary Elements

A discussion of primary elements in the media system takes us "where the action is." Built on a firm foundation of media, personnel, facilities, and financing, and structured by the supportive elements of management and technical services, the primary elements bring the LMC program to fruition.

The primary elements in a comprehensive media system are 1) planning and implementing curriculum, 2) instruction and in-service, 3) design and production, and 4) guidance and consultant services. These are interrelated service elements which often defy clear definition.

1. Planning and implementing the curriculum refers to the involvement of LMC personnel in the educational process from the inception of a specialized program through the modifications and refinements made in the school on a continuing basis. While we imply the interaction of teaching professionals and library media specialists, it should be pointed out that students and citizens are also becoming participants in this vital area.

2. Instruction concerns activities designed to improve the individual student's ability to function effectively in the library media center and to use media and equipment efficiently in the learning process. In-service, the other side of the coin, relates specifically to teacher improvement. This aspect of the program focuses on teacher utilization of media and the LMC in instruction.

3.   The design and production element is service-oriented. It is concerned with the design of new media and the modification of media for teaching-learning purposes. The service is extended to students and teachers alike.

4.   Guidance and consultant services refer to fairly distinct services to students and teachers. Guidance is a term that covers a broad range of individual and group services to students, while consultant services are those that reflect assistance given by library media personnel to teachers.

The LMC may be a centralized facility with a service system that reaches out into the school. It may also be decentralized, with satellite centers strategically located throughout the school. Another alternative is an integrated media system, which loses its physical identity in a school facility that operates on an open space concept (see Fig. 1-2). Fig. 1-3 depicts the extensions of the media system. Regardless of the physical surroundings, the media system extends beyond the walls of the LMC.

In addition to the basic foundation, support, and primary elements that form the media system, there are five conditions that must be applied to any media system at any level:

1.   a central purpose, which is the unifying factor in the system;

2.   clearly defined patterns of responsibility for the diverse elements;

3.   clearly defined operational procedures, which unify collections and services;

4.   an effective communications network linking the media systems elements;

5.   a continuing public relations program or information service, which keeps the system in focus.

Expanding the Media System Concept

The individual school LMC may be considered one subsystem in a total media system within a school district or region, when a central "system media center" is a part of a district or regional plan (see Fig. 1-4). Some general considerations should be applied to the development of the service base of a school district or regional educational "system media center":

1.   provide those service elements that are too costly for individual school units but that are necessary for comprehensive media services;

2.   provide those service elements requiring specialized equipment and personnel;

Fig. 1-2. The School Library Media Center May be Centralized, Decentralized, or a Totally Integrated Media System

Centralized Media System

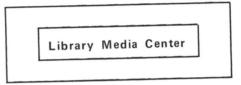

Decentralized Media System (Satellites)

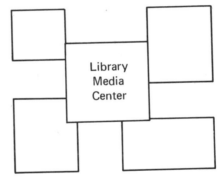

Integrated Media System

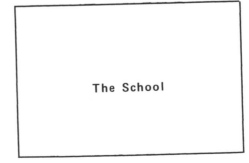

Fig. 1-3. Extensions of the Media System

Gymnasium

Auditorium   Classrooms

Large Group   Seminar, Conference
Instructional Areas   Areas

Language Laboratories   Library   Departmental Resource Areas
                         Media
                         Center

Radio, Television Studio   Lounge Areas

Cafeteria   Field Services

Student and Teacher Homes

Fig. 1-4. The School District "System Media Center"
Provides Supplementary Services

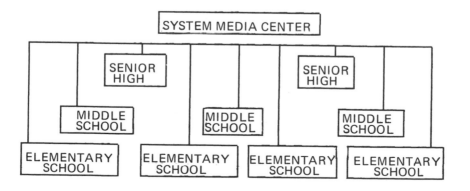

3. provide those services having a broad district-wide or region-wide application;

4. provide those services requiring a large amount of space.

Some examples of the types of services meeting these criteria are: centralized cataloging and processing, closed circuit television, preview and evaluation of collections, professional media collections, comprehensive production services including printing and duplicating, graphics and photographic departments, in-service programs involving personnel from several schools, and consultant services.

Other System Inputs

Beyond the essentially locked-in educational media system, which has articulated components and clearly defined levels of authority, there are other systems and discrete units in the community, region, and state that can greatly enhance the level of performance of the school LMC. Public libraries, offering parallel services to the community, have moved rapidly to develop regional and state networks for more effective service to patrons. Museums, art galleries, theaters, nature centers, planetariums, and other educational and recreational centers ordinarily operate as individual service units. They can, however, provide extraordinary teaching-learning experiences when brought into the purview of the school (see Fig. 1-5).

Fig. 1-5. Expanding the Media Service System Concept

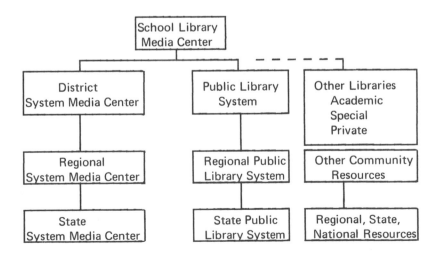

Cox[12] provided a "total system" view that covered the library media center, the LMC's parent administrative body, and ultimately the total society. As depicted, the system moves outward from the student in concentric circles: school, local school system, state educational regulations, national educational policy, total system.

In this concept, the total system represents society at large, which influences the development of national educational policy. In turn, national educational policy influences state educational regulations, where authority is expressed. State regulations directly influence activities in the local school system, where policy-making and supervisory responsibility resides. The school provides the focus for the interaction of several systems surrounding the library media center.

It is apparent that the close relationship between subsystems in the school district governed by direct administrative authority cannot apply to a situation where several independent systems and units interact for the general good. Reality is recognizing the limitations imposed by various agencies based on conditions within their organizations and, in some cases, the limitations of their vision.

Any consideration of expanding the individual school media system requires that the following be done:

1. Examine your own program needs and objectives. As a corollary, consider also what your media system has to offer any other system or institution.

2. Examine various sytems and institutions in the community, region, and state to determine what are desirable inputs for your system based on needs determined in Step 1.

3. Engage in a dialogue with administrators and governing bodies of institutions to determine the feasibility of applying a system concept to institutions participating in discussion. This dialogue will reveal constraints imposed by these systems and institutions. You test out their capacity to deliver any reciprocal services anticipated.

4. Accept the temporary constraints imposed, recognizing the conditions causing restrictions; and, with the institution administrators and governing bodies, consider alternative ways of providing expanded reciprocal services.

5. Select a strategy for improving conditions which will make feasible the desired service, and move to implement the strategy.

6. Evaluate this effort in terms of the degree of success in implementation, and

7. Modify the strategy employed to correct for any deficiencies noted.

SUMMARY

♦ The LMC program does not operate in isolation. It functions in the context of the total educational program and reflects the philosophy of the district and school. If the library media specialist is to do an effective job, he must become thoroughly familiar with the external and internal forces that affect his capacity to perform.

♦ The program of the LMC must be responsive to the educational and personal needs of students and teachers. The comprehensive program develops from an assessment of these needs in the individual school.

♦ The effective LMC program can best be described as a media system composed of foundation, support, and primary elements designed as a network of comprehensive services to improve teaching and learning opportunity. The system extends to students and teachers wherever they work: in the school, in the field, or at home.

♦ Beyond the individual school, the LMC is considered a subsystem in a total system that may include district, regional, and state educational media centers; public library systems at local, regional, and state levels; and other educational and recreational service units at various levels.

LITERATURE AND FIELD INVESTIGATIONS

1. Trace the history of school library and audiovisual program development and cite areas of overlap, merging, and major cooperative efforts.

2. Investigate national and state legislation dealing with school library media center development. Describe the impact of such legislation.

3. Review the activities of national, state, and other professional organizations directed to developing unified school media programs.

4. Explore the ramifications and implications of the terminology problem in the media field.

5. Review the literature to identify student and teacher needs that are being met by a library media center program.

6. Identify elementary, middle, and senior high school LMC's in the area that would provide suitable locations for field investigation. Briefly describe the elements of the media system in the various schools.

7. Compare school media standards and guidelines with those available for academic and public libraries. Discuss similarities and differences.

NOTES

[1] American Association of School Librarians, *Standards for School Library Programs* (Chicago: American Library Association, 1960); American Association of School Librarians and Department of Audiovisual Instruction, *Standards for School Media Programs* (Chicago: American Library Association and National Education Association, 1969); American Association of School Librarians and Association for Educational Communications and Technology, *Media Programs: District and School* (Chicago: American Library Association and Association for Educational Communications and Technology, 1975).

[2] American Association of School Librarians, *Realization* (Chicago: American Library Association, 1968); American Association of School Librarians, School Library Manpower Project, *School Library Personnel Task Analysis Survey* (1969); *Occupational Definitions for School Library Media Personnel, 1971; Behavioral Requirements Analysis Checklist* (1973); *Curriculum Alternatives: Experiments in School Library Media Education* (1974).

[3] American Association of School Librarians and Association for Educational Media and Technology, *Media Programs: District and School* (Chicago and Washington, D.C.; American Library Association and Association for Educational Communications and Technology, 1975).

[4] Donald Emory, "Show Me a Poor Library—I'll Show You a Poor Educator," *Nation's Schools*, March 1966, pp. 86, 87.

[5] American Association of School Librarians and Association for Educational Communications and Technology, *op. cit.*, pp. 110, 111.

[6] Ralph Ellsworth and Hobart Wagner, *The School Library: Facilities for Independent Study in Secondary Schools* (New York: Educational Facilities Laboratories, 1963), p. 25.

[7] American Association of School Librarians and Association for Educational Communications and Technology, *op. cit.*, pp. 5, 6.

[8] American Association of School Librarians, *School Library Personnel Task Analysis Survey* (Chicago: American Library Association, 1969), p. 8.

[9] Edward Chapman, Paul St. Pierre, and John Lubans, *Library Systems Analysis Guidelines* (New York: Wiley-Interscience, 1970), pp. 11-14.

[10] *Webster's Third New International Dictionary* (Springfield, Mass.: G. & C. Merriam Co., 1971), p. 2322.

[11] American Association of School Librarians and Association for Educational Communications and Technology, *op. cit.*

[12] Carl Cox, "View of the School Library," *School Media Quarterly*, Fall 1972, pp. 36-40.

REFERENCES

American Association of School Librarians. *School Library Personnel Task Analysis Survey*. Chicago: American Library Association, 1969.

American Association of School Librarians and Association for Educational Communications and Technology. *Media Programs: District and School*. Chicago and Washington, D.C.: American Library Association and Association for Educational Communications and Technology, 1975.

Bender, David. "Cooperative Planning for Media Program Development," *School Media Quarterly* 3:225-120 (Winter 1975).

Bender, David. "State Educational Agencies: Roles and Functions," *School Library Journal* 22:27-29 (December 1975).

Chapman, Edward, Paul St. Pierre, and John Lubans. *Library Systems Analysis Guidelines*. New York: Wiley-Interscience, 1970.

Corbin, John. "Library Networks," *Library Journal* 101:203-207 (Jan. 1976).

Cox, Carl. "View of the School Library," *School Media Quarterly*, Fall 1972, pp. 36-40.

Ellsworth, Ralph, and Hobart Wagner. *The School Library: Facilities for Independent Study in Secondary Schools*. New York: Educational Facilities Laboratories, 1963.

Ely, Donald, and Chisholm, Margaret. "Reflections from a Crystal Ball," *Audiovisual Instruction* 21:8-11 (January 1976).

Hannigan, Jane. "The Promise of Media Programs: District and School," *School Media Quarterly* 2:9-14 (Fall 1973).

Vagianos, Louis. "Today Is Tomorrow," *Library Journal* 101:147-156 (January 1976).

PERSONNEL REQUIREMENTS

OBJECTIVES

Identify the types and numbers of personnel needed for effective service in the school library media center program.

Design a personnel deployment pattern for a library media center program in a selected school.

Write job descriptions for media personnel in various positions in a selected school.

SOME STAFFING CONSIDERATIONS

A Paragon of Virtue

In the past, the literature defined the role of the school librarian in glowing terms. He was a reading specialist, curriculum generalist, subject specialist, guidance counselor, and administrator. He was at least this and usually much more. Adding to this the qualifications of the audiovisual specialist (curriculum generalist, subject specialist, instructional technology expert, and teacher) gives us the library media specialist. Although it is possible for an individual to prepare for this role, it usually is not possible to perform all of the tasks envisioned on a continuing basis.

The profession has only recently come to the rational conclusion that if one individual is required to assume the total burden of the LMC program, he cannot do an effective job. Unfortunately, library media personnel have always willingly assumed new program responsibilities without knowing how they would deliver. It is time to redefine, clearly enunciate, and effectively implement LMC staffing patterns, which can provide an impact on the educational program of the schools. We are just beginning to have the tools, in the way of research, to accomplish clearly defined objectives and to implement adequate staffing arrangements.

The Service Concept Influences Staff Needs

There are two concepts of service that provide opposing views of the media service concept. In actuality, the opposing concepts arise in most cases from necessity rather than from a distinct polarization of views. The fact is that one can provide for realistic alternative staffing patterns by changing the service concept.

For example, the national guidelines[1] have recommended a staffing pattern predicated on a high degree of interaction between the professional staff and students and teachers in the instructional process. This means interaction in curriculum development, instruction and in-service, design and production, and guidance and consultant services, which represent the principal primary elements of the media service system. This is the leading concept in the LMC and the one that demands our greatest interest and attention. However, without a sufficiently large qualified professional staff, this concept can be implemented only on a very limited basis and only superficially.

The opposing concept is not educationally defensible in the modern school. This concept is embraced where LMC staffing is inadequate or when a judgment (knowingly or not) has been made to limit the interaction of media professionals with students and faculty by limiting the staff size. This concept sees LMC staff involvement only in planning foundation elements and structuring support elements geared to acquiring, organizing, and distributing media. The consequence of this service pattern is a sorely handicapped program.

In practical terms, different staffing models should result in quite different program expectations in a school of 1,000 students. A single media professional in a school of 1,000 cannot function in the same manner four professionals would. The basic problem in our schools today is that neither an adequate professional staff nor sufficient supportive staff is employed in the LMC. Consequently, the library media specialist performs his primary function to a limited extent, and performs a supportive role to a much greater extent.

Guidelines for Media Personnel

The terminology of the 1975 guidelines provide a generalized view of the number and types of people recommended to operate a comprehensive LMC. It should be kept in mind that the numbers and types of staff people cited are based essentially on the consensus of the two national groups involved in formulating standards. The basic relationships among staff size, media collections, size of facility, and financing are again predicated primarily on consensus.

Personnel needed to staff a modern unified LMC program include:

Head of School Media Program: A media specialist with managerial competencies who is designated as responsible for the media program at the individual school level. Qualifications vary with such factors as the size of the school, size of media staff, and type of program.

Media Professional: Any media person, certificated or not, who qualifies by training and position to make professional judgments and to delineate and maintain media programs or program components. Media professionals may include media specialists, television or film producers, instructional developers, radio station managers, and technical processing (cataloging) specialists, whose duties and responsibilities are professional in nature.

Media Specialist: A person with appropriate certification and broad professional preparation, both in education and media, with competencies to carry out a media program. The media specialist is the basic media professional in the school program.

Media Technician: A member of the media staff with technical skills in such specialized areas as graphics, production and display, information and materials processing, photographic production, operation and maintenance of audiovisual equipment, operation and maintenance of television equipment, and installation of systems components.

Media Aide: A member of the media staff who performs clerical and secretarial tasks and assists as needed in the acquisition, maintenance, inventory, production, distribution, and utilization of materials and equipment.[2]

The 1969 standards for personnel recommended a fixed ratio for the school: one professional, one technician, and one aide for each 250 students. The new guidelines, however, provide a range for each category of personnel, thereby allowing for options based on local conditions. Assuming adequate financial support to develop an optimum program in the school, the specific staffing pattern would be influenced by both the national guidelines and the local requirements. For example, a school with an enrollment of 1,000 students and a comprehensive LMC program would have a designated program head, two to three professionals, three to five technicians, and three to five aides (see Fig. 2-1).

Fig. 2-1. Representative Staffing Patterns*

Enrollment	Professional Personnel		Support Personnel	
	Head	Professionals	Technicians	Aides
500	1	0-1	1-2	2-3
1,000	1	2-3	3-5	3-5
2,000	1	4-7	5-8	5-8

*Adapted from American Association of School Librarians and Association for Educational Communications and Technology, *Media Programs: District and School* (Chicago and Washington, D.C.: American Library Association and Association for Educational Communications and Technology, 1975), pp. 34-35.

Can it be assumed that the ratios proposed in the guidelines for media personnel are correct for a particular school? This assumption can only be made if all other LMC program components are provided in the proportions recommended. We are faced with the need for a school-by-school analysis of staff requirements in terms of program expectations, with due consideration given to resources and services provided by other agencies in the system.

Bringing this need for analysis into the foreground is today's major emphasis on accountability in education. In those school districts which are on the "cutting edge" of education—the innovators, the progressive districts—accountability means program analysis in terms of performance criteria. There is a real concern for the application of program criteria that are attainable, observable, and measurable. Should LMC personnel be held accountable for their performance? We believe the answer has to be an unqualified yes. But this does not mean accountable for a specific increment in learning on the part of specific students. We do not have the tools at this point to measure adequately the LMC's contribution to incidental increments in students' learning.

Accountability usually relates program to costs. Looking briefly at Fig. 2-2, we see the cost range of staffing an LMC for a school of 1,000 students if we used the ratios suggested by the guidelines. A minimum of $76,000 and maximum of $132,000 is a likely salary package. It should be obvious that these costs require justification. How do we define a staff position in order to measure its contribution to the total LMC effort and the educational effort of the school?

Fig. 2-2. Estimated Minimum and Maximum Costs of LMC Staff in a School of 1,000 Students

	Salary Range	Total Cost Range	
		Minimum	Maximum
4 Professionals	$9,000–16,000	36,000	64,000
4 Technicians	6,000–10,000	24,000	40,000
4 Aides	4,000– 7,000	16,000	28,000
		$76,000	$132,000

The School Library Manpower Project[3]

The Manpower Project, initiated by the American Association of School Librarians and funded by the Knapp Foundation, was designed to determine the kinds of media personnel that would be needed to operate school library media centers. The goals of the project focused on recruitment, analysis and education. Phase I of the project dealt with a task analysis of school library positions; Phase II was concerned with education and recruitment for school librarianship and provided for six experimental programs in higher education for the preparation of media personnel. Phase III provided for a comprehensive evaluation of the experimental education programs of Phase II.

The Task Analysis Survey, a School Library Manpower Project effort, was conducted in 694 elementary and secondary schools, public and private, in the United States. These schools were judged to have quality library media center programs that met the "Criteria of Excellence" developed for the survey. This diagnostic study has provided a great deal of information. Twelve duty categories were developed for the study.[4]

Development of the Educational Program	Production
Administration	Preparation of Materials
Instruction	Organization
Special Services to Faculty and Students	Circulation
Selection	Maintenance
Acquisitions	Clerical and Secretarial Tasks

Some 300 tasks were developed to fit the duty categories. When presented to survey respondents, the tasks were in scrambled order. It was theoretically possible that any of the personnel servicing the LMC program—clerks, technicians, audiovisual specialists, assistant librarians and the head of the LMC—could perform any of the tasks in any duty category.

The principal advantage of this study is that the data gathered provide direct evidence of what was being done by personnel in quality LMC programs. The evidence of specific performance is available. Like the national guidelines, the survey data leave much to be desired. Perhaps it is because the evidence is not as we would like it. The authors' in-depth study of the survey results has revealed a great deal of overlapping of performance by the various classes of personnel questioned.

For the purpose of collecting data for the study, the library media specialist function was divided in traditional fashion into two distinct positions: assistant librarian and audiovisual specialist. It should be noted that these functions were later merged in the development of a single job description. The audiovisual specialist's responses showed that none of the tasks performed called for any direct contact with students. Of a total of 38 tasks enumerated for audiovisual specialists, 24 were completed to the same degree or extent by assistant librarians, while at least 13 of the tasks could readily be assigned to competent technicians or clerks.

Assistant librarians performed some 140 tasks, 24 of which were completed to the same degree or extent by audiovisual specialists. After reviewing the tasks performed, it would appear that at least 27 of the tasks could be performed by competent technicians or clerks.

Our observations about the technicians surveyed in the study showed that they performed tasks which were, almost without exception, audiovisual activities. Of the 31 tasks performed by technicians, at least two could readily be assigned to the clerical staff. It appears also that probably an additional 23 tasks should be assigned to the technician groups from other personnel categories.

The aides surveyed in the study performed 75 tasks in the various duty categories to at least the same extent as other members of the LMC staff. It would appear that an additional 19 tasks could be assigned to clerks.

The Behavioral Requirements Analysis Checklist (BRAC)[5], another School Library Manpower Project publication, provides a compilation of competency-based job functions and task statements for library media personnel.

Jobs in Instructional Media[6]

The Jobs in Instructional Media study, conducted by A.E.C.T. (formerly D.A.V.I.—Department of Audiovisual Instruction), had as its main objective the creation of a pool of information to be used to restructure existing media jobs and to suggest programs of training needed for those jobs. Unlike the Task Analysis Survey, which used a questionnaire approach, the J.I.M.S. personnel directly conducted 110 job analyses and identified over 1,200 tasks that could be classified.

The study used a modified form of Functional Job Analysis (F.J.A.), which has been used by the U.S. Department of Labor, and an adaptation of the Domain of Instructional Technology (D.I.T.) to develop a two-dimensional matrix (see Fig. 2-3). The F.J.A. technique provided data in three areas: Worker Functions, General Educational Development, and Worker Instructions. Only worker functions are depicted in the matrix illustrated.

Kenneth Silber developed the Domain of Instructional Technology model to describe the media field and serve as a base for job and training guidelines. Instructional Technology was defined as "1) the organization and 2) the application of 3) resources—men, materials, devices, procedures and ideas—in a systematic manner in order to solve instructional problems."[7]

Fig. 2-3. F.J.A./D.I.T. Matrix

What Gets Done in the Media Field (Field-Specific Skills)

		Management	Personnel	Research	Design	Production	Evaluation	Utilization	U/Dissemination	Support/Supply
What	Data Significant									
Workers	Data/People Significant									
Do	People Significant									
General	People/Things Significant									
Skills and	Things Significant									
Knowledge	Things/Data Significant									

Source: Association for Educational Communications and Technology, *Jobs in Instructional Media* (Washington: National Education Association, 1970), p. 18.

STAFFING REQUIREMENTS

Position Classification and Job Descriptions

Accountability is possible only if there is a clear delineation of each position on the media staff roster. It is only when we know precisely what a person is supposed to do that we can measure his performance in that capacity. Until very recently, there was little research evidence in this area.

A growing requirement in school districts is the development of job descriptions—an attempt to agree about what school personnel of various types are supposed to do. This is a common practice in business and industry, and it has been employed to a degree in school districts.

Job descriptions usually result from an analysis of the tasks an individual performs when carrying out a specific job. The description includes four basic parts: job title, distinguishing characteristics or responsibilities of the job, a summary of major duties, and a summary of qualifications needed for the job. As a result of the Task Analysis conducted by A.A.S.L., and a manipulation of data required to reconcile existing practice with what personnel should do, comprehensive occupational definitions were developed for the following library media positions: technician, library media specialist, head of the LMC, and director of a district program.[8] Although the study analyzed the tasks completed by aides or clerks, no description for this position was included, since the position does not require an education beyond high school. (See Appendix A for the occupational description developed for the library media specialist.)

The job description, besides clearly defining the parameters of the job, also indicates its relative position in a larger scheme of position classification for the district. In the position classification scheme we can visually scan the hierarchy of positions, from the job requiring minimal skills and minimal educational background to the most complex job with the highest qualifications. We can also see other jobs rated in the same fashion according to level of responsibility, experience, and education. The position classification scheme is used for general personnel purposes, such as developing salary schedules.

The generalized position classification scheme in Fig. 2-4 merely illustrates the vertical and horizontal dimensions of a classification scheme. Once it has been agreed that the description fits the job, the position is ranked vertically by level of responsibility and difficulty, and horizontally with other types of jobs in the district that have similar general characteristics. This is the way a total scheme for a district is developed. Since the library media specialist is the first professional position in the LMC, then the position is ranked relatively higher than clerical and technician levels in the vertical dimension. The library media specialist can be equated with other instructional personnel whose responsibility and educational attainment are essentially the same and whose positions are governed by state certification requirements so these positions fall into the same classification and appear on the same horizontal level on the classification scheme. Teachers of English, social studies, and science, for example, fall into this class. Non-certificated personnel having equal responsibility and educational attainment may also appear in this class.

Fig. 2-4. Generalized Position Classification Scheme

Class 4	Head of LMC	Department Heads Science Social Studies
Class 3	Library Media Specialists	Teachers
Class 2	Technicians	
Class 1	Aides, Clerks	Clerks, School Office

If a multiple staffing pattern is employed in the LMC, a director or head library media specialist is assigned and is made responsible for the entire media system. This position is usually classed with those of other department heads. Some school systems pay an additional stipend for a position at this level of responsibility based on numbers of individuals in the department. Certification for department head status is not ordinarily a state requirement, though the school district will ask for higher qualifications for these positions, including more education and more years of experience.

Clerks or aids are usually classed with others in the clerical ranks who have similar qualifications. Large school districts have various grades for clerical and secretarial positions. Employment in these categories is dependent upon education, experience, and various examinations. Some school districts class these positions under Civil Service.

The technician at the school level is ranked with technicians at the district level and with various other jobs requiring similar education, experience, and responsibility. It is within the realm of possibility that the technician would be ranked horizontally with skilled maintenance craftsmen (unless, that is, these craftsmen have a strong bargaining agent, in which case their salary rank may be superior to that of the library media specialist and teacher).

It should be clearly recognized that the library media specialist, technician, and aide jobs as viewed in the position classification scheme, and those occupational definitions developed as a result of the Task Analysis are generalized. Position classification groups jobs in broad classes governed by responsibility, experience, and educational qualifications. Job descriptions discriminate between the jobs performed by personnel in each class. There may be several job descriptions for library media specialists who are expected to perform different functions, and this is true of other media personnel as well.

Career Ladder

It is interesting to note that three major publications of recent vintage have cited the same position levels for the staffing of a media program. National guidelines,[9] the Task Analysis,[10] and Jobs in Instructional Media (J.I.M.S.)[11] all arrived at the same conclusion regarding the specialist, technician, and aide positions. Beyond this basic staffing pattern, additional non-certified personnel are suggested.

The formulation of a career ladder, offering an employee the option of entering the field at various specified levels and to advance to the next level when qualified, is a promising new direction. The employee may elect to remain at the initial level or to leave. A second component at each level would be an in-service program to guarantee the type of training and experience needed by the individual on the job. The in-service program at levels above the introductory level may simply reinforce skills developed in an educational component.

Educational growth, as a third component of the career ladder will probably mean that an individual employed at the aide level will be enrolled in an adult education program to earn a high school diploma. The passing of a High School Equivalency Test could shorten the time considerably for many students. The employee then has the option of stabilizing in a clerical position which he has been trained for, or continuing up the educational ladder. He may elect to move into an essentially terminal program in a community college geared to producing technicians, then transfer to a four-year college program in a related or non-related field; or to enroll in a four-year college program on an extension basis. While employed and enrolled in the career ladder program, the employee may be extended release time for school attendance and may work only 25 to 30 hours a week.

The fourth component is a limited one because it relates to the marketplace. The option is always open for the individual who has gained skill and experience through education and continuous employment within the school district to leave and secure employment in business or industry at a level commensurate with the training, education, and experience attained in the initial employing structure.

The existing position classification scheme in most school districts negates the employment of this pool of workers because minimal educational entrance requirements generally call for a high school diploma. If we can recognize two related factors, 1) that many disadvantaged, unemployed, poorly educated people have the potential to succeed if given an opportunity, and 2) that the employment of high school graduates to perform many of the tasks required in the LMC program is in effect underemploying these people, we have a basis for considering a career ladder.

What are the basic components required for an effective career scheme? The first component is an articulated career ladder beginning with a minimal entrance level below that of a clerk, requiring less than a high school diploma, and ending at the top management level in media programs (see Fig. 2-5).

Fig. 2-5. Career Ladder

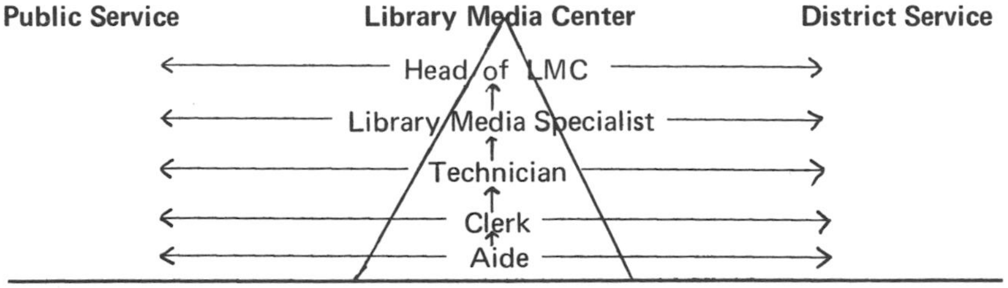

Public Service   Library Media Center   District Service

Both the employment opportunity and the job function of the entrance position might be equated with the position of a "page" in the public library, though the academic requirement would of necessity probably be lower. This position may arbitrarily be called an "aide" position. The general tasks performed provide assistance of a primarily mechanical nature. Articulated above this position would be the media clerk, media technician, library media specialist, and head of the LMC. At any career level the employee has the option of seeking other positions within the school district, in library and educational institutions, and in business and industry.

The aide who can perform mechanical tasks can assume many of the functions cited in the Task Analysis for the media clerk. The following is an enumeration of tasks that a person with minimal education and skills can readily perform.

A. Technical Services
    1.   Acquisitions
            Opens new books and collates pages

    2.   Preparation of materials
            Reinforces books, magazines, paperbacks
            Shellacs book spine
            Covers books with plastic jackets
            Pastes pockets and date-due cards
            Stamps ownership mark
            Sprays maps and pictures with plastic fixative for preservation
            Inserts correct issues of periodicals in plastic covers
            Clips designated items for newspapers and magazines
            Labels library materials such as pamphlets, pictures, clippings
            Puts current newspapers on rods

    3.   Organization
            Sorts and shelves books
            Reads shelves and information files and maintains them in order
            Assists in inventorying all materials
            Assists in inventorying audiovisual and other equipment

    4.   Maintenance
            Inspects print materials for damage
            Inspects nonprint materials for damage
            Repairs books and printed materials

B. Circulation
            Delivers and collects materials and equipment
            Charges, discharges and renews materials and equipment
            Cards or slips books and other materials
            Reviews circulation records to write and send notices
            Pre-stamps date-due cards

    Routes materials according to pre-established lists or records
    Calls in materials on loan when required elsewhere
    Issues student library cards
    Takes attendance in library
    Performs messenger service
    Assists in sale of paperback books

C.   Production
    Duplicates or copies print materials for instructional use

Student Assistants and Volunteers

It has been noted in the literature time and again that volunteers and student assistants should in no way be construed to be legitimate substitutes for employees. The use of students as unpaid clerks cannot be rationalized as a wonderful learning experience for children or as an opportunity for them to contribute to the service program of the school. There can be tremendous value for students in an LMC club, which enables them to learn more about the operation of the LMC. They can make a realistic contribution to the school by assisting in the selection of media. They can participate in literary discussion activities and indeed sponsor this type of activity or film-oriented programs and activities. But shelving, shelf reading, pasting and stamping, and pushing projection carts are LMC tasks that should be performed by paid personnel. If students are employed in this capacity so that the library media specialist can simply survive, then one should freely admit that this is the case.

Some volunteers have Ph.D.'s and some have library degrees. Indeed, some volunteers have better credentials and are more capable than the media professionals they assist. What is unfortunate is the fact that many intelligent, well-intentioned volunteers have rarely functioned as a power bloc in the school district to improve LMC programs and secure media personnel through direct action with Boards of Education. The volunteer library "social clubs," which gather together mothers who help out for two hours a week each in the LMC, have probably contributed to the poor growth pattern of elementary school libraries simply because they are "available" as substitutes for legitimate media personnel.

Volunteer programs of many kinds have been and will continue to be employed in the schools.[12] Many have been designed to use high school and college students and parents as tutors or as teacher aides, emphasizing their direct interaction with students under the supervision of professionals. When comprehensive school volunteer programs are structured, the LMC becomes a resource for teachers and volunteers carrying out an assigned function.

The special-function volunteer—a creative storyteller, artist, or teacher who can enhance an LMC program but who for some reason is not available for employment—is a desirable asset. But the P.T.A. mothers enlisted to "man the library" in the absence of staff are a definite liability.

Exclusive Prerogatives

In many professions there is reasonable doubt as to just what tasks should be assigned to personnel of varying backgrounds and abilities. More and more, an effort is being made to free the professional from tasks that can be performed by paraprofessionals who have less education and experience. This is certainly the case in the library field and in the related field of educational communications and technology.

In the past, our school libraries had only two personnel categories: the professional and the clerical. The professional librarian had at least a four-year college education and the clerk a high school diploma. There was usually a minimum of position exchange. Although the professional frequently became involved in so-called clerical or mechanical functions, only infrequently did the clerical assistant perform professional tasks. A major reason for this pattern was the vast amount of clerical and mechanical work involved in operating a library. The school audiovisual specialist at one time performed only tasks related to equipment distribution and maintenance, and indeed expected to do only that. (Here we have the classic image of the librarian as "clerk" and the audiovisual specialist as a "nuts and bolts" man.) Times have changed. We recognize the fact that the existing situation in many professions, not merely the library media profession, caused many professionals to be underemployed—that is, they performed tasks and jobs considerably below their ability and expectations. Training programs today are rapidly expanding to produce technicians of various kinds[13] for jobs in the school and related areas. Questions arise as to what tasks non-certified, non-professional personnel should perform.

One purpose of the job description is to provide a measure of security for the incumbent. It tells the universe what tasks the holder of the job may reasonably be expected to perform; at the same time, it prevents the individual from being forced into tasks above the stated capabilities of the job or tasks below the level of competence stated for the job. In part, this is what governance on the part of professionals is all about and what collective bargaining agreements are about. While it is generally desirable to encourage personnel to grow in stature and competency on the job, two factors mitigate against extensive activity outside the job description defining the parameters of the individual's work. These factors are simply job security and what we have termed exclusive job prerogatives.

A person who is assigned to a specific job level and who performs competently is a person with a sense of security. Asking a licensed television technician to "push a broom" 50 percent of the time would be to demean him in terms of both his educational background and his level of competence. On the other hand, assigning him the task of producing and directing instructional television programing in the school would probably take him into a situation beyond his capabilities. If the extraordinary technician who is capable of producing and directing at a level of competence beyond his specific job function actually does so, he soon becomes frustrated because he is performing a higher-rated job without being financially compensated at the level of performance.

The job description endeavors to cite the exclusive prerogatives of the employee assigned to the job. Through a combination of education and experience the individual has attained certain skills and talent needed to perform a job. These are the exclusive prerogatives of the holder of the position. When the professional performs clerical and technician functions, he is in one sense denigrating his own position. Also he may be keeping trained people out of the job market. Likewise, the volunteer in the school is in a very real sense "keeping the lid on" the employment situation.

Selecting Personnel for the LMC

It is in the best interest of the school to employ the head of the LMC in advance of all other media personnel. The stated qualifications for such a position are available elsewhere in this chapter. A highly qualified professional who presents evidence of competency and educational background in library science, instructional technology, and curriculum is needed. Leadership ability is extremely important because of the ramifications of the job and the need to relate to people in various subject disciplines and with various personalities. Before one can lead his own staff, he must know what must be accomplished by a staff. One cannot begin program planning at any level without knowing what jobs must be performed in order to accomplish an objective.

Assuming that the head of the LMC has been employed and has the confidence of his administrative superiors, he should be delegated responsibility for staffing. In most school districts this is a cooperative effort involving also the school principal, a district LMC director, and a personnel director, who may be an administrator with several other functions. The head of the LMC should have a clear understanding of the educational program of the school as well as a clear understanding of the media system required for optimum service to students and teachers. It is desirable to structure a staffing pattern with this optimum service function in mind. This is a "system planning" exercise that should be accomplished totally. When it becomes obvious that the staff required will not be forthcoming immediately, then a review of alternatives is required. Some obvious alternatives are: 1) Endeavor to operate a comprehensive program in spite of a lack of personnel. 2) Exclude specific system components until staff is available to effectively carry out the job. This is usually done in LMC programs other than school programs. 3) Change the service focus. A lack of professional staff means users must somehow do for themselves.

In every case an attempt must be made to employ a "balanced staff" having the overall competency needed to provide optimum service. For example, if the intent is to employ media specialists with subject competencies in English, science, social studies, and modern foreign languages, but it is not possible immediately to employ specialists in science and the languages, it would be better to leave the positions open for a time and endeavor to recruit the personnel needed. If coverage is needed, substitutes are usually available and can be trained to perform a holding action. They can also be dismissed at any time.

The national guidelines have offered some suggestions on typical staffing patterns for elementary and secondary schools. The idea a unified program in a school can be begun by organizing staff work according to type of media is, quite frankly, a poor one. It probably was suggested to satisfy those currently operating such programs and to protect them from the traumatic experience of disruption. If there are two professionals operating separate programs, and two is the number required for the LMC program in the school, then the more qualified person should be selected to head the program. If the person selected is not fully qualified, a condition of employment should be that he become qualified. The loser has the following options: to work cooperatively in the system or to leave the school or district.

A recommendation that elementary schools develop specialties according to grade level has met with success. For example, at the Mark Twain Elementary School, Hartford, Connecticut, one professional assumed primary responsibility for K-4 programing, while a second professional assumed similar responsibility for grades 5-8. There was no attempt to limit the interaction of professionals with students and teachers on a continuing basis, but rather an effort was made to define a pattern of emphasis.

A secondary school recommendation of assignments along subject lines is rational to this degree: if a multiple staffing pattern is to be employed, it is desirable to select professionals whose educational backgrounds reflect a variety of subject strengths regardless of the organizing structure. Broad media competency for every professional is essential.

Actual procedures for selecting and employing personnel vary from district to district. Vacancies should not be advertised only locally unless one is sure that the only pool of talent is to be found there. One would expect the district personnel office to be in contact with college and university placement offices as well as specialized schools of business and technology. Other sources would be a state employment office, or in some cases a state department of education. Advertising of positions in newspapers and professional journals is a common practice. Prospective candidates should file a formal application, supply college placement papers if appropriate, and file transcripts and letters of recommendation. State certification would be one requirement for the position of professional media specialist. For many types of positions, particularly clerical, written examinations are a must. Personal interviews are usually conducted by one or more members of the district staff. The head of the school LMC should review pertinent data about the candidate and, if possible, conduct an on-site interview. Since the LMC operation is one that requires close contact and cooperation among the staff, both the candidate and the LMC head should have an opportunity to judge whether or not the candidate is suited to the position and vice versa.

Reality Staffing

Sometimes it is obvious that an optimum staffing pattern will not be achieved in a particular school in the near future or in any future. There are some alternative staffing patterns available today for such situations.

Administrators have spent at least a part of their education in studying the utilization of staff. Generally, however, they have not done a very good job in utilizing the best talents of media personnel—for example, take the case of an elementary school LMC staffed by one professional, with classes scheduled each half hour of each day. In this type of situation there is essentially a single-purpose media program based on instruction. If there is a recognition of the potential in a media program, but at the same time staffing for effective service is a critical problem, alternatives are usually available in the school.

At the secondary level, a practical utilization of subject specialists would be to assign one or more teachers in each subject area to the LMC on a continuing basis. For years schools have utilized teachers' talents as cafeteria supervisors and study hall supervisors. Now here is a professional-level challenge to both the administration and the teacher. Involving them on a continuing basis in media selection, reference, and reading guidance in areas related to their own subjects provides an opportunity to expand the service base for students and faculty members in the specialists' own departments.

Another alternative in both elementary and secondary schools would be to examine thoroughly the roles of specialists such as reading teachers and consultants and "resource teachers," whose function may be defined in various ways but who work essentially with a few students at a time. These people are prime candidates for service emanating from the LMC. Too frequently these professionals are closeted in separate quarters and their skills are minimized, because the possible benefit from these skills is reserved for special cases. If the LMC is seen as the principal service center for all media, the school can capitalize both on these resources in relation to student needs and on the skills of these professionals as they relate to a broader population in the school.

The LMC program generates a vast amount of clerical and mechanical work, which should be assigned to personnel below the rank of professional. Because of teacher pressures and related factors in the schools, we have had aides of various kinds supervising cafeterias, playgrounds, study halls, and street corners. Administrators have recognized the need to release professional teachers from these duties, but they persist in allowing library media specialists to paste and stamp, shelve and mend. If some of this non-professional assistance were to be diverted to the LMC program, the practical consequence would mean the application of the media professional's time to media-related activities.

There are also programs to employ the disadvantaged in public schools today. Many of these programs channel people into the schools as teacher aides. All too frequently, however, the training is a dead end; the people are trained only to perform certain tasks such as counting milk money, helping children with their coats and boots, correcting papers, and in some cases working with small groups of children assigned to improve some basic skills. While these programs usually have an education component, which means attending adult education classes or a community college, the marketable skills learned are minimal and have little or no transfer potential to work outside the school. If the intent of these programs is to provide an educational advantage to the school by having additional personnel available and also to provide the individual with a marketable skill, this can readily be accomplished in an LMC. Here, specifically transferable clerical and other business skills can be learned, and library skills open out to the public library, academic or special libraries, and the labor market in general.

Today's reality may well demand the implementation of an adult volunteer program or expansion of a student aide program to perform continuing, essential tasks. In either case, in-service training should be provided and tasks clearly delineated.

Reality may also mean a redirection or reduction of services provided to students and faculty. This process should be initiated only after a personal assessment of staff strengths and a student-faculty assessment of preferred services and/or levels of service. The services to be retained should be those which clearly make a difference in the educational program of the school.

Deployment of Staff

Because there are many variables to consider in dealing with the LMC, it is extremely difficult to arrive at an optimum pattern for the deployment of personnel. One must consider potential services from the school district, the technical services structure of the organization, the administrative configuration designed for the total media system, and the types of services required.

The LMC staff of a school of 500 pupils is usually 50 percent smaller than that of a school with 1,000 pupils, yet the LMC staff will be expected to perform the same functions to the same extent or degree as the staff of the larger school. It is obvious that the jobs of individuals in smaller schools are more generalized and comprehensive.

In any deployment pattern, the major focus of professional personnel should be on primary elements where there is a direct relationship with users. As much as possible, technical services functions should be performed by non-professional personnel under the supervision of a professional.

Figure 2-6 provides a view of a possible deployment pattern for a school with 1,000 pupils. Assuming that there are four professionals for a standard program, exclusive of comprehensive television and computerized laboratories, the professionals would be assigned responsibilities rather than fixed locations.

Fig. 2-6. Deployment of Media Staff in School of 1,000 Pupils

Management	Primary Elements	Support Elements
P1	P2, P3	P4
	T1	T2, T3, T4
	C1	C2, C3, C4

Professionals	P
Technicians	T
Clerks	C

Professionals: Four required. One professional becomes the head of the LMC and performs the management function. One professional is assigned responsibility for support elements, excluding management. He is also assigned other responsibilities, such as media selection, faculty interaction, and so on. Two professionals assume responsibility for primary program elements. One has direct responsibility for design production.

Technicians: Four technicians are required. Three are assigned to support elements in technical services, one to circulation. One technician would be assigned to the design production function. They work under the supervision of a professional and assume major responsibility for completion of the tasks required. These are essentially fixed-location jobs.

Aides: Four aides are required. Three are assigned to support functions: two in technical services, one in circulation/distribution. One is assigned to the design production function. Although these are essentially fixed-location jobs, other tasks may be assigned such as typing of correspondence. They work under the supervision of a technician and a professional.

Modification of the pattern suggested can readily be made. In a decentralized LMC, change would be mandatory. Any pattern initiated for the first time in an LMC should be considered a trial run. A continuing program of evaluation should be made to verify the degree of success or failure of the pattern.

SUMMARY

* There are two concepts of service—which qualify as opposing views— that are prime determiners of staffing patterns. The first concept is geared to a high degree of interaction between the LMC professional staff and students and teachers in the instructional process. The second concept is directed to minimal interaction of media professionals, with a high orientation toward support functions and a minimal staffing pattern.

* Job descriptions are becoming increasingly important because of a general focus on accountability in education. The job description includes title, responsibilities, a summary of major duties, and qualifications needed for the job. *Media Programs: District and School*, the *School Library Personnel Task Analysis Survey*, and *Jobs in Instructional Media* recommend three classes of positions: specialists, technicians, and clerks or aides.

* A new direction for schools and LMC's is the "career ladder," which permits entrance into the field with minimal education and experience. Through a combination of education and in-service work, the individual may eventually become a library media specialist or may at any time select options to move into related school jobs or out into public service.

* Staffing for an LMC should be planned at the same time that the comprehensive media system is developed. A systems approach is used initially regardless of whether the school district can employ all of the staff required.

* Reality staffing means seeking reasonable alternative staffing patterns through the utilization of "resource teachers," reading specialists, and teachers, as well as various types of paraprofessionals who may be assigned to the school for other purposes.

* Deployment of staff is based on a realistic appraisal of system elements. An evaluation of any deployment pattern is needed to adjust to program changes.

LITERATURE AND FIELD INVESTIGATIONS

1. What background information is needed to determine the personnel requirements for an LMC program? Discuss the implications of such information.

2. Investigate alternative educational programs for the preparation of various types of school media personnel.

3. Investigate the present status of state certification requirements for media personnel.

4. Compare job descriptions for school media personnel to those for personnel in academic and public libraries. Discuss similarities and differences.

5. Compare staff deployment patterns in school LMC's to those in academic and public libraries. Discuss similarities and differences.

6. In various selected schools, review staff utilization practices. Discuss the rationale for such practices.

7. Investigate the use of the career ladder (lattice) in various occupational fields. Compare the findings to activity in the school media field.

8. Compare the use of volunteers in school LMC's to their use in other areas of education or other fields.

NOTES

[1] American Association of School Librarians and Association for Educational Communications and Technology, *Media Programs: District and School* (Chicago and Washington, D.C.: American Library Association and Association for Educational Communications and Technology, 1975), pp. 34, 35.

[2] *Ibid.*, pp. 109, 110.

[3] American Association of School Librarians, *School Library Manpower Project (Phase I—Final Report)*, (Chicago: American Library Association, 1970); *Curriculum Alternatives: Experiments in School Library Media Education* (Chicago: American Library Association, 1974); *Evaluation of Alternative Curricula: Approaches to School Library Media Education* (Chicago: American Library Association, 1975).

[4] American Association of School Librarians, *School Library Personnel Task Analysis Survey* (Chicago: American Library Association, 1969).

[5] American Association of School Librarians, *Behavioral Requirements Analysis Checklist* (Chicago: American Library Association, 1973).

[6] Association for Educational Communications and Technology, *Jobs in Instructional Media* (Washington, D.C.: National Education Association, 1970).

[7] *Ibid.*, p. 288.

[8] American Association of School Librarians, *Occupational Definitions for School Library Media Personnel* (Chicago: American Library Association, 1971).

[9] American Association of School Librarians and Association for Educational Communications and Technology, *op. cit.*

[10] American Association of School Librarians, *School Library Personnel Task Analysis Survey*.

[11] Association for Educational Communications and Technology, *op. cit.*

[12] For the interested reader, see cases 4 and 27 in *School Media Programs: Case Studies in Management* (Metuchen, N.J.: Scarecrow Press, 1974).

[13] See *Jobs in Instructional Media* for samples of two-year level programs for the training of technicians.

REFERENCES

American Association of School Librarians. *Behavioral Requirements Analysis Checklist*. Chicago: American Library Association, 1973.

American Association of School Librarians. *Curriculum Alternatives: Experiments in School Media Education*. Chicago: American Library Association, 1974.

American Association of School Librarians. *Evaluation of Alternative Curricula: Approaches to School Library Media Education*. Chicago: American Library Association, 1975.

American Association of School Librarians. *Occupational Definitions for School Library Media Personnel*. Chicago: American Library Association, 1971.

American Association of School Librarians. *School Library Manpower Project (Phase I—Final Report)*. Chicago: American Library Association, 1970.

American Association of School Librarians. *School Library Personnel Task Analysis Survey*. Chicago: American Library Association, 1969.

American Association of School Librarians. *Task Analysis Survey Instrument*. Chicago: American Library Association, 1969.

American Association of School Librarians and Association for Educational Communications and Technology. *Media Programs: District and School*. Chicago and Washington, D.C.: American Library Association and Association for Educational Communications and Technology, 1975.

American Association of School Librarians. Certification of School Media Specialists Committee. *Certification Model for Professional School Media Personnel*. Chicago, American Library Association, 1976.

Association for Educational Communications and Technology. *Jobs in Instructional Media*. Washington, D.C.: National Education Association, 1970.

Galvin, Thomas. "Change in Education for Librarianship," *Library Journal* 101:273-277 (January 1, 1976).

Kingsbury, Mary. "Education for School Librarianship: Expectations vs. Reality," *Journal of Education for Librarianship* 15:251-257 (Spring 1975).

Minder, Thomas, and Benjamin Whitten. "Basic Undergraduate Education for Librarianship and Information Science," *Journal of Education for Librarianship* 15:258-269 (Spring 1975).

Prostano, Emanuel. *School Media Programs: Case Studies in Management*. Metuchen, N.J.: Scarecrow Press, 1974.

Stone, Elizabeth. *New Directions in Staff Development*. Chicago: American Library Association, 1971.

3

MEDIA COLLECTIONS

OBJECTIVES

Identify and describe the types of media suitable for use in the schools.

Design a media evaluation and selection program for a selected school library media center program.

Select media to meet specific learning needs in a particular school.

Modify media to accommodate specific learning needs of students.

After the library media center (LMC) staff has been organized and has set in motion the activities needed to fully structure the media system, other foundation elements—resources, facilities, and financing—receive their initial attention. This chapter deals with the resources needed to make the LMC program operational. The LMC by its nature can accommodate broad variations in instructional practices in the school. However, the optimum instructional design should reflect two major changes in how education is carried on in the school. The first is a role change for the teachers, from lecturer to diagnostician and master planner of student learning experiences. The second is a role change for the student, from passive learner to that of a self-directed individual capable of using the learning tools available to him effectively and efficiently. In order for the student to become the unique personality that educators agree he should become, he must be totally involved in learning experiences designed to capitalize on his unique learning style, interests, and abilities. The first illustration in Fig. 3-1 shows a typical locked-in, teacher-directed experience: content, objectives, and method are pre-set and the student is a passive receiver of information. The change suggested, shown in the second illustration, opens up a new relationship between teacher and learner; options are open to both in terms of content, method, activities, and media.

VARIETY ABOUNDS

Various terms are used to describe mixed collections of informational and recreational resources which convey varied messages to users. Some of the terms that have been used are:

1. Print and non-print materials. Perhaps the reverse of this should be audiovisual and non-audiovisual, though some insist that the term audiovisual is sufficiently broad to include printed sources.

Fig. 3-1. Changes in Instructional Practices

1. Teacher-Directed Experience

Content ———————⟶ Teacher ———————⟶ Learner
   —objectives
   —method

2. Suggested Teacher-Learner Relationship

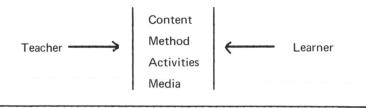

Teacher ——————⟶ | Content Method Activities Media | ⟵—————— Learner

2.   **Materials.** Used independently or with other terms for resources stored and distributed by libraries.

3.   **Resources.** Used synonymously with materials.

4.   **Carriers.** Used by Ellsworth[1] to encompass all forms.

5.   **Media.** In Webster,[2] used as the plural of medium, meaning "through or by which something is accomplished, conveyed or carried on."

In this work, technology and furniture are treated in a separate chapter.

Media Requirements

The function of the library media specialist is to coordinate the selection, organization, and utilization of media as instructional system components in the teaching-learning process and as they serve the individual in his private quest for knowledge. Fig. 3-2 shows national quantitative recommendations for media. While the national guidelines presented recommendations for a base collection and expanded provisions (access beyond the school), only selected items from the base collection are cited.

The media resources of an LMC will be of two types: primary sources and secondary sources. Primary source media consist of the record of events in original form, whereas secondary sources represent media developed from the primary sources. Examples of primary sources are original manuscripts or documents, taped interviews, on-the-scene filmed or videorecorded experiences, real objects, and

Fig. 3-2. Representative Quantitative Standards for Media*

BASE COLLECTION FOR A SCHOOL WITH 500 OR FEWER USERS

TOTAL COLLECTION: At least 20,000 items, or 40 items per user

Books: 8,000-12,000 volumes, or 16 to 24 per user

Periodicals and Newspapers: 50 to 175 titles

Filmstrips (Sound and Silent): 500 to 2,000 items, or 1 to 4 items per user

Slides and Transparencies: 2,000 to 6,000 items, or 4 to 12 items per user

Graphics (Posters, Art and Study Prints, Maps and Globes): 800 to 1,200 items

16mm and Super 8mm Sound Films, Videotapes and Television Reception: Access to 3,000 titles

Super 8mm Films, Silent: 500 to 1,000 items, or 1 to 2 per user

Audio Recordings (Tapes, Cassettes, Discs and Audio Cards): 1,500 to 2,000 items, or 3 to 4 per user

Games and Toys: 400 to 750 items

Models and Sculpture: 200 to 500 items

Specimens: 200 to 400 items

---

*Adapted from American Association of School Librarians and Association for Educational Communications and Technology, *Media Programs: District and School* (Chicago and Washington, D.C.: American Library Association and Association for Educational Communications and Technology, 1975), pp. 70-86.

---

specimens. Secondary sources are represented by a secondhand reporting of the original. Secondary sources form the major portion of school LMC collections.

Printed media are generally well known and are sometimes treated as a single medium because of the mode of presentation. The book, however, although it is a printed medium, appears in both hardbound and paperbound formats, which in the eyes of the user are quite dissimilar. Fader,[3] for example, would provide only paperbound books in library collections.

Types of books that have unique qualities or purposes include bibliographies, reference sources, general fiction and non-fiction of the trade book variety, and textbooks (which, incidentally, do have a place in LMC collections). A book may contain many of the elements usually classified as audiovisual: opaque pictures of many types, transparent overlays, graphs, diagrams, charts, cartoons, comics, maps, and programed material. Books may be utilized in a cross-media approach with records, tapes, and other media in an instructional system.

Magazines and newspapers record information not considered stable enough to be formally incorporated in book form. As carriers of new information, they can play a vital role in the LMC collection. Used in conjunction with the basic indexes available, they are a principal vehicle for use in student investigative experiences. Pamphlets, government documents, and related ephemera provide a way to expand the range of experience through the printed word.

There is no single "best" way to classify and discuss the various types of audiovisual media that are available. The following discussion represents one method of organization and presentation.

Field Experience. There has always been a desire to expose the learner to all of the universe through lifelike experiences, but the limitations are obvious. The field trip is an attempt to provide firsthand experience of one aspect of life. From the kindergarten trip to the post office and fire station, through visits to museums, aquariums and observatories, to the summer trip to Europe and the planned year of study abroad, the school has tried to capture the essence of the world for the learner. While no recommendation is made here that the LMC staff begin conducting world tours, certainly a file of potential field experiences can be maintained.

Realia. The medium of animate or inanimate real things covers a wide field. Realia usually refers to objects and specimens that can be gathered through extensive field experiences. An object is a real thing, as is the specimen. They differ in that the specimen is representative of a class of like objects. Gerbils, baby chicks, and "resource people" who make themselves available to the school may also be classed as realia. The LMC should maintain a file of the names of resource people.

Three-Dimensional Media. In the absence of the real thing or experience, the LMC can provide three-dimensional representations of the real. We refer principally to models, mockups, and dioramas. Models provide a visual and manipulative experience for students. A model of a space capsule, an ear, or a human torso (capable of being disassembled and reassembled) can provide the student with the opportunity for a realistic appraisal of things as they are. Mockups are usually operating, full-scale models developed for specific training purposes or analysis; a school does not necessarily need a full-scale mockup. Dioramas are miniaturized scenes in depth that incorporate a group of modeled objects and figures. All can be purchased commercially or produced in school by students and teachers.

Still Pictures. Two types of still pictures are available for use in the schools: opaque and transparent. Opaque media such as art prints, study prints, posters, and book illustrations can be used in the original form or modified by means of an opaque projection device. The term transparent media refers to a group of visual media whose image is viewed when light is passed through them. Included here are filmstrips, which consist of a series of images in sequence on 35mm film; the photographic slide, which includes mounted 2 x 2 inch film up to the 3¼ x 4 inch Polaroid variety; the microscope slide, which has the potential for use with a microscope or as a projected medium; microfilm (reel-to-reel) and microfiche, which are photographs in miniature form; transparencies, which are becoming increasingly popular today; and the stereodisc, which provides three-dimensional viewing through a stereoviewer. These are available commercially and, in most cases, they can also be produced in schools if the equipment is available.

Graphics. Used in the context of the school media program, graphics refers to a variety of visual forms including graphs, diagrams, charts, posters, cartoons, and comics. Occasionally graphics are described as non-pictorial, in an attempt to differentiate between the still picture and graphics. They can be used in numerous ways, either in the original or as projected media. They may be purchased commercially or produced in school.

Maps and globes are technically also graphics, though they are usually treated separately. Globes are spherical models of the earth, and three principal types are generally found in schools: political, physical political, and slated-outline globes. Maps are flat representations of the earth's surface, and again three principal types are found in the school: physical, political, and special purpose. Many combinations and variations of these basic types are available and in use.

Audio Media. Essentially, two methods are used to convey sound to a listener: disc recordings and magnetic tape. The disc recording and/or transcription had the distinction for years of being a staple of both schools and libraries. The use of magnetic tape in schools has had a significant impact on the market. Tape is available in both reel-to-reel and cassette formats. Reel-to-reel tapes in popular sizes (3, 5, and 7 inch, each operated at varying speeds, 1 7/8, 3 3/4, and 7 1/2 inches per second) have for years provided schools with both a recording and a playback capacity. The versatility of the reel-to-reel tape has made it the basis for both language laboratory and dial access systems. The cassette in turn is beginning to revolutionize the market because of its ease of handling.

Motion Pictures. The motion picture may be silent, implying only visual application, or with sound, which combines both audio and visual potential. The 16mm film has been an important educational and recreational medium. The 8mm format has made dramatic strides in recent years as both silent and sound films. The cartridge filmloop single-concept film, ranging in length from two to five minutes, has had an impact in the visual field equivalent to that of the audio cassette. The 8mm silent and sound film, available in reel-to-reel or cartridged format, is beginning to challenge the 16mm film for many purposes. The potential for school-produced 8mm films is beginning to be realized at this time.

Programed Media. Initially, programed learning was synonymous with teaching machines. Emphasis was on hardware. While the potential of the medium was never realized, interest remains high for programed media as instructional system components. The hardware emphasis has generally declined in favor of less costly processes. Programed instruction is usually described as a means by which information is provided for the user in bit-by-bit, step-by-step sequences. Each segment leads logically to the next step and the user proceeds at his own rate of speed. Immediate feedback is available to the student.

Instructional Kits. A kit may include any number of related media geared to a particular subject. Kits, which in some school districts may be boxed for distribution, may incorporate 8mm filmloops, filmstrips, records, audio and video tapes, 16mm films, three-dimensional media, books, pamphlets, and teacher guides. Instructional kits are available commercially or may be developed in the schools.

Videotape. Television has aptly been termed an audiovisual synthesis because of its potential to incorporate, in any programing segment, any of the media previously described. As with audio tape, video may be used for both recording and playback purposes. The availability of reasonably priced portable equipment will undoubtedly increase use of this important medium in the schools. The potential of videotape in dial and random access systems is just beginning to be tapped. Recent developments, such as electronic video recorders that use tape cartridges and discs, have left the market in a somewhat confused state. Least confusing and probably most practical for schools and small school districts for some time will be portable equipment.

Cross Media. This is a method of media utilization. Two or more media, either commercially produced or produced in the school, are combined. Examples are filmstrip and record or tape cassette combination, slides and tapes, book and record or tape. The method is also called a multi-media approach.

Information Needed Prior to Selection

The key to developing media collections that will meet the instructional and personal needs of students and teachers is found in one word, "awareness." This goes beyond merely being aware of what is needed. It is the ability to translate knowledge about these needs into action, through an evaluation, selection, acquisitions, and organizational process that will provide almost immediately for these needs. What must the library media specialist be aware of if he is to perform the extremely vital function of collection building?

☐ The curriculum of the school and district is one of the first points of information relative to media needs.

1. If courses of study or curriculum guides are available and current, they provide a convenient way to analyze the school's instructional programing quickly. At the very least, the course of study provides an overview of subject matter for various subjects in grades or levels of the school program. Frequently, these guides provide a variety of other information, including some of the activities a teacher can plan for the class, textbooks, and other instructional devices.

2. If resource units or teaching units have been developed district-wide or within the school, they provide an expanded analysis of the types of activities and media that teachers can use in a problem-solving approach to teaching and learning.

3. If the district and/or school is oriented toward student-directed learning, perhaps Learning Activity Packages or Unipacs have been developed, or are being developed, by teachers for student use.

4. If standard textbooks are being used, an analysis of the various series provides direct information about subject matter content and, in most cases, bibliographies of related materials. Media personnel should be aware of these bibliographies because in many cases they represent the sum total of the teacher's knowledge of what is available beyond the text material itself.

5. Teacher methodology in the context of the instruction program, such as team teaching or continuous progress plans, provides insight into the potential use of media forms and related services.

6. Also helpful is an analysis of the range of related activities, such as club programs, guidance functions, and special pilot projects in academic or non-academic areas, or potential changes in the curriculum.

☐ A knowledge of the publishing field, obtained generally through bibliographic study and experience in the field, is an essential factor. One must be able to see instructional and personal needs in relation to the market. A library media specialist must continually review the tools of selection available and preview materials not included in the standard selection sources. Although much has been accomplished in terms of providing usable evaluative sources for some forms of print media, much remains to be done to bring the audiovisual field up to that standard. In general, evaluative tools provide only minimal security for the selector. Relating the school's known needs to the marketplace is one of the principal tasks of the entire media selection process. If it is found that commercial media are not readily available, the options are to produce media locally or to modify commercial or locally produced media for instructional or other purposes.

☐ A knowledge of the technology available and suitable for use with audiovisual media is as vital to the program as the "software" considered for selection.

☐ A continuing analysis of innovative practices in various subject fields (content and methods) that have implications for instructional programing in the school is essential. Besides making available information about innovative practices, the library media specialist must make judgments about implementation of new practices as they relate to the LMC program. This is one way the library media specialist can act as a catalyst for instructional improvement.

☐ Basic to the process of procuring media suited to the needs and interests of students is a thorough analysis of the abilities and interests of students in the school. This is done in part by a study of generalized patterns of behavior and a study of guidance records and test scores.

☐ Continuing dialogues between media staff, students, teachers, and others in the school and district are essential to update knowledge of the total school program.

☐ One should have full and detailed knowledge of the budgeting process for the school and district, including allotments for the LMC program, specific areas covered in the budget, and the flexibility of the budget in terms of transfer of funds.

☐ A complete package of information, for participants in the selection process, should spell out in some detail the media selection policy for the school and district, criteria for selection of media, and procedures required for the preview, evaluation, and selection of media.

Typical Poor Practices

Despite the fact that there is much educational emphasis on training competent media selectors, there are many instances where either untrained or incompetent individuals take responsibility for selecting media for school programs. Some examples of poor selection practices and collection building are:

1. Selecting and purchasing audiovisual or printed media from publishers' catalogs or as a result of a ten-minute conversation with a persuasive salesman.

2. Scanning the catalogs produced by commercial vendors and making selections based on a generalized need. Resulting from the push to purchase commercially cataloged and processed books, this practice was particularly observable during rush times, such as meeting deadlines for the expenditures of E.S.E.A. Title funds. In a way, the simple checklist is a great inducement to the person already overburdened with work.

3. Using a single standard tool, such as the *Senior High School Library Catalog*, for the purpose of selection, and slavishly ordering until every item in the catalog is a part of the collection.

4. Regularly purchasing only single copies of items in an endeavor to broaden the scope of the collection.

5. Purchasing only those materials formally requested by faculty.

EVALUATION AND SELECTION

The evaluation and selection of media is of primary importance and is carried on in relation to planning and implementing the curriculum and in relation to guidance and consultant services. As previously noted, media should not be selected and evaluated by the LMC staff alone, isolated from a knowledge of all the factors needed to make rational judgments and isolated from the people who are expected to utilize the media collected.

Media Policy

A written policy statement of the official school position on selecting media to be purchased is a necessity. A district-wide media policy should be developed by representatives of the media staff, teaching staff, administrators, school board members, student representatives, and community representatives. It should become official Board of Education policy.

The purpose of the written policy is to enunciate clearly what the school and district can and will do in this field. A typical policy statement will:

1. Be compatible with the philosophy of education for the school and district.

2. Recognize nationally stated objectives for media selection, such as the School Library Bill of Rights for School Library Media Center Programs (see Appendix B).

3. Recognize specific community and student needs. An excerpt from the policy statement for the Hartford public schools may clarify types of positive statements required in individual situations: "The diverse multi-ethnic population of the Hartford community places a specific responsibility on libraries for providing educational materials about minority groups which tend to uplift the self-concept of these groups."[4]

4. Recognize the right of individuals and groups, both within and without the school organization, to question and challenge media policies, procedures, and specific items selected for inclusion in the collections of the schools. Usually this right is recognized and specific procedures for filtering questions and challenges are established. The National Council of Teachers of English has had a questionnaire form available for some time which may be incorporated into this section of the policy (see Appendix C).

5. Include both the philosophy and the criteria used for the selection of media.

Many schools and school districts simply do not have a media policy. Also, in many schools only the knowledge of an impending crisis and/or evaluation of the school for accreditation purposes motivates administrators and school boards to develop a policy for the district.

There are sometimes media policies that, although they are not official statements approved by boards of education, do state administrative policy for day-to-day operations of the schools. In this case, official board sanction is neither requested nor given and the policy remains "in the family." There are other situations in which general administrative reaction to the development of a policy is simply negative. School administrators and boards of education, already under attack for textbooks and for policies and practices related to the purchase of multi-ethnic materials, are often unwilling to create new policies that will be subjected to public scrutiny and reaction.

The fact remains, however, that the media policy provides a blueprint for action in the schools and at the same time openly states the school district's best thinking on the subject. It provides media personnel with needed information on the why, how, and for whom of selecting. For others involved in the selection process, it provides a clearer understanding of the relationship of parties as well as definitive guidelines for involvement.

Who Selects and Why

Media selection is a multi-faceted operation that should involve many people at many different levels. The pattern and process vary from school to school.

Media Professional. Responsibility for media selection and the leadership role in selection must be assumed by the individual who will ultimately be responsible for the total LMC program and budget. He is uniquely qualified by training and experience and by total involvement in the school curriculum to coordinate this program function. More than anyone else, he can balance a knowledge of school needs with a knowledge of existing media collections and the availability of media on the market. In addition to generalized skills in selection through a knowledge of bibliography, he and his staff ordinarily represent subject matter strengths in special disciplines.

A primary responsibility of the professional is to create a balance in expenditures for various subjects in various media forms. Related to this responsibility might be that of making a judgment about adding a new medium to the collection. Such judgments must weigh factors of financing, space, equipment, and projected scope and depth of collections.

A common problem concerns introducing periodicals on microfilm into the collection. Beyond a simple desire to include microfilm and a knowledge of the availability of a variety of information in that format, a decision to develop this area requires consideration of some of the following factors:

1. If storage is a main factor, how much space can be saved by converting the back issue collection? Should only recent periodicals on microfilm be purchased, or should the process begin by converting the back holdings, thereby releasing space in the stacks for more recent materials?

2. Is it possible to purchase all periodicals on microfilm, including back issues, or would the cost be prohibitive? If it is too costly, what periodicals should receive priority for purchase and how many years' worth should be provided?

3. If periodicals were formerly bound and circulated, is that procedure to continue?

4. How many and what type of storage units should be purchased? Where should they be located?

5. What equipment must be purchased for use with microfilm? Will a few inexpensive microfilm readers do the job? Are microfilm reader-printers, which have the capacity for printing out a copy of a single page, needed immediately for effective service, and how many should be purchased? Should microfiche attachments be ordered immediately?

6. Where can hardware be located in the LMC? Once a suitable location is found, is electrical wiring available or must a work order be made out for this phase of the operation?

7. How will this new medium be treated in the budget? Is the cost to be absorbed in existing allocations or will additional funds be forthcoming? Since the equipment budget is separate from the media budget, are funds available to purchase equipment? If funds must be taken from an existing allocation for equipment, what equipment items must then be deleted to make room for microfilm equipment?

Teachers. There are some obvious reasons for including teachers in the media selection process. They are generally knowledgeable about the content of their fields; they should know their students' capabilities better than LMC personnel ordinarily do; and they are primarily responsible for programing student activities in the school. Both students and teachers need to be aware of the resources available for teaching and learning. Teachers will tend to use, and assign students to use, media with which they are familiar. It seems reasonable, then, if teachers are to assume responsibility for structuring an extensive media approach to learning, that they should also share a degree of responsibility for the selection of media.

Students. Students can be involved in the selection process in a variety of ways. Since one function of the LMC program is to provide for the personal needs of students, there should be considerable student participation both through individual recommendation and through a group structure. If time permits and media are available for preview purposes, actual try-outs in a teaching-learning situation can be most helpful in making selections.

Whether or not students are actually more sophisticated today than they were in the past, the fact is that students of varying abilities are being involved in curriculum development projects in the schools. At the very least, students have the capacity to make a judgment about what is interesting and what appears to be within the range of their abilities. Some would also add that students know what is relevant to them.

Parent and Community Groups. Whether to involve parents and the community in school affairs is rarely considered a matter for debate today. Broad moves have been made in major cities to decentralize school districts in order to make boards of education more responsive to community needs. Community school advisory councils have sprung up, which have wide interests and powers. There have also been nationwide reactions of parents and communities to educational programs dealing with sex education, drug abuse, and other social concerns. It would appear that a meaningful dialogue must be created with parents and the community relative to the most precious commodity of the community—its children. Although it is not recommended here that parents select media on a continuing basis for the schools, it is suggested that parents participate in establishing the guidelines or policy for media selection in the schools. They should also participate as observers of and reactors to district and school curriculum projects.

Other Specialists. It is desirable to include in the media selection process such specialists as school administrators, district coordinators and supervisors, university and college personnel, and private citizen specialists whose experience may go somewhat beyond the ordinary. Beyond accepting their recommendations for the consideration of specific media, it would appear that their best contributions would be made in the context of curriculum development as consultants or reactors.

Organizing Personnel for Selection

The LMC staff can facilitate the evaluation-selection process by carefully structuring committee activities. They should provide selectors with information about reviewing sources, the media selection policy, criteria and procedures for evaluation, and the availability of funds for purchasing needed media. This type of information should be available in printed form. At least one in-service meeting should be devoted to clarifying roles and procedures. On a continuing basis the LMC staff should provide selection committees with an overview of various fields or areas of interest through bibliographies and other means. In many cases their recommendations, based on several standard reviews of media, will be sufficient to warrant a recommendation to purchase.

The fact remains, however, that much of the material produced is not adequately reviewed, is not reviewed at all, or is simply reviewed late. For example, typical library reviewing sources have concentrated on "trade" publications to the exclusion of the entire textbook publishing field, which each year turns out large quanitities of supplementary resources that would be suitable and desirable inclusions in the LMC collection.

In the school where space can be found to store media being considered for purchase, procedures should be established for direct shipment of media for preview purposes. This can be done item by item, as needed. Where there is a potential that large sums of money might be spent, publishers and producers are usually more than willing to direct-ship any part of their existing inventories for evaluation purposes.

In a secondary school of 1,000 pupils that has a professional LMC staff of four, each professional would be assigned to work with specific instructional departments in regard to selection and other purposes, such as curriculum development. Media selection is one facet of the job. As shown in Fig. 3-3, a reasonable structure would include selection committees of teachers based on departmental lines, with representation from the LMC staff. This would provide for both horizontal (grade level) and vertical (within the subject) considerations. Student committees would meet the LMC staff on a continuing basis. The LMC staff would have two functions: working with established teacher and student committees in evaluation, and working to gather reviewing sources and media for consideration by the selection committees. The final review of selections made by committees may be done by the LMC staff as a committee, or a formal coordinating committee may perform that vital function. The coordinating committee, through the LMC, would be responsible for advising the selection committees of purchases to be made.

The basic structural difference in an elementary school is that there would be an option to have grade level or subject area committees. Most elementary schools are still organized along traditional grade level lines. Many also have grade level chairmen or coordinators. In this case it would be advantageous to organize along

Fig. 3-3. Media Selection Structure for the Individual School

1. Secondary Schools

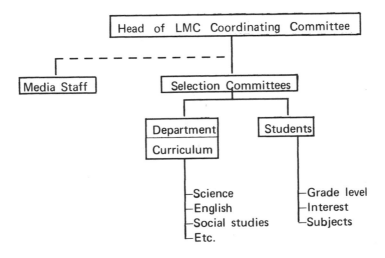

2. Elementary Schools

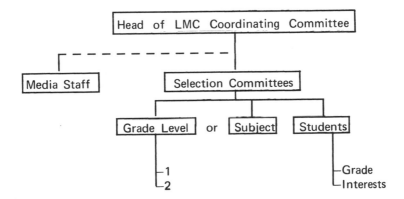

grade level lines and leave articulation vertically in the subject areas to a coordinating committee. If a non-graded program has been established for the school, it would be advisable to organize along subject area lines in a manner similar to the secondary school model. Fig. 3-4 details briefly the functions of the coordinating committee, the LMC staff, and the selection committees.

Fig. 3-4. Evaluation and Selection Process Function

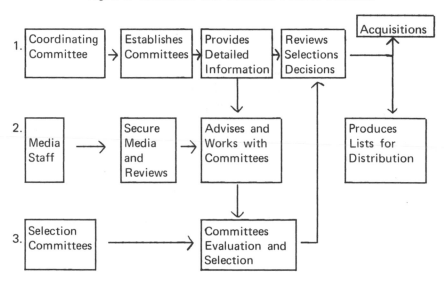

Media Selection Coordinated at the District Level

In school districts that have a system media center, one aspect of the district program may be a department devoted to the preview, evaluation, and selection of media. A highly structured program would have carefully detailed policies and procedures for selection and a firm organizational plan for committee work, culminating in the selection of a comprehensive list of media suitable for purchase in the schools. There are alternative ways of handling the interaction of committees in a school district. One pattern would provide for a district coordinating committee and two sub-committees: curriculum and general review. The curriculum and general review committees coordinate the activities of many selection committees. For school districts with a total school enrollment of up to 30,000 students, the pattern suggested in Fig. 3-5 can be satisfactory. This operation makes use of a district coordinating committee that relates directly to individual school coordinating committees. Resource specialists and community representatives are available to help with curriculum development projects. The internal committee structure operating out of individual schools provides a direct benefit to the parent school as well as a generalized benefit to the district.

Fig. 3-5. District Evaluation and Selection Process

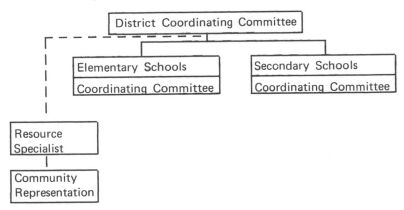

The well-organized district media center may also have a preview and evaluation center with established procedures for making available to committees the latest media from representative publishers and producers. Since few districts have the physical space available to store collections of this type for long periods of time, collections would change constantly as newer media are produced. Some of the work of evaluation and selection would be handled by committees in the district media center, while delivery service would be provided to ship media directly to the schools for evaluation purposes.

The principal objective of the evaluation and selection process at any level is, of course, to guarantee that only media that can meet the evaluative criteria of a school or district will actually be purchased. The school that operates independently in this activity may do an extremely competent job, but it will be limited by the capacity of its staff to deal with the problem. On a school district or regional basis, coverage of the media market is considerably more extensive.

Direct Evaluation of Media

The direct critical evaluation of all media considered for purchase in a school or district would be desirable. In most schools or districts, however, this is not possible. Selectors must rely heavily on reviewing tools, where available, in making their decisions.

With the theme of accountability clearly in mind, it becomes necessary to make some decisions about evaluation, selection, and actual procurement of media. Books reviewed in so-called standard selection tools—for example, the H. W. Wilson Standard Catalog series are pre-selected and are generally considered acceptable for purchase. Media that are merely listed in other guides, such as the NICEM *Index to 16mm Educational Films*, a non-evaluative guide, must either be checked against available evaluative sources or evaluated directly before purchase. Some schools or districts require three positive written reviews before purchase, others insist on direct evaluation for any medium that costs more than a fixed amount determined by the school or district. Any LMC must set up the mechanism for receiving media for evaluation and the rapid return of media to the producer upon completion of the evaluative process. Most media are also sold "on approval," thereby providing the purchaser with the option of returning media promptly.

Criteria for Selection

Criteria established for the direct evaluation of media should be compatible with the media selection policy of the district. Prior to the initiation of direct evaluation, both the policy statement and criteria should be reviewed. If the ground rules are clearly understood, evaluation and selection can proceed in an orderly fashion with a minimum loss of time.

Although one can expect to find variations in criteria when moving from one medium to another, essentially the same broad criteria can be applied to all media. Any medium that is put to the test must be subjected to scrutiny predicated on the following generally agreed-on criteria:

1. **Authenticity**: Is the medium accurate and up to date? What are the qualifications of the author or producer?

2. **Appropriateness**: Is the medium appropriate to the subject matter? Are the vocabulary, content, concepts, theme, suited to the intended audience?

3. **Content**: Does it have an organized, well-balanced presentation? Does it relate to the needs of students? Does it provide outlines, charts, graphs, etc., that will be helpful to the user?

4. **Interest**: Will the message contained in this medium hold the attention of the user? Is it stimulating? Imaginative?

5. **Technical Quality**: Is the quality of production adequate—format, audio and visual qualities, ease of handling, use of color?

Although it would be possible to develop an evaluation form for each medium to be evaluated, such an approach would soon leave one totally enveloped in paper. A variety of forms are in use today; some are extremely comprehensive (presenting more of a challenge than the actual evaluation of media), and others require only that the evaluator indicate purchase or no purchase. Somewhere between these two we can find a relatively simple multi-purpose form that provides the reviewer, who makes the ultimate decision on purchasing, with enough information to make a valid judgment. Fig. 3-6 is a generalized data-gathering tool. Forms should be accompanied by a direction sheet that includes an explanation of the criteria to be used in the evaluation process. Since the forms will become a "consideration" file, it is recommended that overall size be limited to 5 x 8 inches for filing purposes. When information is organized in this fashion, a rapid scanning

Fig. 3-6. Media Evaluation Form

Type of Media _____ Subject Area(s) _____

Author or Producer _____ Grade Range: K-3, 4-6, 7-9, 10-12

Title _____ Purchase: Yes___ No___ Hold ___

= =

Media Profile—Grade on a scale of 1 to 5. One is poor, five is excellent.

Authenticity	1	2	3	4	5
Appropriateness	1	2	3	4	5
Content	1	2	3	4	5
Technical Quality	1	2	3	4	5
Interest	1	2	3	4	5

= =

Comments—Please add on back of form.

Evaluator _____ School _____ Date _____

of the top section provides the reviewer with the most important immediate facts. For filing purposes, one may elect to file by type of media (for example, filmstrip) or by subject, or may elect to file first by medium, then by subject. A media profile is used here rather than a grading score (excellent, average, poor) because a charting scheme provides a higher visual impact on the reviewer. Comments are placed on the back of the form. Although written comments are extremely valuable to the reviewer, they have a way of crowding out other information provided.

BUILDING MEDIA COLLECTIONS

Some Basic Problems

The library media specialist must always be concerned with the needs of students and teachers in relation to existing collections and media available on the market. There is also concern when new curriculum offerings necessitate new directions in collection building. A program change in social studies at a particular grade level, for example, to include the study of Africa, usually requires a concerted effort to secure the quantity of media needed for extensive use by students and teachers, and it also requires a reallocation of funds. It may be assumed that, prior to these new directions, a small quantity of material was available merely to "cover" that area of the world.

A more serious problem arises if a comprehensive curriculum change is made that will affect all grades and all levels of instruction. An example in this case might well be a total school and district focus on environmental and ecological studies in each grade. While there might be a lack of commercially available media initially, the void is usually filled rapidly because of the publishers' alertness to the market's needs. The problem for the media professional is usually that he must spend for this single area a sum of money that is equivalent to the total budget allocation for media expenditures.

If curriculum planning were paced so that new media needs coincided with the fiscal year, an attempt could be made to request a justifiable increase in special project funds. In the absence of such funds, it appears appropriate to emphasize this area of need but practical to phase the buying over a period of time to allow also for the purchase of needed media in other areas. Media selection and acquisitions must then be carefully coordinated with teachers involved in the instructional program.

Media Collections in the New School

It is imperative that collection building for a new school be started at least a year in advance. It would also be to the advantage of teachers and students to have a minimal initial collection of at least one-third of the total potential collection for the school. While it is fairly common practice today to purchase pre-selected "opening day" collections fully processed, no generalized collection can fully suit the needs of a specific school. Each school develops a personality of its own based on the community, types of students, faculty, educational methodology, and so on. Therefore, even though a pre-selected collection may cover a broad range of topics and may be generally curriculum-oriented, this is not the way to build a media collection for a specific school and program. If one is given a "blank check" for media purchases, packaged "opening day" collections may suitably be combined with other carefully screened selections.

A pattern followed in Montgomery County, Maryland, where there is a district media system, provides for three phases in the development of collections for new schools. In the first phase, one-third of the budget is expended by the central agency for basic materials prior to the appointment of the school staff, in order to meet processing deadlines and to have materials in the LMC the first day of school. In the second phase, the next third of the budget is also expended by the central agency based on recommendations of the principal and other professional staff members directly concerned with the opening of school. In phase three, the final third of the budget is spent by the media specialist of the school in conjunction with teachers and students.[5]

The school media collection must begin with as comprehensive a reference collection as is possible with the funds available. Collection building begins with such traditional media as dictionaries, encyclopedias, almanacs, and other general purpose reference tools. The one possible exception to this guideline would be in the building of collections for K-4 elementary schools, where reference sources suited to the needs of these youngsters are less plentiful. The fact remains, however, that an LMC designed to serve both students and teachers should concentrate on reference sources first.

If funds are reasonably adequate, the selection of reference tools should be coupled with the purchase of media needed by teachers in instructional situations. Perhaps viewing these as parallel directions reflects more clearly what is intended here. Maps, globes, transparencies, and filmstrips are vital to teachers if they are to do even a minimal job of teaching. In other words, if nothing else is available, teachers can carry on a program through directed instruction. Teachers will rely on the media program only if every effort is made to satisfy their immediate needs.

Beyond these two basic areas, selection should proceed to develop collection strength in scope and depth. A focus on the curriculum should lead naturally to a concentration of effort, subject by subject, to bring together those media best suited to teaching and learning. In most subject areas, both printed and audiovisual media for individual student use are available on two or more levels of difficulty. This means that the initial purchase of reading matter about simple machines should include not merely one title but perhaps three titles, written at three levels of reading difficulty. This approach provides initially for the needs of students at three different levels of reading ability. It also allows for a natural progression in understanding on the part of students who can begin reading in books that provide information but with a minimal challenge in terms of vocabulary and comprehension, then move to more difficult work as the need arises. Coupled with this approach is a specific need for more multiple-copy purchasing than we have generally had in the school LMC. Items of proven value should be purchased in multiple copies. This is much preferred to expanding the scope of the collection by purchasing single copies of media that may or may not move from their storage areas, when at the same time there are long lists of students waiting for an important item. A rule of thumb used for reserve collections in college libraries is one copy for 15 students. It would not be unreasonable for the LMC to provide one copy of a particularly valuable or popular item for every 10 to 15 students having a need for such information.

Collection building beyond the initial stages calls for a constant assessment of student and teacher needs in relation to curriculum, existing collections, and the market availability of media. It is therefore desirable to focus on a given subject and search for those media that make a definite contribution to the area. Each medium has a unique set of attributes which determine its appropriateness to the task at hand. Committee interaction is vital if the areas selected for building and the learning activities designed are actually going to meet instructional needs.

A degree of both qualitative and quantitative control can be added to the analysis and evaluation of collections through the use of standard retrospective selection tools, such as the H. W. Wilson series, *Children's Catalog*, *Junior High School Library Catalog*, *Senior High School Library Catalog*. It would be less valid, however, to use a single tool for both collection development and quality control.

Bonn[6] cited several techniques of evaluating collections for a number of purposes. The techniques which have been applied independently or in conjunction with one or more other techniques, are as follows:

1. compiling statistics on holdings, use, expenditures;
2. checking lists, catalogs, bibliographies;
3. obtaining opinions from users;
4. examining the collection directly;
5. applying standards, using various methods above, plus testing the library's document delivery capability and noting the relative use of several libraries by a particular group.

Balance in the Collection

There are those who dismiss the concept of balance in the collection, stating that there is no such thing, and who move ahead to other considerations. Equating balance with equilibrium, however, provides a meaningful concept to deal with. It suggests that there is an equilibrium (balance) in collections, just as there is in human beings and society, even though the elements or components may not be perfectly weighted. There is, then, a state of equilibrium at any given moment. Perhaps the simplest way of stating the case is to say that a collection is in balance if it:

1. Is sufficiently broad to meet the basic informational and recreational needs of students and teachers with any medium required, and

2. Is sufficiently specific in content and media to meet the direct instructional needs of the school with due regard for the age-grade-ability levels of students.

It would be inaccurate to cite the quantitative media recommendations of the national guidelines as an example of perfect balance. One could, for example, cite specific percentages for books and filmstrips, based on these recommendations, but such percentages would probably not reflect the balance or equilibrium needed for any given school.

Inventorying and Weeding

There is a growing trend to omit the inventory from standard operating procedures in libraries and LMC's. The inventory used to be the highlight of the year. There was a total book count, lost book and reorder lists were prepared, subject strengths were analyzed, and accurate records of holdings were provided. This was often the time when collections were screened for binding and mending and when the bulk of "weeding" took place. As collections grew and the time-consuming inventory presented a major obstacle to providing service to users, alternatives were developed. Various sections of the total collection were inventoried during slow periods in order to decrease the year-end chore. The next development was to inventory only a part of the collection each year on a rotating basis. The next step was to eliminate the inventory altogether. Considering the enormity of the job in large public and academic libraries, where collections may range from 500,000 items to several million, it is obvious that the annual inventory may be impractical. Additionally, user studies in large libraries reveal that only about 20 percent of the collection represents media in movement. User studies in other libraries and LMC's may show similar results. If this is the case, then support is provided for the idea that the comprehensive inventory is not only time-consuming, but may also be a waste of time.

In the LMC where an inventory can be made in a reasonable period of time—a week or two, for example—it would be advantageous to continue the procedure. The means must be available to gather the kinds of information needed for school district reports, basic data required for budget preparation and for the evaluation and selection of media. One aspect of the media professionals' work as a subject specialist is continual evaluation of the part of the collection that is considered his specialty. If a cooperative relationship exists with departments in the school, or if the selection committee is structured along subject lines, then collection analysis and evaluation can be a fringe benefit. Attention to demand as a factor in providing needed data is essential. Demand provides information about what media are most used on a continuing basis and what kinds of media are requested for what purpose. While many think that gathering circulation statistics is a senseless and meaningless chore, an analysis of circulation records nonetheless indicates what types of media are being used.

Weeding the collection to remove outdated, unused, and worn media should be a continuing task. A rule of thumb for weeding books has been approximately five percent annually. Estimates for the replacement of audiovisual media range from 10 to 15 percent based on normal wear, accidental damage and curriculum revisions. In situations where subject specialists periodically survey the LMC's holdings, weeding should be a part of the task.

Storing Media

The concept of the LMC as a unified program implies an integrated collection of printed and audiovisual media. There is today a range of interpretations of the meaning of integrated collections. On the one hand are those who interpret this to mean merely providing access to printed and audiovisual media under one roof. Audiovisual media are housed in a separate room or area with equipment needed for use. Frequently, printed media are located through the use of a card catalog and audiovisual media are indexed in a book catalog format. The opposite interpretation of integrated collections attempts to place all media dealing with the same subject together on the shelves. In this plan, books, 8mm films, filmstrips, realia, and 16mm films are assigned to the same shelf location.

Neither of these approaches is completely satisfactory. Generally, the first approach is thought to have no philosophical merit. Operationally, however, there is a great deal of evidence in academic and public libraries that effective service to users can be provided when the collections are divided on the basis of media format. This has been one of the principal traditional methods—separate shelving for periodicals, books, microforms, records. The second approach—shelving all media together—is in tune philosophically with the concept of the unity of knowledge. Practically speaking, it is also possible to shelve selected media forms together in one order (books, 8mm films, reel-to-reel tapes). For collections that are extremely modest in size and that are not expected to grow and expand, this may be desirable. Two factors are decidedly against this approach: first, shelving a substantial collection of media takes much more space than does separate shelving of audiovisual resources, for which compact storage is available; and second, media forms are incompatible in size and shape. Until it is somehow practical to store together all media, including study prints, art prints, transparencies, audio and video cassettes, and records, a partial attempt accomplishes very little. A discussion of the storage of media will be provided in Chapter 5.

SUMMARY

+ In this work, the term media is used to encompass all printed and audiovisual forms. The technology required for using audiovisual media is treated in Chapter 5.

+ A great deal of information must be assembled prior to the selection of media: curriculum and methodology, the marketplace, technology available, budgeting procedures, and student interests and abilities.

+ A media selection policy for the school and district should be formulated by a committee consisting of media professionals, teaching staff, administration, board of education members, students, and the community.

+ Criteria for the selection of all media should be based on such qualities as authenticity, appropriateness, content, interest, and technical quality.

+ A formal committee structure should be used in the school or district for the selection of media. In the secondary school, the structure would provide for a coordinating committee and selection teams organized on a subject basis; at the elementary school level, either a grade level or a subject approach may be used.

+ Balance means an established equilibrium in the collection, not a fixed pattern. The collection should be broad enough to meet basic informational and recreational needs, and specific enough to meet instructional needs with due regard for age-grade-ability levels of students.

+ There are many ideas about the best way to store media collections. These range from a traditional pattern of providing separate quarters for various media forms to placing all media forms together on the same shelves. Neither extreme is suitable. Alternatives will be discussed in Chapter 5.

LITERATURE AND FIELD INVESTIGATIONS

1. What background information is needed for the effective selection of media? Discuss the implications of such information.

2. Prepare a bibliography of basic selection tools suitable for use in the development of a media collection for a selected school.

3. Examine media utilization practice in selected schools. Identify teacher purposes and student needs.

4. Design a media selection policy for a selected school.

5. Investigate media preview and evaluation centers to determine: clientele, policies, media, staffing, services, financing and related business processes.

6. Compare the media selection process in the school LMC to that used in academic and public libraries. Discuss similarities and differences.

NOTES

[1] Ralph Ellsworth, and Hobart Wagner, *The School Library: Facilities for Independent Study in Secondary Schools* (New York: Educational Facilities Laboratories, 1963), p. 39.

[2] *Webster's Third New International Dictionary* (Springfield, Mass.: G. Merriam Co. 1971), p. 1403.

[3] Daniel Fader, *Hooked on Books* (New York: Berkley, 1968), p. 52.

[4] *Libraries: Policies and Procedures* (Hartford, Conn.: Hartford Public Schools, 1967), p. 3200.2.

[5] Frances Dean, "Design of Initial Media Collections for New Facilities," *School Media Quarterly* 2:234-236 (Spring 1974).

[6] George Bonn, "Evaluation of the Collection," *Library Trends* 22:265-304 (January 1974).

REFERENCES

Allen, Kenneth, and Loren Allen. *Organization and Administration of the Learning Resources Center in the Community College*. Hamden, Conn.: Shoe String Press, 1973.

Bonn, George. "Evaluation of the Collection," *Library Trends* 22:265-304 (January 1974).

Carter, Mary, and Wallace Bonk. *Building Library Collections*. Metuchen, N.J.: Scarecrow, 1974.

Cohen, David. *Multi-Ethnic Media: Selected Bibliographies in Print*. Chicago: American Library Association, 1975.

Dean, Frances. "Design of Initial Media Collections for New Facilities," *School Media Quarterly* 2:234-236 (Spring 1974).

Fader, Daniel. *Hooked on Books*. New York: Berkely, 1968.

Gillespie, John, and Diana Spirt. *Creating a School Media Program*. New York: Bowker, 1973.

Hansel, Evelyn, and Peter Veilette. *Purchasing Library Materials in Public and School Libraries*. Chicago: American Library Association, 1969.

Johnson, Jenny. "Appraisal of Educational Materials for AVLINE," *Audiovisual Instruction* 21:22-27 (January 1976).

Lyle, Guy. *The Administration of the College Library*. New York: H. W. Wilson, 1974.

Rogers, Rutherford, and David Weber. *University Library Administration*. New York: H. W. Wilson, 1971.

Rowell, John, and M. Ann Heidbreder. *Educational Media Selection Centers*. Chicago, American Library Association, 1971.

4

LMC FACILITIES

OBJECTIVES

Describe major alternatives in the design of facilities for the school LMC.

Write educational specifications for LMC facilities in a selected school.

FACTORS IN PLANNING

Two factors are at work in the planning and construction of a new school. The first is that the school must be compatible to a large degree with the external and internal organization of existing schools in the district. This is usually deemed essential because of general community sentiment and typical management practices in the district. The second is that educational planners and architects must build with an eye for the future. Flexibility of design is imperative, so that present and potential innovations can be incorporated. The planning and construction reflect a compromise of ideals and ideas, and it is within the context of this atmosphere that the LMC is developed.

Rationale for Space

An attempt to plan the LMC so as to create effective patterns of use by the media staff, teaching staff, and students requires considerable effort. More is involved than simply transplanting national guidelines to the school planning situation. Many questions must be answered before the architect can move ahead with his work, and these questions can be answered only if the library media specialist is involved in total school planning and in writing educational specifications as they relate to the total school concept. In this day of rapid change and innovative educational development, it is advisable not to have a fixed, single concept about the form of the LMC before involvement with other school personnel and their ideas. Rigid thinking and the rejection of other ideas will limit the library media specialist's involvement and his opportunity for leadership. A person with a "one-track-mind" working in an educational situation will probably find that he is either excluded from further participation in planning or that he is playing a minimal role.

Besides a knowledge of educational philosophy, of the external and internal organization of the school, and of the relationship of the LMC to other areas of the school, other factors pertain to organizing the spaces needed to operate a program effectively. Some questions to be answered are:

—   What numbers and type of staff will be available to operate this program?

—   What hours will the facility be open for use?

—   What spaces are required?

—   How will spaces be used?

—   What media will be included in the collection?

—   How will media be organized for use?

—   What specialized equipment will be required?

—   What areas are to be shared by students and teachers?

—   What areas are reserved for the exclusive use of teachers and/or students?

—   How should spaces relate to each other?

—   How should each space be programed for use?

The national guidelines which appear to have their greatest impact on the design of facilities in new schools, state what "should be" in schools. The same quantitative standard is applied to schools at any level, elementary through secondary. The one qualifying factor, often overlooked in the quest for guidance in planning, is that the guidelines are directed to the LMC *as it should be* in the context of the school *as it should be*. In other words, the guidelines make an assumption about educational programing—that the internal organization of the school has been structured to incorporate the ultimate in teaching and learning conditions.

A brief outline of what must be done in planning a new facility is presented here. The architect selected to plan a school usually discusses the concept "form follows function." In other words, he intends to base his plans for the physical structure on the building's function as detailed by educators. School districts may have a special planning team of their own to do preliminary work concerning size of building, general configuration, and cost estimates. This might also be the task of educational or architectural consultants, who work with school people to get the job done. In most school districts, teachers and other professionals participate in the development of educational specifications for a new school. The term "educational specifications" is synonymous with "building program," a term used in other fields. Planning a new school facility means planning for the future. Every effort should be made to provide for changing concepts in education.

Library Media Specialist's Function

While it is unlikely that the library media specialist can know all there is to know about facilities planning, he must at least know what his role is in the planning of a facility. He must be familiar with the fields of education and library media service if he is to perform his function with distinction. If the media specialist can do this, the architect can creatively translate his ideas into action.

What is the function of the library media specialist in facilities planning? He should be a part of the planning process from its inception. His responsibility is to coordinate all media and communications systems throughout the school, including language laboratories, multi-media instructional installations, auditoriums, public address systems, and so on. Focusing specifically on the writing of specifications for the LMC, the planner looks first to the objectives, policy, and program that make up the school's philosophy. Without this information, no adequate media program can be formulated. The library media specialist who knows curriculum and is able to make a contribution at this point can help to set the direction for educational programing in the school for many years.

Educational specifications for the LMC, then, are compatible with the total school program being developed. Specific areas to be considered are as follows:

1. Introductory matter:

    a. A statement of the philosophy and objectives of the library media center as it relates to education in the school.

    b. A statement defining the LMC's orientation to the entire educational plant, whether it is one building or several.

    c. A statement providing general directions relating to all areas. One might mention here requirements such as carpeting, ventilation, the need to provide flexibility of space, and conduit or raceway for future electrical or electronic inputs.

2. Definition of each space required: At this point, national, state, and local standards or recommendations will be of value. The guidance provided by regional accrediting groups will also be helpful, as will authoritative literature. For *each* space the following information is needed:

    a. Name of the space

    b. Size of the space

    c. Type and number of occupants of space

    d. A description of the function of the space. This will include:

    — relationship to other spaces in the LMC

    — activities anticipated for the space

    — any special considerations such as the environment or atmosphere intended

    — problems (such as security, and the need for special locks)

3. Built-in equipment: This is a separate list of what is required for each space, such as clocks, cabinets, shelving, and sinks. These items are usually part of construction costs and are handled by the building contractor.

4. Furnishings and equipment: The selection and purchase of furnishings and equipment may be included in an architect's contract for an additional sum, or may be a responsibility assumed by the educational staff of the district. No matter how the question is handled, the library media specialist should prepare a separate list of movable furniture, such as desks, carrels and audiovisual equipment.

5. Personnel requirements: A separate list of staff requirements will be prepared as a part of the total package of information prepared for the new school.

The Architect

The architect selected either will have had experience in school building design or will have educational consultants available to him. The architect does not simply sit back and translate the planners' ideas into form. Frequently the educational concepts incorporated in the new school actually come from the architect, because his experience in the field gives him a broad picture of a building's potential. This can be a benefit to unimaginative educators or it can be a serious detriment, depending on the architect. Educational facilities planners must be aware of existing and projected innovations in education and must be ready to listen to new ideas and to manipulate them to fit the situation.

The architect[1] assists in the development of the building project in three essential stages—decision, design, and delivery. In the decision stage, he may participate in feasibility studies, financial analysis, programing, and research required as preliminary work. The design stage calls for planning and developing all of the project details and the preparation of construction documents. The delivery stage calls for the administration of the construction contract and may call for management of the actual construction project and services related to furnishing the building.

The basic services provided by the architect are as follows:

Schematic Design Phase. Through conferences with various school personnel, the architect studies and analyzes the educators' requirements. He then prepares schematic design studies; these are drawings and other documents that illustrate his initial efforts to translate the educational requirements. The architect also provides as much information as possible about construction and materials. After the educators have reviewed this phase and approved the work, and the architect has submitted a statement of probable construction costs, this phase is considered complete.

Design Development Phase. This phase provides for the refinement of schematic design studies. The architect prepares more detailed drawings and provides data about the appearance of the structure, electrical and mechanical systems to be used, the types of materials to be used, and a more refined statement of construction costs. Again, review and approval by educators is required before the architect moves on to the next phase.

Construction Documents Phase. In this phase the architect prepares working drawings and specifications based on the design documents that have been approved. The work to be done is described in technical language: the materials and equipment; type of workmanship required; structural, mechanical and electrical work; site work; and special equipment requirements. This is also the phase in which the architect assists in the preparation of bidding information, proposal and contract forms, and so on. At this point any additional adjustments to probable construction costs will also be made.

Bidding or Negotiation Phase. The architect provides the educators with advice and assistance in obtaining bids or negotiated proposals and in awarding the construction contracts.

Construction Phase. The architect administers the construction contract by:

— preparing needed supplementary drawings

— reviewing the construction schedule, materials, samples, and so on

— periodic visits to the site to review progress and see that work is proceeding according to the contract

— issuing certificates of payment for the contractor

— preparing change orders in work approved by the educator

— determining the date of project completion, providing the educator with the written guarantees prepared by the contractor, and issuing a final certificate of payment to contractors

Alternatives in Facilities Organization

The typical, traditional, and most common organizational pattern for physical facilities has been the single, centralized library media facility. In the past, the school library has almost invariably suffered from three basic faults: First, it has had perimeter shelving to house collections, with seating in the center of the room; this creates distractions for users. Second, the circulation desk has often been located on one side of the reading room, which leads to considerable noise and confusion in the LMC. Third, students have had to walk through seating arrangements or completely around seating to reach media. These very real problems add to the general inadequacies found in media, personnel, facilities, and budgets.

What are the major alternative organizational patterns for library media facilities? Let us first consider the fact that there is a great deal of physical difference between a self-contained library media facility and one that is a part of an academic building. The self-contained facility usually offers the educational planner and the architect broader opportunities for design. The facility that is developed within the physical structure of the school starts with many design problems simply because it must fit, like a jig-saw puzzle piece, into the total school.

Among alternative patterns of organization in use today are the following:

1. **School as an LMC Concept**. The optimum organization of a library or LMC has long been conceived of as a totally integrated exchange: the LMC as a school—the school as an LMC. Although this concept is never fully translated operationally in terms of using media for learning, physically the translation has been made. The trend toward the learning center or multi-instructional area concept in elementary school design has been responsible for a pattern that includes open space instead of traditional classrooms that accommodate 25 students each, team teaching and flexible grouping for instruction, and media integrated totally into the teaching-learning space. Fig. 4-1 is a generalized representation of the pattern intended. An elementary school with an open interior design provides space for three major areas: primary grades, intermediate grades, and media resources. Although the figure shows a rectangular shape, squares, circles, octagons, and other forms are also used. The concept is intended to provide total flexibility of space, personnel, and media.

Fig. 4-1. School as an LMC Concept

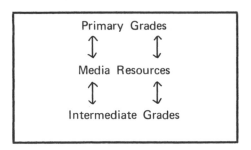

2. **A centralized media system**. Usually, centralization of an LMC program means physically combining the system elements that are most compatible and interrelated from a service point of view either in one area of a school building or in one part of a campus. A pure or absolute translation of the media system concept on a centralized basis would physically relate language laboratories, multi-media instructional facilities, and the LMC in one defined geographic area. The instructional direction of the school would be based on a high orientation to this

centralized learning core. Other spaces, commonly referred to as teaching stations, would be distributed geographically and would provide for other forms of teacher-student interaction.

A less absolute but more common interpretation of centralization merely dictates the physical unification of traditional library/audiovisual elements in the facility called an LMC. The organizational pattern arranges basic services functionally, providing space for reference services and distributing other media by form (books, periodicals, filmstrips, etc.). Ordinarily, planners of facilities are cautioned to limit seating in general use areas to no more than 100 in one space. This means simply that if a facility is to seat 150 users, it should be organized into at least two distinct supervisory areas. Actually, evidence and experience provide us with a better gauge of the number of students to be accommodated in a single area. A maximum of 50 students is recommended; 20 to 30 would be even more desirable. Fig. 4-2 provides a generalized view of a typical centralized LMC.

Fig. 4-2. A Centralized LMC

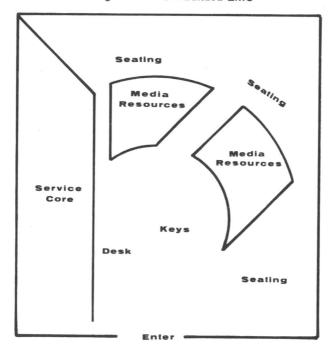

3. **Centralized divisional or resource center schemes**. Divisional and resource center schemes are principal variations in large centralized school LMC facilities. They provide ways to handle large numbers of students and also to concentrate space, media, and personnel on a single subject or related group of subjects studied in the school. Using one of these approaches provides some flexibility in the types of media housed in a specialized collection.

The division collection has been used with varying degrees of success in colleges and public libraries. Collections may be limited to books or may encompass other printed and audiovisual forms as well. Decisions about using this approach may be made arbitrarily by the media staff, with due recognition of the interrelationship of media housed together and student-faculty needs, or it may be the result of a compromise with administration and teaching staff in establishing priorities. The more common approach is to group two or more subject disciplines, such as math and science, languages, and social sciences, into divisions. The allocation of space to the various divisions is usually arbitrary, and divisions are separated by double-faced shelving or other types of readily movable dividers rather than by permanent walls. Space allocations for the divisions will ultimately be governed by an evaluation of space requirements based on the quantity and types of media housed in a division, in addition to actual use by students and teachers; sometimes a reorganization of the divisional structure will be called for.

Fig. 4-3. Centralized Divisional and Resource Center Schemes

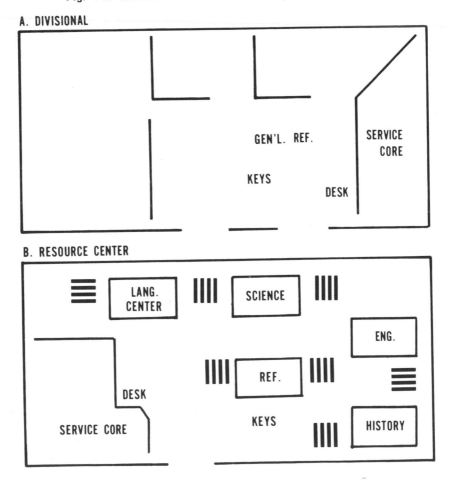

The "resource centers" approach differs slightly from the divisional approach. It refers to carving seating space out of a standard arrangement of shelving for media. For example, a resource center in science would mean providing seating for 25 to 30 students among the 500—600 range of the Dewey classification; an English resource center, among the 800s, and so on. This is a simple, effective technique for patterning seating in a large facility. Fig. 4-3 depicts these two alternatives in a generalized scheme.

4. **Decentralized LMC Facilities.** There has been a trend in recent years to decentralize the physical space and service program of the school LMC. Although this seems to be rational and within the concept of a media system, the pattern has resulted in some confusion and conflict of purpose, since many view the space and services split under this arrangement as essentially related and not to be thought of as separate entities. A decentralized LMC would have a modest central facility or service core, with satellites (which are also called centers, departmental resource centers, or learning centers). The satellites may house general collections selected to serve the needs of a particular grade level or they may be subject-oriented, in much the same manner as the divisional or resource center plans considered above. The pattern has received its greatest promotion at the secondary level, under the strong influence of the professional educator rather than media personnel. In fact, decentralized centers may not even be a part of a service system coordinated with the LMC.

Usually decentralized facilities are seen in senior high school facilities and, to a lesser degree, in intermediate or middle schools, which may house any grade combination from five to eight. The philosophy behind the pattern, however, arose from the idea of a classroom collection of printed and audiovisual media at the teachers' fingertips. This "fingertip" principle is difficult to overturn; only rarely does the alternative concept of "sharing resources" succeed in replacing it. At the secondary level, where many teachers do not have a permanent room as a base, the departmental office has provided the requisite fingertip control. It is a logical progression from the classroom, to the departmental office, to the departmental resource center. If teachers of the same subject are physically concentrated in specific areas (often located a fair distance from an existing LMC), an understandable interest in a center to serve the department is generated. This interest is even stronger if the media system operating in the school is inadequate; conditions become ripe for change.

Whether to provide centralized or decentralized facilities for student and teacher utilization of media and services is an important consideration today. For decentralized facilities, the existing patterns of organization and control are:

1. A resource center fully supported and operated by a specific department in the school. Total responsibility is in the hands of the department chairman.

2. A resource center supported and operated jointly by a given department and LMC. Each has clearly defined responsibilities for programing.

3. A resource center supported and operated by the LMC as a media system component.

Fig. 4-4. Decentralized Facilities

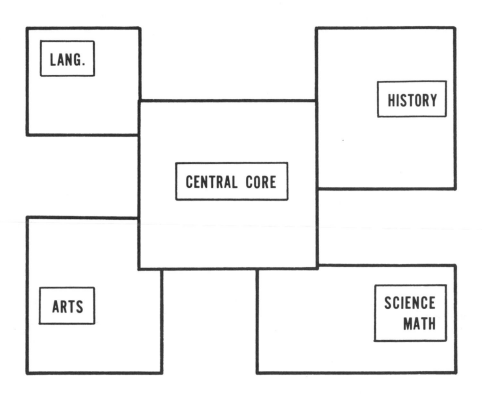

What are the advantages and disadvantages of decentralized LMC facilities? Ahlers and Sypert[2] cited some of the advantages and disadvantages of decentralization when the satellites are a part of the media system.

Advantages cited:

1. Access to materials is faster and easier from the teaching areas and study centers.

2. The librarian is responsible for the auxiliary resource center, serves fewer teachers and students, and gets to know them better.

3. The librarian may easily visit classrooms and become identified with the faculty of the subject or grade level that is his special responsibility.

4. It is sometimes easier to add auxiliary resources than to expand existing library facilities.

5. Auxiliary resource centers may become independent study centers or the major part of such centers.

6. More space dispersed throughout the school encourages independent study and use of materials.

7. Professional librarians can be assigned according to their competency in specific subjects or areas of work.

8. Auxiliary resource centers provide the flexibility of access needed for team teaching, ungraded groups, and large schools' enrollments and physical facilities.

Disadvantages cited:

1. A larger budget for duplication of material is needed, since most materials in the auxiliary resource centers should also be provided in the central library and possibly in more than one auxiliary center.

2. More professional and clerical library personnel are needed to staff each center.

3. Problems in cataloging, since the user should be helped to find which materials are in that particular resource center, which are in other auxiliary centers, and which are in the central library only. Each auxiliary resource center must have a catalog and the center library's catalog must indicate locations of all materials.

4. Dispersing materials tends to fragment knowledge and limit the user of a subject center in his search for information.

5. Breadth of opportunity for browsing may be curtailed for the user who visits only one resource center.

Location of the LMC

Consideration of the centralized facility can give one a better understanding of the relationship of the LMC to the remainder of the school. Centralization in this context has been defined as the organization of the LMC facility and program in one defined area. The centralized facility may occupy one or more floors of a building, but the parts of the facility will be physically connected.

It is usually recommended that the LMC facility be located in an area of the school or campus directly related to instructional areas. The private residential school should choose a site orientation on campus that relates to both academic facilities and student residences, thus splitting the travel distance for users. A major issue in the location of the LMC in any school will be the time and distance one must travel to use the facilities. For some, this factor overshadows any other consideration, so it is highly desirable to make the LMC as accessible as possible. If the centralized facility is to be an integral part of the school, it is recommended that the facility be near major academic areas; also, it should be located on the main floor relating to the main entrance to the school. Attempting to do both of these things may be contradictory. If the LMC is to be used after school hours, then provision must be made for direct access to the media facility while the remainder of the school is closed to the public. Direct access does not necessarily mean first floor. The main problem with trying to get a "first floor front" location is that many other school departments seek the same space. The school business office, health suite, guidance suite, auditorium, and gymnasium all might choose the same location. Since the principal concern is access to the LMC after school hours, an architect can meet the requirement in several ways. For example, if the LMC is located on a second floor of an academic building, a direct-access staircase can lead to the facility or a lobby at the main level can route users of the building to various locations, including the LMC.

It is usually recommended that the LMC not be located in proximity to playgrounds, a gymnasium, music areas, shops, of other areas that might generate a great deal of noise. This obviously limits possible locations. It would be a pleasure to be able to say that location does not matter if the LMC plays a vital role in instruction; but this is unfortunately not the case at all.

Provision should be made during the planning stages for expansion of the facility. Various options are possible during this time, such as expanding within the school building by adding spaces initially programed for other purposes. In order to allow for potential expansion, the facility should not be bounded by corridors which, because of fire or other regulations, could not be used for expansion. Other problem areas could be stairwells, heating plants, or other permanent obstacles. Whether the philosophy of the school will permit expansion of the facility at a later time is immaterial at the planning stage; providing the conditions for future expansion is important.

Relating Space to Program

One way to study the various spaces needed in an LMC is to categorize them into the system structure already discussed in Chapter 1. Decide which spaces are provided essentially for support functions and which are necessary to primary functions. If the intent and purpose of each of the functional spaces is known, a simple classification scheme can provide for two basic areas based on support and primary use. Fig. 4-5 provides an adaption the space program recommended in the guidelines.[3] In cases where square footage was cited as a range of figures (for example, Workroom—300-400 square feet), the largest figure has been used here. Note that support space amounts to 41 percent of the grand total.

It is true that the role of media specialists in the planning of a new facility or a renovation is not to develop plans. However, it is helpful to test out visually the relationships required in planning. It can be helpful to cut out squares, ellipses, or other shapes, to label them and move them around on a board simply to test out relationships based on the functional requirements of the media system. Using the basic support and primary spaces provided, one can begin to test out the relationships between individual spaces.

Fig. 4-5. Space Allotments, School of 1,000 Students

Support Space	Sq. Ft.	Primary Space	Sq. Ft.
Entrance, circulation and distribution	800	General function space: reading and browsing, individual viewing and listening, individual study and learning, storytelling, information services (15% @ 40 sq. ft. per student)	6,000
Administration: 4 @ 150 sq. ft.	600		
Work space	400		
Maintenance and repair	200		
Stacks	400	Conference rooms (3 @ 150 sq. ft. each)	450
Magazines and Newspapers	400	Small group viewing and listening	150
Equipment distribution and storage	400	Group projects and instruction in research	1,200
Television			
Studio 40' x 40'	1,600	Media production laboratory	800
Storage	800		
Office with workspace	150	Dark room	200
Radio 20' x 25'	500	Center for professional materials for faculty	600
Storage and control center for remote access (est.)	1,000	Computerized learning laboratory	1,000
Total Support Space	7,250	Total Primary Space	10,400

Grand Total: 17,650 square feet

Fig. 4-6 shows one way of relating the types of spaces required for the LMC. The LMC is first broken down into its smallest functional components, then restructured to form a composite picture. In this illustration the smallest functional space is called a unit. Two or more related units are then merged to form a cluster of related functional units. Two or more clusters are merged to form either the support or the primary space program. The LMC is a composite of related support and primary space. This pattern does not imply that it is possible then to separate physically the two types of spaces defined (for example, one cannot assign all of the primary space to one floor and all support space to another floor). Support spaces are what the term implies. They support the primary space program where the principal activities of users are carried on.

Fig. 4-6. Relationship of Spaces

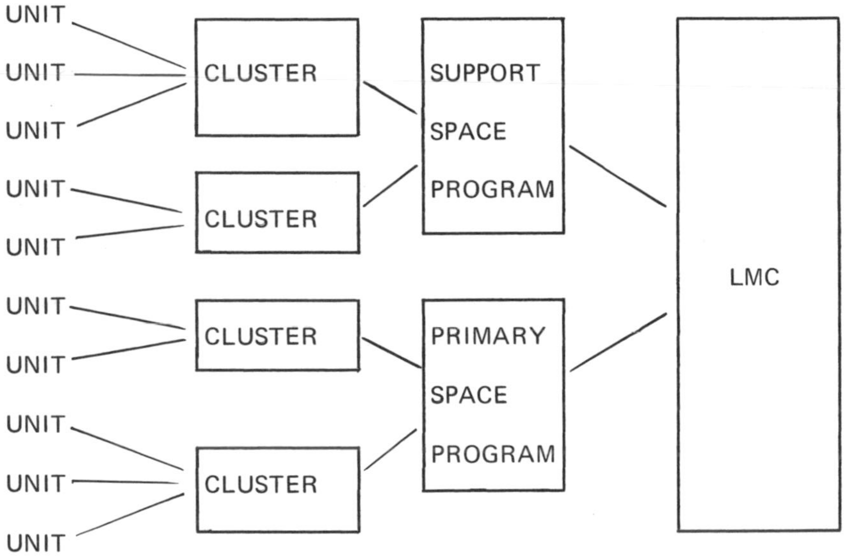

Flexibility

"Flexible" is defined by Webster's Third as "characterized by ready capability for modification or change, by plasticity, pliancy, variability, and often by consequent adaptability to next situation."[4] It is a term that has been used in educational circles in reaction against the former rigidity of space, curriculum, and personnel. It is a key concept in educational facilities planning. It is used, used, and overused. Gross said, "There is some truth to this criticism: flexibility is a high abstraction and only gets its meaning when broken down into specific requirements to fit particular cases."[5] He cited architect William Caudill, who abandoned the term in favor of words with a high degree of specificity: expansible space, which can allow for ordered growth; convertible space, which can be economically adapted to program changes; versatile space, which serves many functions; and malleable space, which can be changed at once and at will.

Although these terms are highly applicable to the entire school, they are particularly appropriate to a discussion of space requirements for a library media center. Terms may be used in various combinations. For example, when considering the need for a facility that can be enlarged as teaching-learning concepts change and as media collections threaten to take over all available floor space, the concept of expansible space focuses the attention of planners more directly on the need to build a facility that by its very nature will grow in size and change in form. One may think of expansible space in two ways; the first is simply a "pushing out walls" idea of getting additional room when needed, the second is to think in terms of expansible and convertible space in tandem. This second approach recognizes the fact that change and innovation can be applied to a facet of a media operation that requires additional space, while another related aspect of the media program is reduced. In creating a new equilibrium, one expands where needed by taking advantage of the concept of convertible space, which implies that because of the use of non-load-bearing walls, it is economically feasible to expand one area and reduce the size of its adjacent area.

School LMC's today are developing what Caudill refers to as versatile space. Most general use space is versatile and can serve many functions simultaneously. In a single area one might see students and teachers reading, viewing, listening, writing, and discussing. Also, use might be made of paper, pencil, and book while random-access audiovideo systems and computer-assisted instruction might be "happening" at the same time, in essentially the same space. To a considerable degree this is possible, and it is a practical solution to the space utilization problem in schools. If space is at a premium, the pattern of assigning specific functions to individual spaces can leave one area unused for extended periods of time while other areas are overcrowded.

The concept of malleable space—that is, space that can be changed at once and at will—while compatible to a degree with the concept of versatility, implies the ability to convert to a totally different pattern of use. For example, adjacent conference rooms that seat six to eight people can become a seminar room seating 16 if a folding partition is moved. The same space, if conditions are properly prepared, can also become a facility for group viewing of television.

Perhaps the term flexibility is the one that will continue to be used successfully in programing educational facilities. Supplying enough descriptive information to make "flexible" meaningful to the reader does not limit the term unnecessarily.

CENTRALIZED FACILITIES

The centralized facility is treated in detail here because it remains the most common way to organize the LMC system. The decentralized and open space plan are treated as extensions of, or deviations from, the centralized approach. As noted, there are two types of space—primary and support.

Primary Space

The total space provided for primary program functions consist of a group of discrete units that can be combined and programed as functional clusters of related service spaces. Fig. 4-7 illustrates a patterning or relationship of the various primary system components, showing six clusters that contain related functional units.

Fig. 4-7. Primary Space Structure

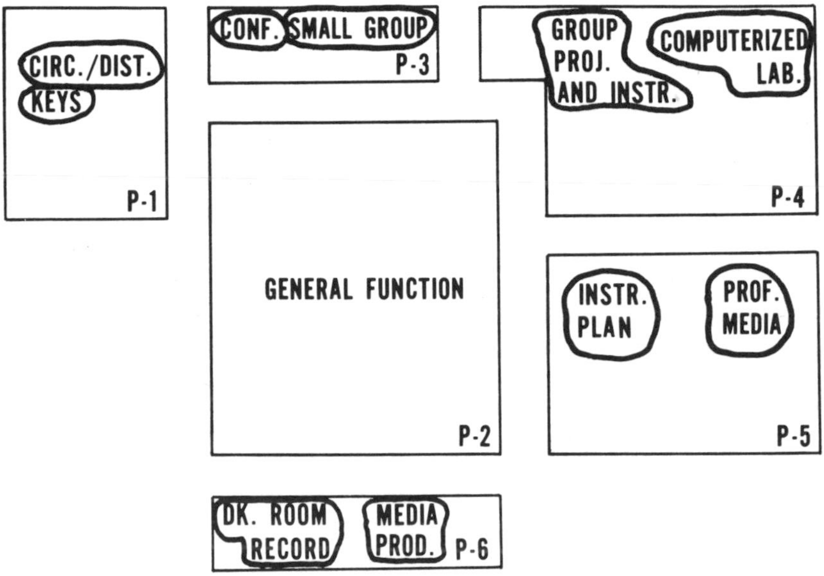

Cluster 1 contains a circulation/distribution unit and a keys unit; these provide a transition to the important business to be conducted by students and teachers in the LMC. The two provide basic information about the location and use of media and about all LMC services.

The circulation/distribution unit may serve as a general security checkpoint. Its major functions include circulating and distributing all media to be used anywhere in the school or community, booking audiovisual equipment for use at various teaching stations (this equipment to be stored elsewhere), distributing portable equipment to be used by students and teachers in the LMC, and handling the reserve media collection.

The keys unit provides two types of informational sources. The card catalog provides information about what is in this LMC collection (an alternative to the card catalog is a printed book catalog). The second part of the keys unit consists of bibliographies that are used as guides to information which exists in the media universe. Obviously, the larger the LMC, the more comprehensive this collection will be. The cluster should be situated so that users who do not have business to conduct at the keys unit can pass by it easily.

Cluster 2 is referred to as a general function area. It should be large enough to accommodate a minimum of 15 percent of the student population at one time. If the school has a high orientation toward the extensive use of media, independent study, and flexibility of scheduling, then it would not be unrealistic to expect the general function area to accommodate as much as 75 percent of the student population. Many unit possibilities exist, and they have been experimented with in school, public, and academic libraries. The idea of storing all media and all activities in one room, assigning resources to perimeter shelving and providing seating for users in the center of the room at six-position rectangular tables, has now passed into oblivion.

Factors that govern specific unit development in individual schools include media storage requirements, media personnel, and student and teacher needs programed for the LMC. The general function area is probably the most critical in the entire LMC operation. Options available for the organization of units in this cluster were defined earlier.

Cluster 3 contains two types of spaces suggested in the national standards: conference rooms, and a small group space for viewing and listening. Unit functions imply a degree of group interaction among students, between students and teachers, among teachers, and among media personnel and these groups. In addition to the free flow of ideas, this concept anticipates the free movement of bodies in a variety of activities. This is an extremely important cluster, one that is rarely provided for adequately. Each conference room should allow for multi-purpose activities, including group discussion, project development, listening, and viewing. Users should not have to move through the general function areas of the LMC to get to this cluster, though it should be situated conveniently to the general function areas. Conference rooms should be grouped in units of two, with movable partitions so that the space can also be used for seminar groups, group viewing, and so on. Another desirable grouping would be four conference rooms that could be used independently, as a large group space, or as any intermediate combination. It is not always possible to arrange for exactly the combination wanted, sometimes due to community fire regulations. In these cases, the term "flexibility" means using options within the conference rooms. Sound-proofed rooms, clearly defined by fixed floor-to-ceiling walls, are required. It should be possible to remove these walls with a minimum of cost and disruption of program if required.

Cluster 4 includes two learning centers, each of which is equivalent in size to a standard classroom in a modern elementary school. Though in practice the units—one for group projects and instruction in research and one for a computerized learning laboratory—represent different use requirements, they are compatible. If we can assume that the space for group projects is one in which classes of students meet to "kick off" individual and group learning projects under the direction of library media specialists and teachers, it is reasonable to assume also that students will be channeled to other learning spaces, such as the computerized laboratory, general function areas, and so on. This unit may actually take two forms: the first as an area in which students may receive formal instruction and also relate to each other and to media organized here temporarily, while the other provides for formal multi-media presentations relating to LMC utilization and/or the specific learning needs of the students. Adopting this latter function for the space would depend in large part on the number and size of multi-media lecture spaces provided throughout the school.

The computerized laboratory envisioned would provide audio-video programing for several different areas of study at the same time. The optimum situation would find teachers creating programs for the system and integrating these programs with independent study aspects of learning. If the LMC is integrated with academic areas of the school, it would be desirable to provide direct access to this cluster from a corridor. In any event, access should be provided so that class groups need not use the general function area as a corridor.

Cluster 5 is composed of two units: professional materials for faculty, and an instructional planning unit. Functions can be mixed or clearly distinguished. The professional media unit would relate to professional collections housed in a system media center. If no central collection exists, the school collection will be larger and more generalized. In any case, media relating to teaching, including periodicals and curriculum guides, would be housed here for teacher use. It would be a place where teachers could relax, catch up on professional work, or meet with teachers from other areas.

On the other hand, an instructional planning unit would be designed to accommodate teaching teams and would be organized around the types of furniture and equipment needed to plan instruction on a day-to-day basis. Long-term planning would also be accomplished here through the preview and evaluation of media related to instruction. This unit could also provide facilities for the design of new media forms.

The last primary space considered here (Cluster 6) should be planned to accommodate both creative and routine activities related to designing and producing new media and to modifying existing media for use in a learning situation. This cluster would include a general production unit and a more specialized unit with a darkroom and recording facilities. A few qualifying comments are needed about the best use of this cluster, since media production is assuming new proportions in school LMC programing. The extent of services offered by the district in a system media center must be considered. Ordinarily, graphics work is one of the first services provided by a district center. If service beyond that offered at the district level is needed, or if this service is not provided at the district level, then a full program of services should be offered at the school level, including typing and duplicating services. Another consideration is the need for darkroom facilities. Generally, film development is handled through a commercial photographic company, even in system media centers for school districts with as many as 50,000 students. If the school photography club needs darkroom facilities, the LMC may be the place for it. If photography is a part of a school graphics arts program or some other program, then sharing facilities might be more practical than duplicating them.

In some schools, students as well as faculty need access to media production facilities. The question is whether students and teachers can use common production facilities or whether separate work areas are needed. If teachers wish to smoke and/or discuss professional business in this environment, they may prefer not to have students in the area. An instructional planning unit for faculty could alleviate problems of this type. Teacher use of the media production unit would then be limited to actual production time, while consultation with media personnel would be carried on in the instructional planning unit. An alternative plan might also provide separate planning spaces in the production unit, with joint use of production equipment. Schools that foster an informal relationship between teachers and students will feel no pressure in this case.

Support Space

The various types of space needed to support primary functions of the LMC program can readily be grouped into clusters of related service units. Fig. 4-8 details the types of support space needed in the LMC and the possible relationship of service clusters.

Fig. 4-8. Support Space Structure

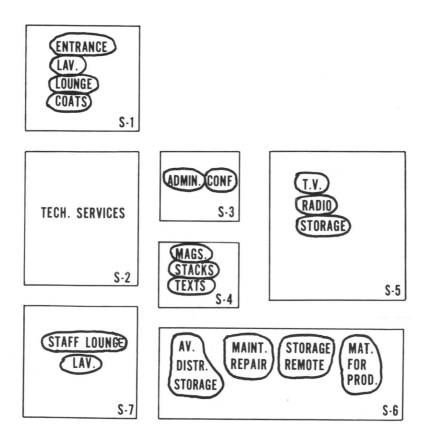

Cluster 1 should contain an entrance lobby and may also contain lavatories, coatrooms, and a student lounge. A centralized LMC that is physically separated from other teaching-learning areas in the school should provide a main entrance that relates externally to high density traffic areas of the school or campus, so long as the complications of potential noise and activity do not preclude such a location. This entrance should be the primary point of ingress and egress, providing a transition point that gives students time to acclimate themselves to a new set of conditions. Exhibits and displays can be provided at this point in wall-mounted or free-standing cases; through tackboards of various sizes and shapes, including floor-to-ceiling tackboard for one or more areas; or by means of various free-standing panel display units. In campus-type schools, public lavatories should be available.

Although coatrooms are apparently being phased out of library media facilities at all levels, the fact remains that students who intend to spend several hours working in and moving about an LMC would appreciate having a place to store coats and books. An area of student lockers could be provided, each of which would have a shelf for books and hooks for coats. Locks could be obtained at a circulation desk, so that security would not be the responsibility of the media center staff. (Twenty such units would occupy only 20 linear feet of space, two feet deep.)

Cluster 1 also provides for the comfort of users by having a lounge unit. The size and actual function of this space must be determined through an evaluation of need. The lounge usually provides casual seating, low tables, lamps, and so on. The furniture groupings serve to structure discussion areas within the unit. This would also be considered a minimal security area. Sometimes the unit serves a dual function; the space is used for a non-circulating collection of media or as a non-circulating reserve collection. In such cases, security is provided either directly or by forcing access through a check-point adjacent to the circulation unit.

If the LMC is integrated in an academic building, then lavatories, coatrooms, and lounge areas may well be omitted, assuming that reasonable proximity to comfort units outside the LMC is available. The security factor is an individual school problem, so the design of the cluster should provide options as to whether the formal supervision of this area is rigid or flexible.

Cluster 2 incorporates the basic technical services units required to acquire media and equipment for the LMC, to provide necessary processing services, and to move media and equipment out for circulation and distribution. Organization of the units should reflect the flow of media through the cluster. Since this is a prime receiving area for media and equipment, it should have direct access to a corridor and to an elevator, if the LMC does not have a first-floor location. The school LMC that occupies a building of its own provides direct access to the outdoors through this cluster.

Cluster 3 houses administrative space for staff and, in larger facilities, conference and secretarial space. There is some difference of opinion about quarters for administrative functions. The guidelines recommend some 600 square feet of administrative space for an LMC in a school of 1,000. Some argue, however, that 150 square feet per professional is an excessive amount, and some point out that not every professional needs office space. The rationale for assigning administrative space is to provide a fixed location for the professional who spends part of his day selecting media; meeting with sales representatives, members of the teaching staff, and students; and working on other administrative tasks related to the center. Considering that some LMC's have an extended-hours program and are open perhaps six days a week and until 9:00 or 10:00 each evening, this space becomes vital. An alternative to providing an administrative unit that houses four professionals is to distribute the administrative space throughout the primary structure, such as an office at the keys unit and/or circulation unit; or offices relating to specific professional work stations in the general function cluster. If the distribution does not in fact reduce the total usable space for general function programing, this pattern is most desirable. Where maximum "flexibility" is required in the general function cluster, office space can be provided by using movable metal units with or without doors. The principal disadvantage here is that the sound level cannot be adequately controlled.

An administrative conference room provides meeting space for the media staff, allows for the continuing review and discussion vital to selection, and provides a suitable meeting space for faculty and student LMC committees. Another option is to provide private administrative space for the head of the LMC (150 square feet would be generous), a conference room of the same size, and secretarial space. Other space could then be distributed throughout the LMC. We can assume that as school LMC facilities and staff size increase, one secretary will be required to handle the administrator's correspondence and much of the typing for acquisitions.

Cluster 4 units are grouped together because of their basic storage nature. The units are magazine storage, stacks, and textbooks. Media stored here are ordinarily those to which only limited access is required.

Magazine storage can be handled in a variety of ways in the LMC. The current trend is away from binding periodicals in school LMC's and toward providing backfiles on microfilm. The equivalent of one year's file of periodicals should be available in the LMC general function cluster for immediate access. Even if backfiles are to be maintained on microfilm, it is desirable to store three to five years worth of periodicals in the magazine storage unit for class projects.

The stacks are primarily a dead storage unit for little-used media that are considered to be of value to the collection. Multiple copies of resource media and kits of media may also be stored here. Direct access to media is fundamental to the modern school LMC, hence these stacks imply limited use and access.

A textbook storage unit is included in the cluster as an alternative. If the LMC is to be the principal location for the storage and distribution of all media to be used in the school, then textbook management also should become a function of the LMC. This function may require additional staff, depending on the number of textbooks used in the school. Limited access to this unit is anticipated; it is desirable, however, to provide access to a service corridor for delivery of texts to teaching stations without passing through the primary structure.

Cluster 5, which houses television and radio units. is supportive in nature because the units are production space, their output being received both in the LMC and throughout the school. They are treated as optional spaces because the extent to which these facilities are needed in each school will be governed in part by the services that the district system media center offers. Because of the nature of the equipment involved, direct access to a corridor is essential and double doors are required. Storage and office space are a part of the cluster.

Cluster 6 units are grouped functionally because they all involve audiovisual equipment service. The materials for production unit provides storage space for the media production unit. Direct access to the primary structure is required.

Maintenance and repair service in the individual school can be gauged only in relation to the services offered at the district level. If the district media center provides comprehensive maintenance and repair services, then only the essential minimal and basic repairs need to be handled in the school. In the absence of services at a district level, facilities for simple maintenance and repair must be provided at the individual school level and, as required, contracts must be made with commercial firms for major repairs and servicing.

The remote access control unit is the heart of the computerized laboratory. It usually requires the constant attention of a technician.

The audiovisual equipment distribution and storage unit in this cluster relates directly to teaching stations. Direct access to a corridor must be provided to move equipment expeditiously to needed locations. Equipment for use in the LMC, however, would be stored in the circulation/distribution unit.

Cluster 7 represents a staff convenience center. If the LMC is independent of other academic buildings and is also open for extended hours, this is an essential cluster. It would also be desirable for those schools in which the LMC is a separate facility in a campus-style arrangement. Any LMC facility that operates on an extended-hours basis needs such a cluster because after-hours access to other school facilities is generally curtailed. The fact that the staff in a large school may number 12 to 20 members gives added weight to the need for convenience facilities.

Fig. 4-9 suggests one pattern for relating primary and support space.

Traffic Patterns

Not enough attention has been paid to the movement of individuals and groups through an LMC of any size. The traditional small school library didn't even warrant consideration of this factor. The basic problem to be solved is how to get users where they want to go in the shortest possible time with the least inconvenience to themselves and other users. Ellsworth developed a generalized traffic pattern whose concept is adaptable to any centralized LMC.[6] Traffic moves from the entrance-circulation to the keys area (or bypass), through the media collection, to various user spaces (see Fig. 4-10).

Internal Physical Environment

The environment for learning that the LMC creates says a great deal about the program philosophy of the school and can be a determining factor in encouraging students and teachers to spend their time profitably in a learning situation. Students and teachers are tired of rigid blocks and spaces in education, of rooms that do not allow air to circulate, of rigid use patterns, fixed color patterns, and drab conditions.

Fig. 4-9. Relating Primary and Support Space

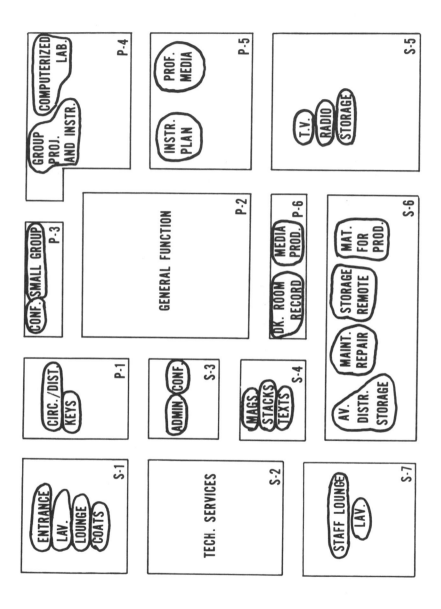

Fig. 4-10. Traffic Patterns

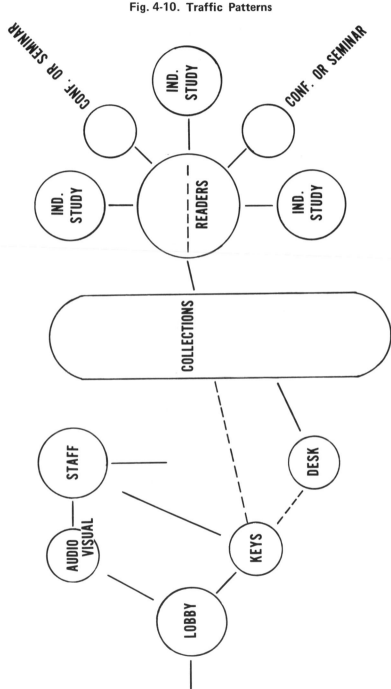

Some general conditions apply to all or most spaces of the LMC:

Temperature control. It should be possible to control conditions thermostatically throughout the LMC regardless of external weather conditions. The LMC needs an integrated heating-cooling system capable of a dual function throughout the year—a total climate-control system capable of automatically adjusting and controlling the temperature and flow of air.

Architects are among the chief proponents of air conditioning LMC's and school facilities in general, for reasons that go beyond pure considerations of comfort. Air conditioning allows the architect wide latitude in interior planning; he can literally "put the pieces together" without concern for windows that must perform a ventilating function. For example, in the case of an LMC that is integrated with an academic building, he can place the entire LMC in an internal location, with no need to provide windows to ventilate the various components in the facility. In the light of experience with typical air-conditioning systems in schools, however, it would be highly desirable to have an environmentally conditioned facility that also provides some manual method of controlling the flow of air, such as windows that open.

A consideration of windows leads logically to a consideration of the architect's use of glass in building schools. The use of glass in schools that are provided with climate control is generally limited to external considerations of aesthetics, general cost factors of building materials, and perhaps "bringing the outside into the building" aesthetically to capitalize on a particularly spectacular view. One should also consider that direct sunlight through glass makes it difficult to control the internal climate and creates other problems because of glare and reflected light. Climate control has been a major consideration in the recent trend away from exterior walls of glass to "schools without windows."

Artificial lighting. No specific prescription for lighting in the various areas of the LMC will be made here, though some observations can be made. A recommendation to avoid illumination levels above 70-80 footcandles, which would tend to bleach out images on computer display terminals, television screens, microfiche projectors, and other rear screen projection, was provided in a position paper prepared for Educational Facilities Laboratories.[7] This provides a degree of guidance for those who are planning space where projection equipment is to be used.

Through the use of artificial lighting, the LMC can create conditions that accommodate the potential needs of users. Both incandescent and fluorescent lighting can be used to provide varying environmental patterns and more interesting ceilings, which are usually bland. At least in the general function cluster, lighting should be zoned and controlled by dimmer switches that control the intensity of lighting in the various areas. Besides meeting specific lighting needs in various areas, this method can also provide interesting environmental conditions.

Ceilings. Although it is not often considered worthy of an aesthetic treatment, the ceiling of the LMC does offer many possibilities. In the self-contained campus-type facility, the architect can design various types of ceilings. The loft plan, which provides large open spaces uninterrupted by load-bearing walls, lends itself very well to extraordinary modifications of traditional flat ceilings. Although the multiple-level academic building generally precludes much in the way of relief from the ordinary, particularly if the LMC has other building levels above it, even here both interesting and practical variations in ceiling height can be planned for various areas. For example, the entrance and catalog keys clusters can have lowered ceilings and lighting that differs significantly from that in the general function cluster. Ceilings in conference and other areas can also be modified to provide a varied pattern.

Acoustical treatment. The best acoustical treatment for an LMC facility comes from a combination of factors, including ceiling treatment, flooring, the heating-ventilating system used, and the size and general configuration of areas. It also helps to arrange book stacks, equipment, and furniture so that the number of students contained in any area is limited to between 25 and 50 students.

Flooring. Carpeting is recommended as a suitable floor covering for the LMC. Although it is initially more expensive than tile, carpeting is much acclaimed as a surface that is both easier to maintain and longer wearing.

Architects and others frequently recommend varying the height of floors. Split-levels, depressions that form storytelling areas, or raised lounge areas visibly defined by three or four stairs are commonly employed. However, there are several reasons to avoid this variation in floor level: 1) Some physically handicapped children cannot readily negotiate flights of stairs or even one or two stairs; this is a consideration not to be taken lightly. 2) Changes in the organization of the facility are difficult to make if a permanent physical barrier has been incorporated. A balcony, whether it is for stack storage or for other student utilization purposes, presents the same problem. Although a ramp or an elevator might solve these problems, such solutions are often not considered during the planning stage.

Wall treatment. The walls—now that they are no longer used primarily for book stacks—can provide special acoustical or visual effects. New and used brick, slump brick, tile blocks with various patterns formed by epoxy paints, paneling, laminated plastic papers, and paints in a variety of colors can be employed satisfactorily.

Internal environment planning should coordinate all factors: acoustics, climate control, flooring, ceilings, walls, and lighting. The interior decorator is frequently cited as a required member of the school design team. The LMC is a prime area for the creative talents of a gifted decorator.

SUMMARY

* The library media specialist plays an important role in the planning of schools in general and of LMC's in particular. The development of educational specifications for the LMC is of particular significance. Educational specifications, also called a building program, provide the architect with a narrative outline of the educational program of the school, which he translates into a functionally and aesthetically designed building.

♦ Alternative concepts of LMC (or media system) planning include a physically centralized facility which may be patterned in traditional fashion, with arrangement by media forms; a divisional or resource center approach, which groups all media related to the same subject; a physically decentralized system, which endeavors to place satellites, or centers, in proximity to potential high use areas within a single building or a group of buildings; and the media system that is totally integrated with instructional spaces.

♦ The entire space requirement of the media system may be viewed as encompassing two fairly distinct types of space: primary space, which includes functional areas for students, teachers, media, and services; and support space, used to provide the "backup" services that make the media system function effectively and efficiently. The smallest functional units are combined with related units to form clusters of space; these clusters are oriented toward either support or primary structures of the LMC.

♦ The internal environment created for the LMC says a great deal about the philosophy of the school. The relationships of such factors as ceilings, flooring, walls, climate control, and acoustics should be considered.

LITERATURE AND FIELD INVESTIGATIONS

1. What background information is needed to design LMC facilities? Discuss the implications of such information.

2. Investigate the roles of educators, architects, and others who would be involved in facilities design.

3. Conduct an in-depth investigation of one or more of the following: lighting, environmental conditioning, interior decorating.

4. Investigate award-winning school LMC facilities. Describe how they relate to the educational program of the school.

5. Investigate state and local building codes. Discuss the implications for school LMC facilities.

6. Investigate state education department regulations or guidelines. Discuss their implications for school LMC facilities.

7. Compare school LMC facilities with those in academic and public libraries. Discuss similarities and differences.

NOTES

[1] Adapted from *A Statement of Professional Services* (Washington: American Institute of Architects, 1968).

[2] Eleanor Ahlers, and Mary Sypert, "The Case for Decentralization," *School Library Journal* 16:42 (November 1969).

[3] American Association of School Librarians and Association for Educational Communications and Technology, *Media Programs: District and School* (Chicago: American Library Association and Association for Educational Communications and Technology, 1975), pp. 95-103.

[4] *Webster's Third New International Dictionary* (Springfield, Mass.: G. & C. Merriam Co., 1971), p. 869.

[5] Ronald Gross, and Judith Murphy, *Educational Change and Architectural Consequences* (New York: Educational Facilities Laboratories, 1968), p. 15.

[6] Ralph Ellsworth, and Hobart Wagner, *The School Library: Facilities for Independent Study in Secondary Schools* (New York, Educational Facilities Laboratories, 1963), p. 52.

[7] *The Impact of Technology on the Library Building* (New York: Educational Facilities Laboratories, 1967).

REFERENCES

Ahlers, Eleanor, and Mary Sypert. "The Case for Decentralization," *School Library Journal* 16:41-44 (November 1969).

American Association of School Librarians. *Realization: The Final Report of the Knapp School Libraries Project*. Chicago: American Library Association, 1968.

American Association of School Librarians and Association for Educational Communications and Technology. *Media Programs: District and School*. Chicago and Washington, D.C.: American Library Association, and Association for Educational Communications and Technology, 1975.

Bender, David, and Estelle Williamson. "State Funding for School Construction," *School Media Quarterly* 2:217-220 (Spring 1974).

Briggs, Paul. "School Media Center Architectural Requirements," *School Media Quarterly* 2:201-202 (Spring 1974).

Ellsworth, Ralph, and Hobart Wagner. *The School Library: Facilities for Independent Study in Secondary Schools*. New York: Educational Facilities Laboratories, 1963.

Erickson, Carleton. *Administering Instructional Media Programs*. New York: Macmillan, 1968.

Green, Alan C., *et al*. *Educational Facilities with New Media*. Washington, D.C.: National Educational Association, 1966.

Gross, Ronald, and Judith Murphy. *Educational Change and Architectural Consequences*. New York: Educational Facilities Laboratories, 1968.

Haviland, David, and William Millard. *Multimedia Classrooms Revisited*. Troy, N.Y.: Center for Architectural Research, Rensselaer Polytechnic Institute, 1970.

Hoffman, Elizabeth. "Ten Commandments for Media Center Planners," *School Media Quarterly* 2:223-226 (Spring 1974).

Kay, Jane Holtz. "Ideals and Axioms: Library Architecture," *American Libraries* 5:240-246 (May 1974).

Miller, Marjorie, and Janet Ankrum. "The Trump School: A Move Toward Recentralization," *School Library Journal* 16:45-46 (November 1969).

Statement of Professional Services. Washington: American Institute of Architects, 1968.

Trump, J. Lloyd. "Independent Study Centers: Their Relation to the Central Library," *Bulletin of the National Association of Secondary School Principals* 50:45-51 (January 1966).

Wedin, Winslow, and Raymond Barber. "An Architect's Theoretical Considerations," *Drexel Library Quarterly* 9:75-82 (July 1973).

5

LMC EQUIPMENT AND FURNITURE

OBJECTIVES

Identify and describe equipment and furniture suitable for use in a school LMC.

Select equipment and furniture for an LMC in a particular school.

INTRODUCTION

Although furniture and equipment could have been discussed in other chapters—and particularly equipment, since the term media by definition includes the technology required for the use of media—furniture and equipment are sufficiently related to warrant joint treatment.

As with every aspect of the development of the LMC, the prime consideration in the purchase of equipment and furniture for student and teacher use is program intent. For example, if students are to listen to audiotapes and to view filmstrips and 8mm films, then the following questions must be considered: Will equipment be used by large groups, individuals, or small groups? Where will equipment be used? Under what conditions will equipment be used?

The analysis of equipment needs for the school and the LMC is related to the expanded use of audiovisual media not merely as teacher tools but as vehicles for the direct personal attention of the individual learner. Beyond the group showing of a 16mm film, we look forward to the possibility that an individual student will be able to select a film for his personal use. The effectively organized LMC will provide the same intimate experience for the student and film that has been provided for the student and the book.

In general, the selection of furniture for classrooms, auditoriums, and large-group instructional areas has been more successful than the selection of furniture for the LMC. Classroom furniture is usually chosen after due consideration of size of students, functions to be performed by students, and maneuverability of furniture. On the other hand, the tables and chairs for the elementary school LMC have, for years, consisted of "standard" four- to six-position tables and chairs to accommodate the largest children in the school. This choice was related to the practice of scheduling class-size groups for the LMC on a formal basis. Little consideration was paid to size of students, and little or no consideration was given to the need for different types of furniture to satisfy student and teacher needs in varied LMC activities. Today, the need to analyze what students and teachers will be doing in the LMC is recognized. Among the questions to be raised are these: What type of seating would be best for leisure reading? What type would be best for equipment use?

LMC Needs Differ

There is a need to differentiate among types of equipment needed in various teaching stations, multi-media facilities, language laboratories, and the LMC. There are three basic considerations: 1) the intent or purpose of use, 2) the medium or media to be employed, and 3) the type of equipment required to convey the message effectively. It may be assumed that most (though not all) classroom use will be teacher-directed group viewing or listening. Team teaching and modular scheduling in schools mean that there will be large group presentations of various kinds for students. The school that has a facility designed specifically for multi-media presentations can use rear-screen projection with slides, filmstrips, and 8mm or 16mm films. Students might be scheduled for a large-group multi-media presentation once each week in a specific subject area. The remainder of the week they might meet for small group seminars and individual conferences with teachers, or work independently in seminar rooms, laboratories, or the LMC. If remote access audio-video systems are provided in a school, the location of installations varies widely—from language laboratories to LMC's. Usually it is anticipated that the teachers will create much of the programing in the school and that student use will be generated by the need to complete assigned work. These systems must have a fixed location, and the furniture chosen must accommodate students and program sources. Remote access audio and video systems assume that faculty members will develop specific listening and viewing experiences, and that students will be scheduled to use the medium at specific times. These fixed carrel positions contain "built-in" equipment, while tapes are stored in a separate location.

Student use of standard audiovisual media in the LMC presents a variety of problems. Equipment selected for use here should differ from models designed for classroom use. An effort should be made to provide the user with the most effective impact of the medium under difficult physical conditions such as lighting, and at the same time to avoid distracting others. There are ways to accomplish this, though none is perfect.

Fig. 5-1 shows the national quantitative recommendations for equipment. Although the national guidelines present recommendations for a base collection and expanded provisions (access beyond the school), only selected items from the basic collection are cited here. One should consider these requirements as absolute only if the media collection is sufficiently large to warrant the equipment specified and only if the potential for use does in fact warrant the quantities recommended. The following discussion of equipment deals essentially with the devices usually available in the schools.

LMC EQUIPMENT

Most of the portable equipment purchased for general use in the school can be modified for use in the LMC. If funds and equipment are in short supply, that may be the only reasonable alternative. Generally, however, there are specific types of equipment that are better suited for use in the LMC. No attempt will be made to describe all types of equipment on the market today.[1]

Fig. 5-1. Representative Quantitative Standards
for Equipment*

BASE COLLECTION FOR A SCHOOL WITH 500 OR FEWER USERS

Microform Equipment: Readers and Printers. 2 readers, 1 of which is portable, plus
1 reader-printer.

Filmstrip Equipment: Silent and Sound Projectors and Viewers. 10 projectors and
30 viewers.

Slide and Transparency Equipment. Slide Projectors: 6, or 1 for every 100 users.
Slide Viewers: 10, or 1 for every 50 users. Overhead Projectors: 10, or 1 for
every 50 users.

**16mm and Super 8mm Sound Projectors and Video Playback and Reception
Equipment.** 6 units, with 2 assigned to the media center, plus 1 additional
unit for each 100 users.

Super 8mm Equipment. 20 Cartridge-Loader Projectors and sufficient Open-Reel
Projectors, plus 1 additional Projector for every 75 users.

Audio Equipment: Tape Recorders and Record Players. 30 audio reproduction
units. Listening units: 1 set of earphones for each reproduction unit and 1
portable listening unit per 25 users.

MISCELLANEOUS EQUIPMENT

Opaque Projectors. 1 per media center and 1 per 500 users (or 1 per floor in a
multi-story building).

Microprojectors. 1 per media center and 1 or more additional per school.

---

*Adapted from American Association of School Librarians and Association for
Educational Communications and Technology, *Media Programs: District and School* (Chicago
and Washington, D.C.: American Library Association and Association for Educational
Communications and Technology, 1975), pp. 72-83.

Devices for the projection of still media in the classroom include: filmstrip
projectors, slide projectors, overhead and opaque projectors. With the exception of
the opaque projector, which requires almost total darkness, these devices can be
used in an LMC where the light can be somewhat controlled. If it is assumed that
work in the LMC will be done essentially on an individual or small-group basis,
there is no need for an opaque projector.

Obviously, filmstrip, slide, and overhead projectors can be used in seminar or
conference rooms using either a screen or a light-colored wall as a projection
surface. If the overhead lighting in the general-function area can be controlled, then
these devices can also be projected on a wall-mounted screen or suitable wall space

in that area. Transparencies may also be viewed by using a light box similar to a slide sorter or by simply placing a sheet of plain white paper behind the transparency as a background.

Use of standard filmstrip and overhead projectors can be modified in several ways: they can be used in a study carrel, with the image projected through a rear screen device (which may be built-in or portable), or by direct projection against the rear or side of a carrel. If there are no carrels, then the projectors can simply be used on a flat table surface and shown on either a portable desk top screen or a rear screen unit (see Fig. 5-2).

Fig. 5-2. Typical Devices for the Projection of Still Media

Devices whose principal viewing method is rear screen projection are recommended for LMC use. Sample rear screen previewers are shown in Fig. 5-3. These models offer considerable flexibility; they can be used by individuals and small groups in a variety of locations in the LMC.

Fig. 5-3. Rear Screen Projection Devices

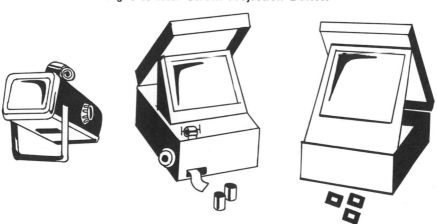

Audio media include records and tapes. Record players and tape recorders are used throughout the school, and they may be used successfully in an LMC with headphones (see Fig. 5-4). Two types of tape recorders are available—reel-to-reel and cassette. Some schools are moving to the cassette tape for all audio media use. Programs can be purchased directly in the cassette format, or the original record or reel-to-reel material can be transferred to cassette and the original stored as a "master" copy. The principal considerations are convenience in use and a reduction in the variety of equipment required to program a school and LMC effectively. Inexpensive cassette tape playback units—that is, those which do not have a record capacity—should have rewind and fast-forward controls, both battery and AC/DC options, and an option for use with or without headphones.

Fig. 5-4. Audio Media Devices

A cross-media approach, combining visual and auditory material, is common in schools today. The sound filmstrip consisted initially of a filmstrip without captions and a record synchronized with the filmstrip. The audio cassette has extended the options; purchasers can buy either the filmstrip-record combination or the filmstrip-cassette. As shown in Fig. 5-5, equipment for either back-of-the-room classroom use or rear screen use with headphones to control sound is available. Again, rear screen is the preferred style.

Fig. 5-5. Cross-Media (Visual and Auditory) Devices

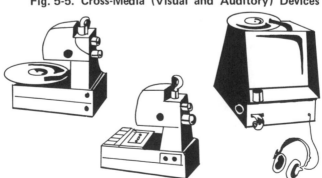

Motion projection, silent or sound and in an 8mm or 16mm format, provides many benefits in the teaching-learning situation. The 16mm and 8mm reel-to-reel projectors suitable for classroom and LMC use are shown in Fig. 5-6. Sound and light control are factors that require attention in the LMC. Conference or seminar rooms, where available, can be readily adapted for use if a wall-mounted screen or light-colored wall can be used as a projection surface. Portable rear screen units and headphones provide additional ways of modifying projector use. The cartridged 8mm silent and sound motion film projectors are offered as both standard and rear screen devices (see Fig. 5-7). Rear screen units whose sound is controlled by the use of headsets are recommended for the LMC.

Fig. 5-6. Motion Projection Equipment

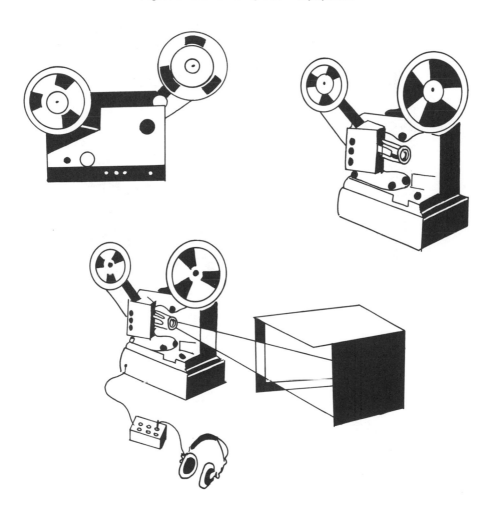

Fig. 5-7. Motion Projection (Cartridge Type) and Rear Screen Units

Microfilm and microfiche are being increasingly used at the secondary school level, for the storage of backfiles of periodicals and in many cases for information that is contained only in this new format. Readers and reader-printers for this medium must be available. Simple readers enable the viewer to read and take notes, while the reader-printer enables him to press a button and receive "hard copy," which he may take away for further study or use (see Fig. 5-8). Although it is possible to purchase a single device that accommodates both the microfilm to microfiche format, if heavy use is anticipated it is preferable to provide separate devices for each.

Fig. 5-8. Microfilm/Microfiche Devices

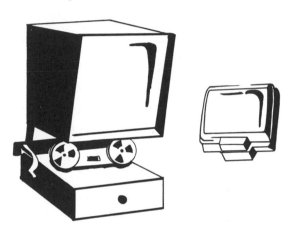

Technology has been cited as the greatest challenge to libraries today because of the changes it has effected in facilities, media forms, and services. Changes stem primarily from three technological inputs: computers, microforms, and communications.

Computers will be utilized in basic library areas such as acquisitions, circulation control, cataloging, and information retrieval. A great deal of pioneering work has already been done in these areas and will continue. At present, computerized acquisition and circulation systems are operating in schools and school districts.

Microforms have already significantly changed research operations in libraries. Although they were initially used as a means of storing and preserving material, their current application has been directed to the miniaturization of technical reports and research information. Microfilm and microfiche have been the microforms principally used in the school LMC for the storage of newspapers and periodicals, as well as for the acquisition of research material not available in book form. The chief obstacle to greater proliferation of microforms is a lack of standardization or compatibility in the field, though it appears that as the field begins to stablize its impact will be significant. Some academic libraries have standardized their holdings by limiting acquisitions to two formats: 35mm microfilm and 4" x 6" microfiche.

The communications field offers a challenge to libraries in that television has made it possible to transmit images of text over long distances (facsimile transmission). This input will eventually provide a new interlibrary loan network. For schools and school districts in general, this is a fringe benefit that will probably be obtainable eventually through a regional system. The use of television within a school or district for instructional programing will be a more direct and significant application of this medium over the years.

It is generally assumed that, as these vehicles become operationally perfected and as costs diminish, school LMC's will begin to acquire them. Meanwhile, innovative school districts have already taken steps to utilize the latest in technology. As long as "flexibility" is the key word in building facilities, the LMC will be able to change physically to incorporate technological advances. The greater challenge, however, is philosophical; it concerns the ability of media personnel to evaluate on a continuing basis the state of technology for assimilation into the field.

To date, two technologically advanced system have been employed in school LMC's with reasonable success: wireless audio systems and remote audio and video retrieval systems (frequently referred to as dial-access systems). Like most technological "miracles," they must be approached with caution and carefully evaluated as alternative means of accomplishing learning goals.

Audio systems have received a great deal of attention in education as a means of providing a learning experience alternative to reading. Foreign language, business, and music departments in secondary schools were among the first to utilize the potential of the medium. The audio system comes naturally to the LMC as a synthesizer of learning experiences.

The wireless audio system is offered as an alternative to the more usual individual or small-group use of audio media in the LMC; in the latter situation a record player or tape recorder was used directly with headsets in a fixed location. The wireless system consists of an AM or FM transmitter capable of sending out four to eight different programs at one time. The LMC or room is "looped" with a perimeter wire conductor placed under carpeting, above acoustical tile ceilings or affixed to the walls, and connected to the transmitter. The transmitter broadcasts the prescribed audio programs over four to eight channels. (The number of channels is determined by need and cost.) The wireless system can accommodate and transmit various sources, such as records, reel-to-reel and cassette tapes, or any combination of these. Each program source is played out over a different channel. Student reception is by headset in any physical location within the "looped" area. All students can dial the same program on the same channel, or they select programs from any channel available. Operationally, the wireless audio system is a "manned" station; a member of the LMC staff must change programs as needed, whether use is provided through a daily or weekly schedule or on demand. The student usually has no control over the presentation of programs.

Remote audio and video systems are a more sophisticated method for the distribution of programing. The trend today, particularly in new school construction, is to secure a total communications system that will provide a single remote control station and decentralized subsystems for language laboratories, business education purposes, the LMC, and other programing needs. Again, this reflects an effort to reduce the piecemeal acquisition of incompatible systems for varied instructional purposes.

A typical, fairly standard approach provides a certain number of carrels for student use. Pre-recorded audio tapes in various subject areas, available on standard tape decks in a remote location, provide the program source. A student can call for any of a variety of programs. He calls for a specific program by dialing (or by pressing touch-tone keys). The program request electronically activates the proper tape and the student receives the information through a headset. When the program has been completed or, the listener stops the program, a rewind mechanism is activated and the tape is stored for reuse. Taped programs are usually in 15-minute segments, and students who want the same program begin listening at the same time.

The optimum situation, available today on a limited scale, is random access to audio and video information. Random access means that each request for information is provided immediately. All programs emanate from a single, central storage and control unit. The three basic components required for this are a storage bank of programs, a computer control unit, and student work spaces (usually carrels). The student carrel has a headset for listening, a video monitor for viewing, and an electrical outlet for a student tape recorder if he wishes to duplicate a program for later use.

A program call to the computer unit initiates the process needed to provide the student with his individually copied program. Master tape programs are stored for rapid duplication. When the program request is made, the computer connects the master copy to a high-speed recording device serving the individual student carrel, and a duplicate of the master program is recorded for the individual's use. These tape recorders then serve as playback and recording units for the individual carrels. The student now has an individual tape; he can start, stop, and restart the program or change programs. He can record his own voice if he chooses.

The principal features of the system are computer control and high-speed duplication of programs. An additional feature of the system is an automatic telephone access capability. When the proper phone inputs are provided, a user at home or in another remote location can dial the computer number and request a stored program. Classroom and other school spaces can be equipped to receive programs stored in the system. Distribution of programs to other schools can also be provided through the system.

A fairly recent development, whose progress should be carefully followed by media personnel, is the electronic videoplayer. This device has been heralded as the technological development that will supersede existing television programing in the school. This concept provides the convenience of an audio cassette or 8mm cartridge, translated to the medium of television. The typical videoplayer consists of a compact, portable play device that can be connected to any black and white or color television receiver. The medium to be played, which may be in cartridge or record format, is placed in the videoplayer, and operation is started by pressing a button. Transmission to the television receiver is direct. A single videoplayer can be linked to as many television sets as required.

The problem once again is the lack of a standard format, since about 20 different companies throughout the world are in the process of developing these systems. There are at present two broad categories to consider: those which have the capacity only to play back material already recorded, and those with a record capacity, both "off-the-air" and with accessories to tape in the school, for later replay. Four different types of media are employed in the various systems: film, magnetic tape, a transparent tape, and a video disc. When the problems of standardization, costs, and software are ironed out, the potential of the medium may be realized.

Selecting Equipment

Both staff and students should participate in the selection of equipment just as they participate in selecting media. Those who are to use the equipment should have an opportunity to evaluate it in the teaching-learning situation. It makes sense to include them in the establishment of policy and procedures for selecting equipment, the development of criteria to be used for various purposes in the school, and the evaluation process.

In the small school, the media selection committee may serve adequately for this purpose. The devices selected, after all, are to provide access to the media collection. If specialized devices are to be evaluated, such as dial or random access systems, it may be desirable to bring in expert assistance. As with any selection process, the basic question is, "What purpose is this device to serve?"

If the district media director coordinates a total school district program, there should be a district equipment selection committee composed of teachers in the field, administrators, and library media specialists.

However, the availability of a district committee in no way diminishes the necessity for individual school action. In order to achieve the best results for a school, the school media staff must be involved actively in the system, with an interlocking relationship between school and district. The individual school media and equipment committee should be the representatives to a district-wide committee.

There are general criteria that can be applied to the devices used in a school media system. Any consideration of equipment should begin with the question of purpose. Beyond purpose the following criteria apply:

1. Is the device portable?
   Compact
   Light weight

2. Is the device sturdy and reasonably attractive in design?
   Constructed of durable material
   Free of imperfections

3. Is it easy to operate?
   Controls accessible and clearly marked
   Few control mechanisms

4. Does the device meet performance standards?
   Does what the manufacturer claims
   Does what it is supposed to do well
   Meets school use requirements

5. Is the device easy to maintain and repair?
   Minor repairs simple, quickly effected
   Parts requiring cleaning easily accessible
   Parts can be replaced

6. Are the manufacturer and distributor reliable?
   Will the manufacturer continue this equipment line?
   Parts available when needed
   Types of services available on manufacturer and distributor agreements

7. What are costs for comparable equipment?

At least two additional criteria apply to portable equipment used in the LMC:

8. Is there a model available from the manufacturer which is designed for use by an individual?

9. What modifications of the typical portable device can be made?

Equipment for use in the schools should be subjected to rigorous evaluation. It is always helpful to consult published evaluations of equipment, such as those found in *Library Technology Report*.[2] It is desirable to consult with other media personnel about the equipment they use, so as to determine their opinions about satisfactory and unsatisfactory performance records. Many do keep maintenance and repair records, which can be valuable.

Evaluation should include a demonstration of competitive equipment under identical conditions. If possible (and, if there is a large sum of money involved, it usually *is* possible), there should be an extensive try-out period under varying conditions by media personnel, teachers and students. These same individuals should be requested to use the directions provided with equipment to check on clarity and ease of operation. A technician, or someone who performs that function, should also go through the motions ordinarily employed in the in-school or district repair and maintenance of equipment.

Usually a school or entire district endeavors to standardize the equipment used. This requires the purchase of the same make and model of a device from a particular manufacturer, and it avoids some of the problems of training teachers and students to use equipment effectively. Maintenance and repair costs may also be significantly reduced. There is another side of the coin, however. Some say that standardization is a myth in the rapidly changing field of technology. To a large extent this is true, since each manufacturer strives to improve or up-grade his product. The result is a situation similar to that found in the automobile industry. The possibility that another manufacturer might develop a far superior product is another cause for concern among those who standardize; also, school district policy concerning bidding procedures can hinder attempts at standardization. While a decision to honor a standardization program may well be forthcoming, price is a very important consideration when little or no variation in equipment specifications is apparent. It is perhaps advisable to stabilize equipment purchases instead of standardizing them. The concept of stabilization is preferred because it recognizes the necessity of limiting makes and models of equipment while at the same time it provides for transition to other equipment that offers significantly improved operation.

Media Production Equipment

The equipment assigned for media production is of two types: portable, which can be taken into the field (including 8mm movie and 35mm still cameras); and fixed position equipment, such as the dry mount press, slide reproducer, and spirit duplicator. It should be noted that such equipment as audio and video tape recorders, although not listed in the guidelines as local production equipment, does in fact double as production equipment. Fig. 5-9 provides a list of local production equipment recommended in the national guidelines. Media most frequently cited for production in the schools—graphics, audio tapes, slides, and transparencies—provide some evidence of need. Copying and duplicating equipment are also considered "standard" today. Beyond this, a determination can be made only by direct investigation of factors in the school.

Fig. 5-9. Representative Local Production Equipment*

LOCAL PRODUCTION: INDIVIDUAL SCHOOL

Camera and copystand	Paper cutter (30"-36")
Copying machine	Super 8mm camera
Dry mount press (18" / 23")	Tape splicer
Duplicating machine	Transparency maker (thermal unit)
Film splicer (8mm and 16mm)	Typewriter for graphics (10-12 pt. type)
Light box	Videotape equipment (portable)

---

*Adapted from American Association of School Librarians and Association for Educational Communications and Technology, *Media Programs: District and School* (Chicago and Washington, D.C.: American Library Association and Association for Educational Communications and Technology, 1975), pp. 84-86.

LMC FURNITURE

The pattern established for student and teacher use of the LMC is based on an estimate of learning needs and is usually programed in the educational specifications for the new school. Various estimates are available for the allocation of user space. Ellsworth[3] recommended that 60 percent of user space be reserved for study carrels, 15 percent for group study (conference) rooms, 8 percent for flat top tables, and 17 percent for lounge furniture. The national guidelines recommend that 30 to 40 percent of seating be reserved for study carrels. Since the LMC focuses on the individual and his needs, 60 percent of seating at study carrels seems minimal, with the remaining divided between standard four-person tables and lounge seating. If adequate conference room space is provided for group work (which includes conversation), there is little need for the standard round and rectangular tables found in libraries.

Carrels. Study carrels are of two varieties, dry and wet. The dry carrel provides a visually private workspace for the individual, while the wet carrel adds at least an electrical outlet for audiovisual equipment use. If carrels are to be purchased, they should be "wet." Ellsworth[4] presented several prototypes of carrels suitable for use in the schools. Many of these types are available commercially, others may be fabricated for use. For example, it is possible to modify existing four-position tables for study carrel use. In any event, the following advice is worth heeding: unless the carrels are finished with a plastic laminate, such as Formica, the problems arising from student graffiti will be very trying. This applies to any age group in any school. Unless it has been actually gouged with a weapon, the plastic laminate can be readily cleaned, whereas plywood and hardboard usually require sandpaper, a block of wood, and a great deal of muscle.

Carrels should be sufficiently high to provide visual privacy. Although most carrels available commercially close the user in on three sides, it is desirable to leave one side open so that the individual does not feel closed in. For example, the typical double carrel should have partitions in front and between users; however, it is desirable to leave the sides open to provide visual change. The different varieties of carrels developed in recent years can be used satisfactorily in many situations.

Carrels arranged in single or double rows along walls or partitions, facing in the same direction, can be used to advantage (see Fig. 5-10). At least four feet should be allowed from the front of one carrel to the front of the following one to provide for access to seating. Another suggested variation is the pinwheel arrangement (see Fig. 5-11). It is suggested that carrels be grouped in clusters of 15 to 25.

It is not unusual to find an LMC that provides a casual corner for recreational reading, with lounge chairs and tables. As noted, Ellsworth cited a need for only 17 percent lounge furniture. Individual seating and two-seater lounge furniture with suitable tables and lamps can be effectively used. Lounges that provide space for three persons are generally not recommended.

Fig. 5-10. Carrels in Rows

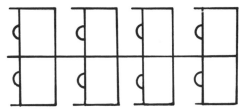

Fig. 5-11. Carrels—Varied Patterns

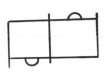
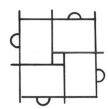
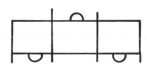

Tables selected for the LMC should seat no more than four students. These tables may be round or rectangular in shape. If several tables are to be used, there should be a mixture of types. Elementary school height of tables will vary from 25 to 28 inches, junior high level from 27 to 30 inches, and senior high from 29 to 30 inches. Tables may be all wood or a combination of metal and wood, or plastic. Table tops should be laminated plastic.

A highly recommended alternative to standard library tables, for conference rooms and other group activity spaces, is the trapezoid table. As shown in Fig. 5-12, trapezoid tables can be arranged in many ways.

Fig. 5-12. Trapezoid Tables

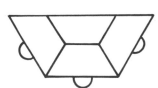

Many kinds of chairs are available for use in the LMC—solid wood, molded plastic, a combination of wood and metal, and with or without arms. Chair height depends on the height of the tables selected for purchase. Elementary level chair height ranges between 14 and 17 inches, junior high level between 16 and 18 inches; senior high chair height is 18 inches.

Other items of furniture requiring attention are the card catalog and circulation desk. The height of the card catalog does make a difference, since the general size of patrons is always a factor. Elementary schools must have a catalog that its patrons can reach. At the secondary level, there is a temptation to provide card catalog units with a counter height work surface above; this limits the catalog to a maximum height of about 42 inches, and the user must constantly bend over to reach the drawers. Any catalog purchased for any school LMC should be expandable. In most cases this means a catalog of at least 15 drawers. The divided catalog, which has an author and title file and a separate subject file, is definitely the trend today.

Somehow the idea has developed that the circulation desk is the heart or "nerve center" of the LMC, instead of the collections or the service personnel. Many libraries have circulation desks that are unnecessarily large. The circulation desk should be compact, made up of modular units that are joined together. At the elementary school level, desk height is suggested, while at the secondary level, the unit should be counter height.

In most school LMC's, the circulation/distribution area is also used to store reserve media, so storage shelving is required. This is also a logical place to store portable equipment that is to be used in the LMC. This area should be staffed by clerical, not professional, personnel. In the LMC operated by a single professional without assistance, there should still be a separate service desk for this person.

Storing Media

The open-stack (direct-access) arrangement is the current pattern for the storage of books and other media in the school LMC. This means that media are located in the LMC, and that users can go directly to the shelves or storage units for items needed. Usually, seating and work space are provided in direct proximity to stored media.

Books. Practices developed over a long period of time have created the book storage pattern in use today. Regardless of the fact that one cannot see authors' names, book titles, or colorful book jackets, and the problem of books falling over, the existing pattern for shelving books has rarely been considered worth challenging. Only the physical storage of paperbacks has broken the pattern.

Some general comments about shelving are in order. Shelving used in the LMC may be wood or metal. Wood has been the standard for open-stack collections, metal used for closed stacks. In the past, wood was considered quality shelving, while metal was considered an inexpensive installation. Today, however, metal shelving has taken its place in open-stack collections on a par with wood because of the many styles available, the use of wood-grain end panels, and the variety of colors available. The cost of metal remains slightly lower.

All shelving purchased should be three feet on center and fully adjustable. It is suggested that consideration be given to purchasing from reputable houses that will continue to produce the specific type of shelving purchased for years to come. It is recommended that top and bottom shelves not be used initially, and that shelves be only two-thirds full. Shelving that is backed keeps books from slipping away. However, in situations where ranges of shelving are used it is preferable not to use backs, because they tend to close the space visually. Adjustable back stops can be used.

The height and depth of book shelving varies with the grade level of the school. It is suggested that shelving height for elementary schools be six feet. Though this is a foot higher than what is ordinarily recommended, the additional height is suggested here for two reasons: 1) the top shelf space can be used for display purposes as long as the book collection remains modest in size; 2) as the collection expands, this becomes the first line of defense. The first area for expansion becomes the top and bottom of shelving units. The recommended height for junior and senior high schools is seven feet.

Depth of shelving varies for different collections. For general non-fiction and fiction collections, the recommended depth of shelving is 8 to 10 inches. We suggest a 9-inch depth as a standard. For an oversized collection, 10 to 12 inches is recommended. Reference book shelving should be 12 inches deep. Although shelving will be adjustable so that space between shelves can vary, recommended space between shelves is 10 to 12 inches. Fig. 5-13 illustrates a 3-foot section with four shelves. The bottom shelf should slope back to facilitate reading call numbers on books shelved here.

Fig. 5-13. Typical 3-Foot Section of Shelving

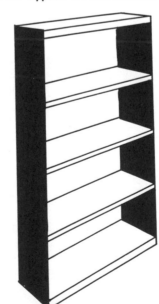

In the elementary school, shelving for picture books should be 42 to 50 inches high, and 12 inches deep. The space between shelves should be 14 to 16 inches. A special feature, and one very much needed, is the addition of upright partitions spaced every 7 to 8 inches to prevent these books from spilling over (see Fig. 5-14).

Fig. 5-14. Picture Book Shelving

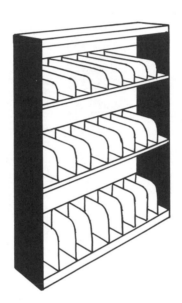

The pattern of shelving all books along perimeter walls is no longer the accepted one. Recommendations today call for free-standing double-faced stacks in ranges. Maximum range length suggested is 15 feet, although occasionally a length of 18 feet can be tolerated. The walking space permitted between shelving is 32 to 36 inches. In a school situation, no less than 36 inches of space between ranges is suggested. If it is anticipated that there will be continued heavy traffic for specific types of books, such as reference or picture books, 5 to 6 feet between ranges would be needed.

Counter height shelving (no less than 42 inches high) is often used to create patterns of use in the LMC. It is suggested that there be only limited use of shelving of this height because it is a nuisance for the user to stoop to read the shelves and to lift books placed at that level. A practical and beneficial trend is the practice of adding a unit of 42-inch-high shelving to the end of each range of shelving (see Fig. 5-15); the user can stand here and can comfortably review books selected before moving on to the seating area.

Fig. 5-15. Counter Height Shelving

Estimates of book capacity for full 3-foot units are: general fiction and non-fiction, 30 volumes; reference books, 18 volumes; and picture books, 60 volumes. A common guide or estimate for general collections is 125 volumes per 7-foot-high section of six shelves.

Other media usually stored on shelves are record collections and periodicals. Fig. 5-16 shows storage of these forms. Periodicals are stored with covers showing, while record storage is similar to that of hardbound books. The rationale for these different approaches is obscure. The assumption is that periodicals have colorful covers, record albums do not. Also, a great many more records are purchased than periodicals, so the space problem looms large. For periodicals, there are two options: 1) Standard periodical shelving, which is 12 inches deep and provides a 16-inch slant shelf. This can also provide storage capacity for several back issues beneath the shelf, which can be raised. 2) The free-standing periodical rack. Options are available for records also: 1) standard record shelving available at a depth of 16

Fig. 5-16. Record and Periodical Storage

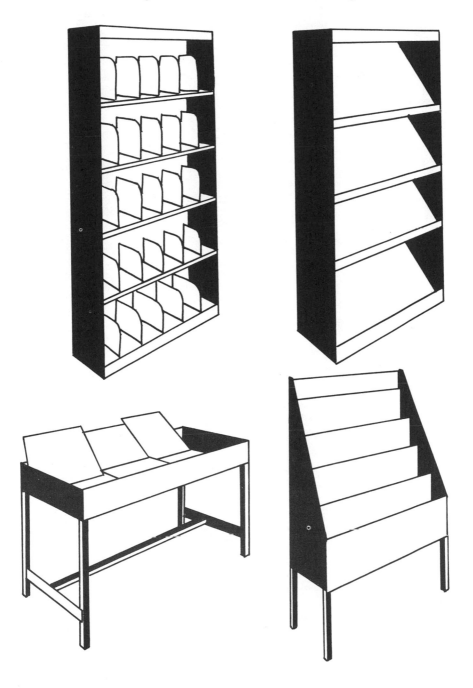

inches, or 2) the record bin. One must weigh the relative advantages of each, such as the coordination of record and periodical shelving with book shelving.

Paperback books are usually shelved with covers facing the user. Wire racks, like those used in drug stores is recommended. These can be either "spinners" or straight-line types with pockets for books. Wood shelving is available that accommodates paperbacks in the same manner, but that is coordinated with other wood furniture.

Vertical files can be used for both **pamphlet materials** and **transparencies.** Generally, legal-size metal files are used. These are available in a variety of colors and may be three or four drawers in height. They are arranged in banks either free-standing or against a wall. Other types of storage are available for transparencies but are not recommended.

Filmstrips may be stored in many ways. The compactness of free-standing stacking units makes this type highly recommended in situations where the collections will grow. The wire sections make it difficult to move the filmstrip cans, particularly if constant adjustment has to be made in the Dewey classification. Slotted units are preferred, so that cans can be moved in either direction to accommodate additional filmstrips.

Filmstrips, audio cassettes, 8mm films, microfilm, and microfiche should be stored in free-standing, stacking units as shown in Fig. 5-17. The units, which are available in metal and in a variety of colors, can expand. Reel-to-reel audio tapes can be stored in the same type of unit or on standard library shelves. If they are stored vertically on library shelves, then upright partitions should be placed 7 to 8 inches apart.

Fig. 5-17. Storage of Filmstrips, Audio Tapes, 8mm Films, and Microforms

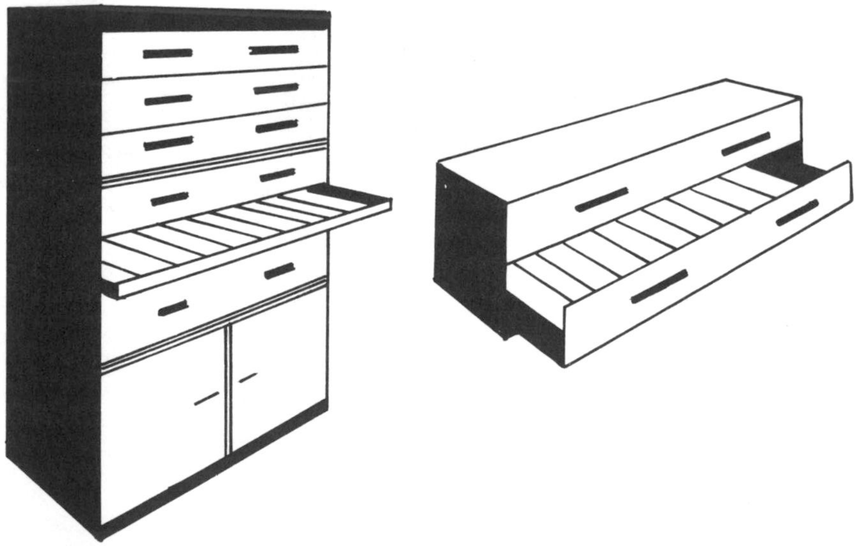

If 16mm films are to be stored in the individual school LMC, either closed cabinet storage or open shelving may be used. Video tapes may be stored on standard shelving (see Fig. 5-18).

Fig. 5-18. Storage of 16mm Films

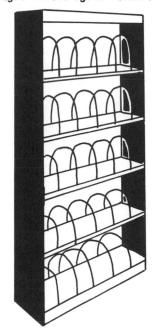

Shelving of the 12- to 16-inch-deep variety should be available to store sound filmstrips and kits, slides (which should be stored in units as they would be used), models, dioramas, and miscellaneous odd-sized media.

Manufacturers are endeavoring to provide a way to store all media forms related to the same subject together in the LMC. Two approaches are being used; the first, illustrated in Fig. 5-19, provides for shelving inserts to be used for various media forms. This method still separates media forms but allows them to be physically stored on shelves in the same general location; the second approach provides varied packaging alternatives for media forms, boxing them in a book format so that they can be shelved in a Dewey Decimal class. Adjustable shelving is supposed to provide for the accommodation of various sized packages to house media.

Fig. 5-19. Shelving Inserts—File Boxes

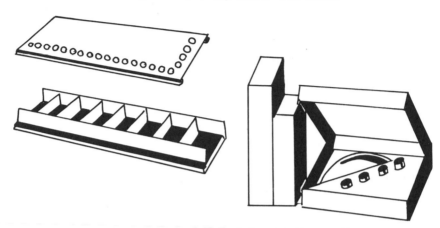

SUMMARY

♦ The selection of equipment and furniture influences the space utilization plans for the LMC. A generalized pattern is followed: student and teacher needs are determined first, then the physical environment needed to house these requirements.

♦ Although classroom equipment may be modified in many ways for use in an LMC, specialized equipment for individual, independent use should be preferred, if it is available.

♦ Equipment selection should be handled in the same way as media selection. Many people should cooperate in selection, using for guidance the prepared policy and criteria statements.

♦ Furniture should be selected on the basis of student and teacher need. Equipment selected for use will help to set up specific requirements for the selection of furniture.

♦ The method chosen for storing media depends on the philosophy of media personnel and others involved in the planning of the LMC. Many storage patterns separate media by form. However, manufacturers are providing the means to store all related media together, regardless of form.

LITERATURE AND FIELD INVESTIGATIONS

1.   What background information is needed to select equipment and furniture for a school LMC? Discuss the implications of such information.

2.   Locate major sources of information about equipment and furniture. Discuss positive and negative factors.

3.   Determine how media utilization practices will influence the equipment and furniture needs of a school LMC.

4.   Compare various storage possibilities available for audiovisual media. Discuss positive and negative factors.

5.   Compare school LMC needs for equipment and furniture with the needs of academic and public libraries. Discuss similarities and differences.

NOTES

[1] See the *Audiovisual Equipment Directory*, National Audiovisual Association (annual), for a comprehensive overview of equipment.

[2] See *Library Technology Report* (Chicago: Resources and Technical Division, American Library Association); annual, by subscription.

[3] Ralph Ellsworth, and Hobart Wagner, *The School Library: Facilities for Independent Study in Secondary Schools* (New York: Educational Facilities Laboratories, 1963), p. 51.

[4] *Ibid.*, pp. 54-69.

REFERENCES

Audiovisual Equipment Directory. Fairfax, Va.: National Audiovisual Association. Annual.

Audiovisual Marketplace. New York: R. R. Bowker. Annual.

Berliner, Oliver. *Color TV Studio Design and Operation: For CATV, School and Industry*. Blue Ridge Summit, Pa.: TAB Books, 1975.

Brown, James, Kenneth Norberg, and Sara Srygley. *Administering Educational Media: Instructional Technology and Library Services*. New York: McGraw-Hill, 1972.

Brown, James, Richard Lewis, and Fred Harcleroad. *AV Instruction: Technology, Media and Methods*. New York: McGraw-Hill, 1977.

Educational Product Report. New York: Educational Products Information Exchange Institute. Monthly, Sept.-June.

Ellsworth, Ralph, and Hobart Wagner. *The School Library: Facilities for Independent Study in Secondary Schools*. New York: Educational Facilities Laboratories, 1963.

Erickson, Carleton. *Administering Instructional Media Programs*. New York: Macmillan, 1968.

Hawken, William. "Systems Instead of Standards," *Library Journal* 98:2515-2525 (September 15, 1973).

Hicks, Warren, and Alma Tillin. *Developing Multi-Media Libraries*. New York: R. R. Bowker, 1972.

Hollowell, Mary, ed. *Cable Handbook 1975-76: A Guide to Cable and Newer Communications Technologies*. Washington, D.C.: Communications Press, 1975.

Kelley, Gaylen. "But Where Do I Plug the Carrel In?" *School Media Quarterly* 2:260-267 (Spring 1974).

Kenney, Brigitte, and Roberto Esteves. *Video and Cable Communications: Guidelines for Librarians*. Chicago: American Library Association, 1975.

Library Technology Report. Chicago: Resources and Technical Division, American Library Association. Annual, by subscription.

Robinson, Richard. *The Video Primer*. New York: Links Books, 1974.

Rosenberg, Kenyon C., and John S. Doskey. *Media Equipment: A Guide and Dictionary*. Littleton, Colo.: Libraries Unlimited, Inc., 1976.

6

THE LMC BUDGET

OBJECTIVES

Identify and describe alternative budgeting systems used in schools and school districts.

Design a PPB System for an LMC program in a selected school.

Design a management system for control of media budgetary processes in a selected school.

Financial support of the school LMC program is a critical factor if comprehensive media services are to be provided to students and teachers. One must recognize that any school or district has a limited amount of money to spend for existing programs and for the initiation of new programs. In many communities, the average school budget increase that will be allowed by fiscal authorities can be predicted, year by year.

What this means is that existing funds must be allocated to many well-conceived educational programs. One may also find substantial allotments for some programs which are neither well-conceived nor operationally sound. Since continued and expanded funding is required for any program initiated, competition for funds is very keen.

BUDGET PREPARATION

The LMC is in a unique position in the school. Its very existence is dependent on other programs. Therefore, the budget allotment for the LMC must rest on the perceived need for the extensive services potentially available to students and teachers in the teaching-learning process. What must be avoided is a pattern in which preparation of the budget and decisions about financial support are totally removed from the school. The media professional in the individual school must be involved in the budget-making process from the beginning.

Information Needed for Development of the Budget

A continuing program of analysis and evaluation should include the following:

Inventories of media and equipment. One must be completely knowledgeable about quantity and quality of existing resources.

State of development of collections. One should know, in terms of both standards and program needs, the relative strength of collections.

Costs of media and equipment. This information is essential for planning expansion of collections and for projecting needed increases in funding.

Past performance. One should have information (for at least a five-year period, if possible) of funds available for the LMC program, plus an analysis of how funds were spent. This provides an opportunity to visualize both a pattern of support for the LMC program and the effectiveness of expenditures in relation to program needs.

Knowledge of state, national, and regional guidelines; and of at least the average media expenditures for the state.

Knowledge of school and district priorities and the relationship of the LMC program to these priorities. One must know if curriculum development has created a priority for expanded science facilities, resources, and methodology. This information becomes essential to effective media budgeting because of an assumed relationship between improved instructional programing and a need for media and LMC services.

Effectiveness of the LMC program in meeting its objectives. Essential to the entire budgetary operation is full knowledge of the degree to which objectives have been established for the LMC program and the degree to which these have been met.

School budget year. Although many school districts operate from July 1 through June 30, other districts operate on a different budgetary year. For example, it is not uncommon to find a budget year that runs from April 1 to March 31 or one that runs from October 1 to September 30. Without discussing the relative merits of these, it is obvious that this information is needed in order to plan effectively for the next budget period.

Beyond the assessment of LMC media resources and the effectiveness of the media system, information can usually be obtained from various school district personnel: principals and their assistants, for information about their priorities and budgetary planning; guidance and/or reading personnel, about student capabilities; curriculum and other district directors, about curriculum development, federal and state funding sources; district financial officers, for budgetary procedures, an historical look at LMC expenditures for past years, and specialized funding for various district programs and projects; and state department of education personnel, for statistics about average expenditures and program comparisons. The program planning method developed by Liesener,[1] discussed briefly in Chapter 8, provides a useful approach to the collection of this information.

National Guidelines

The guidelines[2] recommend that the annual per pupil expenditure for media and equipment in the school district should be at least ten percent of the national per pupil operational cost, based on average daily attendance. The per pupil operational cost includes the cost of administration, instruction, attendance services, health services, pupil transportation services, operation of plant, maintenance of plant and fixed charges.

It is estimated that this sum would support the total media system for a school district, including individual school programs, a district program, and various contractual arrangements made with other service agencies. The figure represents an estimate based on an assumption that a comprehensive, unified media program actually operates in a district, and that education is guided by a focus on individualization, inquiry and independent study.

The district usually has a clearly defined budget planning period. In most districts, this is a final aspect of the planning which has gone on during the year. In other words, during the last few months of a given fiscal year all budget work will be completed for the following year. In some districts, a great many people will be involved in budget planning, including media personnel at the school level. This is most desirable and reflects a philosophy which recognizes the need for a broad perspective of financial need related to educational programing. Other districts still restrict budget planning to a central core of administrative personnel. In the former situation involvement in budget building becomes an integral part of the media professional's job, while in the latter case he may have to intrude on a pattern of long standing in the district and, in effect, upset the existing equilibrium to create a new ordering of budget-making procedures and priorities.

For many years, school districts used *Financial Accounting for Local and State School Systems*[3] as an accounting guide. In this handbook, each category of expenditure was assigned to a specific numbered series. For example, the 100 series dealt with administration, the 200 series with instruction and so on. The chief criticism of this system has been that expenditures for salaries, services, supplies and materials are meaningless unless they are related directly to the service areas and units for which they are purchased.

The revised handbook "is designed to be a vehicle or guide for 1) program cost accounting or for 2) accounting for programs in a program, planning, budgeting and evaluating system."[4] The new handbook provides the means for relating a specific expenditure to all *dimensions*, thereby providing for complete accountability. Fig. 6-1 shows excerpts from the handbook.

The three most important dimensions for financial record keeping are: fund, object, and function. Other dimensions recommended for use are: operational unit, program, source of funds and fiscal year. Having a copy of the guide available will provide a broader understanding of the system.

The library media specialist who has learned to function in a leadership capacity usually does not stand alone at budget time. He has the support of the administration, teachers, and students in his school, as well as the support of many sources outside the school. Support within the school is gained by effective participation in the principal's advisory council, by involving teachers and students in committee work relating to the LMC program and budget, and by coordinating an effective media system throughout the school. Support outside the school is gained by creating an awareness program through the news media, through favorable reports by children to parents, and by direct and continuing contact with the community as it relates to the school. Support at the school district level is gained through the cooperative participation of LMC personnel in curriculum development and related professional activities. The LMC budget that begins with

Fig. 6-1. Summary of Expenditure Accounts*

A

FUND
1 General Fund
2 Special Revenue Fund

B

OBJECTS
100 Salaries
  110 Regular Salaries
300 Purchased Services
  360 Printing and Binding
400 Supplies and Materials
  410 Supplies
  420 Textbooks
  430 Library Books
  440 Periodicals
  490 Other Supplies and Materials
500 Capital Outlay
  540 Equipment
  550 Vehicles
  560 Library Books

C

FUNCTION
1000 Instruction
  1100 Regular Programs
    1110 Elementary Programs
    1120 Middle/Junior High Programs
    1130 High School Programs
2000 Supporting Services
  2200 Support Services—Instructional Staff
    2210 Improvement of Instruction Services
    2220 Educational Media Services
      2221 Service Area Direction
      2222 School Library Service
      2223 Audiovisual Services
      2224 Educational Television Services
      2225 Computer-Assisted Instruction Services
      2229 Other Educational Media Services
3000 Community Services
  3400 Public Library Service

D

OPERATIONAL UNIT
001 XYZ Elementary School
501 ABC Middle School
701 DEF High School

E

PROGRAM
1100 000 Regular Programs
  1110 000 Elementary Programs
    1111 001 Program No. 1—XYZ
      Elementary School

F

SOURCE OF FUNDS
1 Local
3 State
4 Federal

G

FISCAL YEAR
1 FY 1972-73
2 FY 1974-75
3 FY 1975-76

H

INSTRUCTIONAL ORGANIZATION
10 Elementary School
20 Middle/Junior High School
30 High School

I

JOB CLASSIFICATION ACTIVITY
100 Official/Administrative
200 Professional—Educational
400 Technical

J

TERM
1 Fall Term—Day
2 Fall Term—Evening

K

SPECIAL COST CENTERS

*Excerpted from Charles Roberts and Allen Lichtenberger, *Financial Accounting: Classifications and Standard Terminology for Local and State School Systems*, Handbook II, Revised (Washington, D.C.: U.S. Government Printing Office, 1973).

this kind of interaction geared to improving media services in the schools has an excellent start.

Cost Estimates

If an intelligent budget presentation is to be made, it must include not only the cost estimates for new media and equipment, but also the replacement of media and equipment, rentals, supplies, parts for equipment and maintenance, and repair costs.

Average costs for books in various subject areas are available in several publications. Dealing with commercial jobbers over a period of time provides a fair gauge of costs minus usual discounts for various types of books. For the inexperienced book buyer, the advertised or quoted discounts can be both confusing and disturbing. For example, advertised discounts of 30 to 35 percent ordinarily apply only to trade books in regular publishers' bindings. Library bindings are a special classification, as are "short discount" items, and the quoted 30 to 35 percent is not applicable. Encyclopedias usually do not have to be estimated because quotations are readily available in most locales through area representatives. If a specific list of books has been developed, and if time is not a factor, most reputable jobbers will provide a quote on a given list and hold the price firm for 30 to 60 days.

Cost estimates for many audiovisual media forms may be obtained in the same manner as estimates for books, using standard tools in the field. When time permits, one can request direct quotes from producers or jobbers.

One can estimate the list cost of audiovisual equipment by using the *Audiovisual Equipment Directory*[5] or the various catalogs of producers or commercial vendors. A local vendor can provide both the list price on items of interest and the probable discounts. Large school districts and state agencies ordinarily have contract discount agreements with two or more equipment vendors. Prices are usually available through the school district business office, through the office of a media director, or by direct contact with the contract vendors.

Various estimates exist concerning the replacement costs of audiovisual media and equipment. Such costs are variously estimated to be from 10 to 20 percent each year based on normal wear and tear, accidental damage, and the need for updating collections. In the absence of specific records for the individual school, which would be the most accurate way to determine replacement needs, it is probably safest to allow for a 15 percent replacement factor until accurate record-keeping procedures are initiated.

Estimates on the frequency of replacing audiovisual equipment in the school range from five to ten years. A fairly simple process would be to use ten years as the estimated life-span of all equipment, compute the cost of the total equipment inventory and use ten percent as a replacement factor. Prices would be computed at current rates.

A thorough maintenance check should be given at the end of each year to all equipment that has been actively used. This can be accomplished at various other times, such as vacation periods. If a qualified equipment technician is employed in the school, or if a district media center staff assumes that responsibility, the media professional has one less problem to contend with. However, in the absence of this service, it is usual to contract this service with a reputable commercial firm. It is becoming common practice for audiovisual equipment vendors to offer complete service facilities. Otherwise, most dealers will provide you with a cost-per-unit range for each type of equipment requiring annual maintenance. To arrive at an estimated total cost for annual maintenance, the cost-per-unit range is multiplied by the average number of units to be serviced.

Wherever possible, and it is possible for most of the estimates discussed, information should be available in tabular form both for record keeping and for presentation purposes in the budget. Fig. 6-2 is an example of a form that can be used for recording maintenance costs.

Fig. 6-2. Annual Contracted Maintenance Costs

Item	Number To Be Serviced	Estimated Unit Cost Range	Estimated Total Cost Range
16mm projector			
Filmstrip projector			
Tape recorders			
etc.			

If actual use figures are not available for the supplies needed for media design and production, estimates of requirements must be provided. Types of equipment available for production purposes must be balanced against anticipated student and teacher demands. The rapidly developing focus on filmmaking in particular and production in general makes necessary a careful assessment of needs. A range of $5.00 to $10.00 per pupil may be used to estimate production supplies needed for adequate-to-quality performance. From a practical point of view, one must begin with a knowledge of the production capabilities of the LMC facility and staff. If filmmaking is considered a student program option or requirement, a more definitive cost factor must be determined.

Rental costs for 16mm films vary widely, depending on both the instructional focus of the school and the collections available in the district, public libraries, and regional education centers. Past performance records would obviously be of assistance here, as in other instances where estimates are required. One may estimate a range of three to five rentals per teacher, at $10.00 per rental, for adequate-to-quality performance. If specialized instructional programs are developed around the film as a principal vehicle for motivation and learning, a major revision of planning is in order. For example, a secondary school level study of humanities that uses major commercial films as a focus would need an entirely different set of estimates. One must be constantly aware of new instructional methods requiring extraordinary financial considerations.

It is frequently considered desirable to project a budget for a three- to five-year period. In this case it is necessary to gather data relative to existing inventories of media and equipment, to establish terminal goals for attainment, and to secure cost estimates for each item to be included in the budget request. Fig. 6-3 provides a tabular representation of estimates to reach projected goals in three years. The format presented is suitable for media and equipment and may be modified for other uses.

Fig. 6-3. (Media) Required to Meet Stated Goals (3 Years)

Item	Inventory 1976–1977	Quantity Needed	Estimated Total Cost	1/3 Budget Each of Three Years 1977–1978–1979 1978–1979–1980
Records Tapes etc. Replace- ment				

Presentation of Budget Information

Many school districts allow limited participation of LMC personnel in budget planning. A standard form is provided for an enumeration of anticipated requirements for the next fiscal year, and no written justification is requested. Central administrative personnel make whatever adjustments are deemed necessary in the figures and incorporate the information provided into the total budget package for the district. The superintendent of schools or an assistant provides an oral narrative report to the school board and, if required, to other agencies that request clarification. This practice has caused much confusion and misunderstanding and has precipitated a great deal of criticism of current budgeting procedures.

Some school districts have developed more satisfactory procedures for clarifying budget requests. One pattern that has been used with some success provides a narrative explanation for each recommendation made in the budget package. The budget request also contains a summary form so the reader can see at a glance the previous year's allotment, the projected increase, the recommendation for the new fiscal year, and a projection for three to five years. A typical summary form is shown in Fig. 6-4.

Fig. 6-4. LMC Budget Summary

Category	Allotment 1976-77	Projected Increase 1977-78	Recommendation 1977-78	Projected 1978-79 1979-80
430 Library Books				
440 Periodicals				
etc.				

PLANNING, PROGRAMING, BUDGETING

The PPB system has been widely acclaimed as a panacea for educational improvement because it is an integrated approach to program development and budgeting. The system received its greatest impetus for development under Robert McNamara and the U.S. Department of Defense in the early 1960s. President Johnson ordered federal agencies to adopt the system in 1965. The U.S. Office of Education has been a strong advocate of the plan and educational use of the system has grown rapidly.

Some of the positive and the negative factors of PPBS are:

It helps schools to:

— improve cost analyses and control

— evaluate programs in terms of objectives, costs, benefits

— identify and analyze alternative ways of achieving the same goals

— establish priorities

— allocate resources in light of total needs and resources

— appraise the performance of those responsible for reaching stated goals

—	coordinate short-range and long-range planning

—	inform the public of the purposes, costs and expected results of school programs

But it also:

—	takes time, money, and skill to develop and operate

—	results in more detailed accounting and budget documents, requiring summarization or interpretation

—	may result in placement of too much emphasis on the costs of programs rather than their benefits

—	may meet with resistance from staff members who resent systemization of the education process.[6]

A school district that adopts PPBS abandons a system that has been used almost universally in this country. The traditional system is composed of functions and objects. Each function (such as administration, instruction) contains several objects, such as salaries and supplies, which are termed line items. The basic criticism of this approach is that individual costs of various programs not only are unknown but cannot be determined. A statement in an N.E.A. publication helps to clarify budget format requirements:

Implementation of a P.P.B. system does not require that the budget format be altered, but it does require that for programing purposes expenditures be grouped in terms of program objectives rather than in terms of the items bought. In some jurisdictions budget formats have been altered.[7]

Through the use of PPBS, a school can meet the goal of accountability. The school district must develop a clear statement of objectives and then use these objectives in planning, budgeting, and evaluating its many programs. Built into the PPBS package is the concept of long-range and short-term planning, analyzing alternatives, and measuring outputs in terms of objectives.

PPBS requires the preparation of a series of documents:

1.	The program structure and statement of objectives.

2.	Program analyses (cost-effectiveness analyses) and memoranda.

3.	The multi-year program and financial plan.

In the preparation of these documents the P.P.B. system requires:

1.	Clarifying and specifying the ultimate goals or objectives of each activity for which a government budgets money.

2.	Gathering contributing activities into comprehensive categories or programs to achieve the specified objectives.

3.	Examining as a continuous process how well each activity or program has done—its effectiveness—as a final step toward improving or even eliminating them.

4.   Analyzing proposed improvements or new program proposals to see how effective they may be in achieving program goals.

5.   Projecting the entire costs of each proposal not only for the first year but for several subsequent years.

6.   Formulating a plan, based in part on the analysis of program content and effectiveness, that leads to implementation through the budget.[8]

Using this system a school district endeavors to determine, for each student, the exact cost of each program or activity that he is involved in during the school year. Analysis of costs can be organized in several ways, but ultimately what should be determined is the cost for each pupil: direct costs (such as teacher salaries, classroom supplies, support services such as the LMC, and curriculum development); and indirect costs (such as administration, maintenance, operating expenses, and debt services). These costs are projected for the current year, the next year, and five years hence.

Each program considered vital to the total educational enterprise is subjected to rigorous analysis before being programed into the budget. Fig. 6-5 illustrates the process required.

Fig. 6-5. PPBS Process

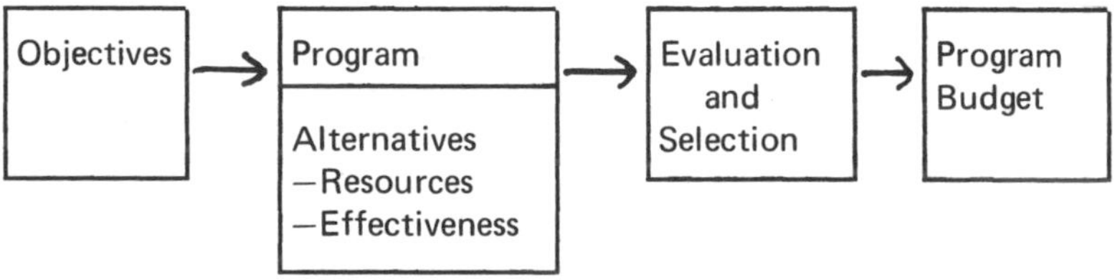

First, quanitifiable objectives must be structured for each program. Behavioral objectives in a format devised by Mager[9] are suitable for this purpose. Each program consists of a group of related activities directed toward achieving the objectives established. A series of alternatives or options is provided for each program, and these alternatives delineate resource requirements and effectiveness. Evaluation and selection of program alternatives to meet the stated objectives are based on costs, the availability of resources, and other considerations. The resulting program budget at least theoretically, will have involved a variety of school personnel, administration, board of education members, and the general public.

What does program budgeting suggest to LMC professionals? Combined with the concepts of accountability and of the LMC program as a media system, it means that media professionals must apply a few basic principles to the entire media system. The budget should be considered merely the climax in the chain of operations. Much of what is required in any budget planning takes place before a budget proposal is made. Preplanning is the key to successful program and budget development.

Under optimum conditions, the LMC program should perhaps be eliminated from consideration as an isolated entity in the budget and the costs of this service should be assigned to other educational areas: that is, a cost factor should be added to each area of school service, including science, math, English or language arts, guidance, health, independent study programs, and so on. Distributing the costs for this program—media, personnel, facilities, services—would accomplish two goals: it would provide an overview of the relative contribution of the media system to each area of concern, and through this assignment the actual program costs in principal areas of study could be determined more accurately. This can be a very practical procedure, since it provides a rational educational basis for the seemingly extravagant rise in media center costs.

If the LMC is to be budgeted as an operational entity, which is usually the case, the perspective cited above should receive due consideration. The media system that operates out of an LMC is for students and teachers, and not for the media staff. Program relationships must be clearly delineated to provide a picture of how, where, and when the instructional program is served.

The PPBS procedure requires the preparation of a document that includes not only dollar values but also a narrative presentation of program relationships. Basic to the presentation is the development of media system goals that will incorporate the ideals of service to teachers and students in terms of the educational program of the school, the individual personal needs of students, and the professional needs of the faculty. Goals that focus on individualization, independent study, and inquiry will probably coincide with the general goals of a modern educational program. If a faculty and student LMC committee representative of the school program has not been in operation prior to this time, there is no better reason for initiating such a committee. If goals are to be meaningful, they should be cooperatively developed.

The next step in the procedure calls for a program description. This section should clearly delineate the parameters of the media system for the school. A recitation of foundation, support, and primary system elements would be provided, as well as a statement of how they are organized, how they operate and the relationship between elements. This section should be limited to two or three pages.

The third ingredient, a system analysis and evaluation, is presented in narrative form and spells out how well the system serves students and teachers. Quantitative deficiencies must be related to qualitative factors. The fact that the book collection does not meet national standards is meaningless; a justification in terms of programing must be made. A deficiency exists only if a need is not being met under present conditions. Knowing how many students during a given period of time will require access to the resources provides quantitative data for use. If a knowledge of the range of students' ability such as reading scores, is added to this, an adequate statement of deficiency can be developed.

Step four of the project requires the development of long-range plans. This is a major strategy designed to bring about constructive, positive change. It requires an analysis of goals, program, and system evaluation already prepared in order to project where the media service system will be three to five years hence. A "rolling" five-year plan should be designed; this is updated each year, based on the most current information available for projecting the subsequent five-year period. Guidelines are of some assistance here because they help to define the direction for media system development. The curriculum of the school is of primary concern. Gauging programed and potential changes in content and methodology requires continuing contact through the LMC committee structure and through departments, and an exploration of district planning.

The principal input into the planning phase is a series of performance objectives for each system element. They must be clearly stated and must be measurable.

The PPBS proposal is a plan for the future. There should be a comprehensive document, which can be used for varied purposes, including public relations work. The actual budget presented should be a summary of the total plan. The format should coincide with standard budgetary procedures for the district.

Administering the Budget

The budget finally allotted to the school LMC program should provide the means for continuing existing services and also improving the operational potential of the media system. Regardless of the dollar outcome, at least three basic factors are available for the media professional to work with: a service plan for the media system, a plan for the purchase of new media and equipment as well as replacements, and a public relations vehicle.

As part of the public relations and service programs of the LMC, the media professional has an obligation to provide teachers and administrators with a review of the LMC's budget allotment and to recommend ways to adjust program expectations to reality. Such information is presented through the committee structure of the school. The professional staff judgments must be considered before final judgment is made by the head of the LMC. If student participation is expected in the evaluation and selection of media, in the formulation of LMC policy and service programs, and if student support of the media system is anticipated, then the students will need facts on which to base their judgments.

Generally, the budget of a school district allows flexibility in the handling of funds. Flexibility is provided so that the administration can meet emergency situations and can structure the most effective use of whatever funds become available. Instructional program changes make this flexibility desirable.

It is, then, perfectly legitimate to make judgments based on new evidence of need. For example, the amount to be spent for 8mm films can be decreased and the sum to be spent for filmstrips can be increased, if necessary. However, an attempt to use media funds for equipment, or vice versa, can rarely be justified. In the same way, it is rarely justifiable to use a book account for the purchase of large quantities of audiovisual media. The budget request represents a realistic appraisal of the needs of the LMC program, and the need for each item and each dollar requested has been justified. The request for a certain amount of money for printed resources says, in effect, "This is what is needed."

If transfer of funds *is* justifiable, however, permission can usually be obtained from school and district administrators, who likewise can recognize the necessity for transfer. If the media specialist has the confidence of the administration, many things are possible.

One possible way of avoiding the transfer problem is to gain the right of budget review prior to final approval and allocation of funds. The right to review allows for the restructuring of priorities in various accounts before allotments are put in final form. Some, however, suggest submitting budgets with priorities already structured.

The LMC is a many-faceted operation. It is in part a business organization responsible for the expenditure, in many cases, of thousands of dollars each year. One can expect that financial officers for the district will have accurate accounting procedures established centrally for the control of funds. Monthly or periodic financial accounting statements are often issued to each department, to provide information about the status of the department's accounts up to that date. If this information is provided on a regular basis and is reasonably up to date, it can be of value. The LMC usually needs a simplified bookkeeping system so that the head of the LMC can be aware of the status of his accounts at all times. In the absence of specific assistance from the central business office, it is suggested that this record be maintained by account number, following the same procedure used for personal checking accounts.

SUMMARY

- ◆ The library media specialist must be well informed about his own school and LMC and knowledgeable about budgeting procedures in the school district. Additionally, he must have available information about existing inventories and must be able to estimate accurately the costs of new media and equipment, maintenance and repair, rentals, and so on.

- ◆ The effective library media specialist must be involved in the budget-making process on a continuing basis.

- ◆ The Planning, Programing, Budgeting system is highly recommended by many fiscal authorities because it provides a method for directly relating programs and costs. The principal elements required are goals, program description, system analysis and evaluation, long-range plans, and performance objectives. The system provides a way to distribute LMC program costs among several academic and special programs in the schools.

LITERATURE AND FIELD INVESTIGATIONS

1. What background information is needed to develop and administer the school LMC budget? Discuss the implications of such information.

2. Investigate present thinking about various types of budgetary systems. Discuss positive and negative factors of each system.

3. Analyze the budgetary process and administration of the budget in LMC's in selected schools.

4. Compare school district budgetary systems with those in academic and public libraries. Discuss similarities and differences.

NOTES

[1] James Liesener, "The Development of a Planning Process for Media Programs," *School Media Quarterly* 1:278-287 (Summer 1973).

[2] American Association of School Librarians and Association for Educational Communications and Technology, *Media Programs: District and School* (Chicago and Washington, D.C.: American Library Association and Association for Educational Communications and Technology, 1975), p. 41.

[3] Paul Reason, *Financial Accounting for Local and State Systems* (Washington, D.C.: U.S. Government Printing Office, 1957).

[4] Charles T. Roberts, and Allan Lichtenberger, *Financial Accounting: Classifications and Standard Terminology for Local and State School Systems*, Handbook II, Revised (Washington, D.C.: U.S. Government Printing Office, 1973), p. 50.

[5] *Audiovisual Equipment Directory* (Fairfax, Va.: National Audiovisual Association, annual).

[6] Carl E. Wilsey, "Program Budgeting: An Easy Guide with the Confusion Removed," *American School Board Journal*, May 1969, p. 17.

[7] Committee on Educational Finance, *Planning for Educational Development in a Planning, Programing, Budgeting System* (Washington, D.C.: National Education Association, 1968), p. 10.

[8] "What Is a Programming, Planning, Budgeting System?," *NEA Research Bulletin*, December 1968, p. 113.

[9] Robert Mager, *Preparing Instructional Objectives* (Palo Alto, Calif.: Fearon, 1967).

REFERENCES

American Association of School Librarians and Association for Educational Communications and Technology. *Media Programs: District and School*. Chicago and Washington, D.C.: American Library Association and Association for Educational Communications and Technology, 1975.

Audiovisual Equipment Directory. Fairfax, Va.: National Audiovisual Association. Annual.

Committee on Educational Finance, *Planning for Educational Development in a Planning, Programing, Budgeting System*. Washington, D.C.: National Education Association, 1968.

Erickson, Carleton. *Administering Instructional Media Programs*. New York: Macmillan, 1968.

Gillespie, John, and Diana Spirt. *Creating a School Media Program*. New York: R.R. Bowker, 1973.

Hannigan, Jane. "PPBS and School Media Programs," *American Libraries* 3:1182-1184 (December 1972).

Liesener, James. *A Systematic Process for Planning Media Programs*. Chicago: American Library Association, 1976.

Liesener, James. "The Development of a Planning Process for Media Programs," *School Media Quarterly* 1:278-287 (Summer 1973).

Magaro, John. "PPBS—A Means Toward Accountability," *Audiovisual Instruction* 20:10-12 (December 1975).

Mager, Robert. *Preparing Instructional Objectives*. Palo Alto, Calif.: Fearon, 1967.

Roberts, Charles T., and Allan Lichtenberger. *Financial Accounting: Classifications and Standard Terminology for Local and State School Systems*, Handbook II, Revised. Washington, D.C.: U.S. Government Printing Office, 1973.

"What Is a Programming, Planning, Budgeting System?," *NEA Research Bulletin* 46:112-113 (December 1968).

Wilsey, Carl. "Program Budgeting: An Easy Guide with the Confusion Removed," *American School Board Journal* 156:16-19 (May 1969).

7

SUPPORT ELEMENTS OF THE LMC PROGRAM

OBJECTIVES

Describe the support elements needed for the effective and efficient management of a school LMC program.

Use a systems approach to design various LMC program elements in a selected school.

Chart technical services and other media system processes in a selected school.

Identify and describe alternative methods for the evaluation of the organization and personnel.

Evaluate the organization and personnel of the LMC in a selected school.

The support elements of the school media system are management and technical services. Combined with the foundation elements of media, facilities, personnel, and finance, they provide what is needed to initiate comprehensive, high contact, primary elements. Since this work is concerned with a management focus throughout, this section will deal essentially with areas not treated elsewhere.

MANAGEMENT

The term management is synonymous with administration; it refers to the act of managing, directing, or controlling. A fairly comprehensive definition was offered by the school library manpower group:

Management is the operational direction and leadership exercised for optimum operation of the school library media program. It includes the identification, acquisition, organization, administration, supervision and evaluation of the use of funds, personnel, resources and facilities to support a program for utilization of recorded knowledge.[1]

Management of the media system requires extraordinary leadership at times, because the media system affects and is affected by a broad spectrum of forces (see Fig. 7-1). It is not management in isolation or in relation to simply the nuts and bolts of equipment. It is the orchestration of diverse parts designed to create an educational climate in which students and teachers can grow. Because each school develops a unique personality, each school media system must be uniquely tailored to that personality. Considerable evidence shows that while some forces exert a

Fig. 7-1. The Media System As It Affects and Is Affected
by Varied Forces

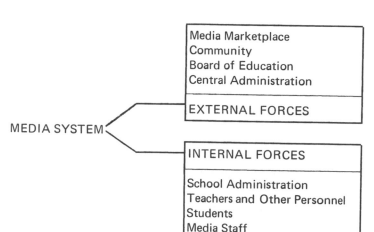

MEDIA SYSTEM

Media Marketplace
Community
Board of Education
Central Administration

EXTERNAL FORCES

INTERNAL FORCES

School Administration
Teachers and Other Personnel
Students
Media Staff

stronger influence on the media system than others and while the media system can influence and affect certain forces more than others, any of the forces can increase or reduce the effectiveness of the operation.

An obvious objective of any LMC manager, though it is often overlooked, is to be effective, to get the right things done. Drucker,[2] in his work on executive effectiveness, noted that five conditions or habits of the mind must be acquired:

1. You must know where your time is spent. Time is always in short supply and there are many pressures toward unproductive and wasteful time. Since time lost cannot be retrieved, the focus must be on accomplishing tasks which make a contribution.

2. You must focus your attention on outward contribution. The focus on contribution is the key to effectiveness. A basic question to be answered is, What can I contribute that will significantly affect the performance and results of the institution? Another question might be, What results are expected of me?

3. You must build on strengths—your own, the strengths of superiors, colleagues and subordinates—rather than weaknesses. It is probably true that no one is strong in every area "Know thyself" is aptly applied here.

4. You must concentrate on the few major areas where superior performance will produce outstanding results. There are always more important contributions to be made than time available to make them. Priorities must be set. To do "first things first," to concentrate on major opportunities gets results.

5. You must make effective decisions. This is a matter of system—the right steps in the right sequence. What is needed are fewer, but fundamental decisions.

Systems Approach

As pointed out earlier, Webster's operational definition of the term system as applied to the media program is "a complex unity formed of many often diverse parts subject to a common plan or serving a common purpose." Further, a system is "a set or arrangement of things so related or connected as to form a unity or organic whole, a set of facts, principles, rules, etc., classified or arranged in an orderly form so as to show a logical plan linking the various parts."[3]

Some time ago the "systems approach" was defined as simply a new term for the scientific method applied to problem solving. It consisted of fact finding and the critical examination of the facts regarding a total system and each of its parts. Emphasizing the analysis and design of the whole system instead of individual elements or parts, this approach encompasses the major themes of educational management today, such as accountability, behavioral objectives for programing, the PPB system for fiscal control, and the development of job descriptions.

Lehman[4] outlines the eight steps of a systems approach to education, developed by PROJECT ARISTOTLE (Annual Review and Information Symposium of the Technology of Training, Learning and Education):

1. Need—the education/training problem

2. Objectives—measurable learning goals

3. Constraints—restrictions or limitations

4. Alternatives—candidate solutions

5. Selection—choice of best alternative

6. Implementation—pilot operation of the chosen solution

7. Evaluation—measurements of results obtained against originally stated objectives

8. Modification—the change of the system to correct for deficiencies noted.

Program Objectives

Program objectives stated in behavioral terms are clearly a part of education today, and it is obvious that they will probably become even more important. The pattern has been developed in an effort to quantify, measure, evaluate, and apply a cost analysis factor to the business of education—both teaching and learning. The procedure is totally compatible with and is an integral part of a systems approach. The practice of writing behavioral objectives is not particularly well understood, though much has been written on the subject. Mager, a prominent expert in the field, said:

> An objective is an intent communicated by a statement describing a proposed change in a learner—a statement of what the learner is to be like when he has successfully completed a learning experience. It is a

description of a pattern of behavior (performance) we want the learner to be able to demonstrate.[5]

Objectives are stated in behavioral terms in order to provide clarity of understanding, observation of processes, and measurement of achievement. Where possible, the following elements are basic to the development of objectives: determine first the terminal behavior sought—that is, the kind of behavior that will be accepted as evidence that the objective has been accomplished; describe the conditions under which the behavior will occur; and state the criteria for level of performance that will be acceptable.

There are three principal advantages of using behavioral objectives. First, the program intent can be stated clearly; the most important operational objectives can be selected and focused on because they are viable; and third, when money is not available to do "everything for everyone," the existence of program objectives sets priorities.

In order to do an effective job of writing program objectives, it is necessary first to define clearly the ramifications of a total system for the school. For most, such a definition will be simply an application of the media system described in this work. From this vantage point, one can select feasible priorities from the myriad opportunities provided, with a high degree of confidence for success.

A Planning Process

Liesener's[6] comprehensive approach to planning for effective school media services is related to the concepts of accountability and PPBS budgeting. Materials are available that incorporate basic guidelines and instruments which can be used, also adapted, in the individual school or district-wide. There are nine steps in the prescribed school media planning process:

1. **Definition of Program Output Alternatives.** This basic step requires the use of a survey instrument called the "Inventory of School Library Media Center Services." It provides for a comprehensive list of potential services, arranged in six broad service categories: 1) Access to Materials, Equipment and Space; 2) Reference; 3) Production; 4) Instruction; 5) Consultation; and 6) Public Relations.

2. **Survey of Perceptions of Current Services.** The "Inventory" is used as a basis for surveying user perception of services, for increasing awareness of potential services, and for stimulating user involvement in the total operation of the media system.

3. **Determination of Service Preferences and Priorities in Relation to Local Needs.** This step requires use of a form called "Form for Determining Preferences for School Library Media Center Services." The process involves representative participation in determining service preferences and priorities. The instrument is essentially an abbreviated outline of the inventory. Output is a statement of priorities that may best serve the needs of users.

4. **Assessment of Resources and Operational Requirements of Services.** This step uses an instrument called the "School Library Media Center Data Collection Guide." The intent is to gather data in such a manner

as to be able to identify the specific resources and staff time required for providing user services at a given level.

5. **Determination of Costs of Preferred Services and/or Current Services**. An instrument called the "School Library Media Program Costing Matrix" is used. Data collected in step 4 are used with salary and materials cost figures to determine the expenditures for current service offerings as well as estimated cost of preferred services at a given level.

6. **Calculation of a Program Capability**. The process requires comparing current available resources with resource costs of preferred services, and calculating the range and level of preferred services presently feasible with resources available. The results of these calculations will reflect how many and to what extent preferred services can be provided with available resources. A picture of additional resources needed to improve service offerings is also given.

7. **Communication of Preferred Services Currently Feasible to Total Client Group**. This step is used to inform users and administrators which of the preferred services can be provided within the constraints of existing resources.

8. **Reallocation of Resources and Implementation of Changes in Operations to Provide the Range and Level of Services Selected**. In this step, judgments are made about the reallocation of resources to preferred services where possible. Also, an effort is made to provide recommendations specifying the changes needed in standard budgetary procedures in order to accommodate change.

9. **Periodic Evaluation of Services Offered and Documentation of Changing Needs**. The process is never entirely closed, since implementation and evaluation lead naturally to renewed systematic planning and modification.

Flow Charting

The process of charting has been devised to illustrate graphically the sequential flow of work and information through a system. When there are clearly defined objectives in mind, charting can be extremely useful. The principal advantage of the process is that it allows one to temporarily halt for scrutiny, operations that may be difficult to understand because of their complexity or because of the relationships that exist within a system. This does not imply that only complex operations can or should be charted. Flow charting is especially useful in either the initial organization or the comprehensive revision of a total system. Another practical and realistic use is to interpret and help others to understand various elements of a system or the total system itself. Dougherty and Heinritz[7] clearly discuss various charting procedures and provide useful examples of flow charts. In order to provide a pattern of consistency, they selected chart symbols used by the American Society of Mechanical Engineers. Probably more commonly used today is the IBM flowchart template, Form X20—8020, used in the development of program and system flowcharts. The IBM program symbols are shown in Fig. 7-2.

Fig. 7-2. IBM Flowchart Template

IBM.

```
+--------------------------------------------------+
|           FLOWCHARTING TEMPLATE                  |
+--------------------------------------------------+
```

FORM X20-8020

The symbols shown on this envelope are recommended for
use in the preparation of system and program flowcharts.

A detailed description of FLOWCHARTING TECHNIQUES
can be found in the IBM Data Processing Techniques manual
by that name (C20-8152).

PROGRAM FLOWCHART SYMBOLS

SYMBOL	REPRESENTS
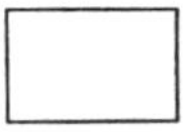	**PROCESSING** A group of program instructions which perform a processing function of the program.
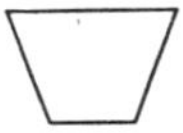	**INPUT/OUTPUT** Any function of an input/output device (making information available for processing, recording processing information, tape positioning, etc.).
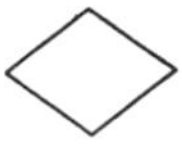	**DECISION** The decision function used to document points in the program where a branch to alternate paths is possible based upon variable conditions.
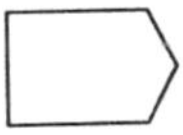	**PROGRAM MODIFICATION** An instruction or group of instructions which changes the program.
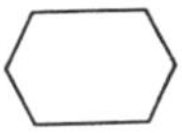	**PREDEFINED PROCESS** A group of operations not detailed in the particular set of flowcharts.
	**TERMINAL** The beginning, end, or a point of interruption in a program.
	CONNECTOR An entry from, or an exit to, another part of the program flowchart.
	OFFPAGE CONNECTOR A connector used instead of the connector symbol to designate entry to or exit from a page.
 ◁ ▷ ▽ △	**FLOW DIRECTION** The direction of processing or data flow.

SUPPLEMENTARY SYMBOL FOR SYSTEM AND PROGRAM FLOWCHARTS

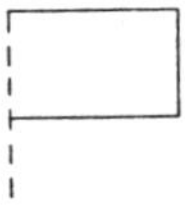	**ANNOTATION** The addition of descriptive comments or explanatory notes as clarification.

Various types of charting procedures are used for different purposes. For example, a block diagram is a simple graphic representation of a process or collection of processes. It may be used alone as a generalized explanatory device or used as the first step in charting the improvement of a given situation. Fig. 7-3 shows a block diagram graphically representing a generalized circulation system.

Fig. 7-3. Generalized Circulation System—Block Diagram

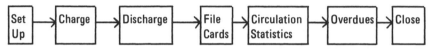

Fig. 7-4 shows an adaptation of Dougherty and Heinritz's flow process charting procedure that can be readily used to chart processes in the school LMC. Once the steps and descriptions are placed in order, symbols are added to complete the chart. At this point a flow diagram can be designed from the data collected, if required.

Fig. 7-4. Flow Process Chart (Teacher Request for Specific Book)

Subject Charted: **Type of Chart:**

Present Method   Proposed Method   Man   Product

        Chart Begins:
        Chart Ends:

Symbol	Steps	Description of Events
 ▽	1	Teacher request
□	2	Check catalog
◇	3	Not available—report to user
□	4	Available—check shelf
◇	5	Not on shelf—report to user
 □	6	Available—charge to user
 ▽	7	Deliver

---

Adapted from Richard Dougherty and Fred Heinritz, *Scientific Management of Libraries* (Metuchen, N.J., Scarecrow, 1966).

Decision flow charting is a means of representing work flows that include yes and no decisions. This type of chart is generally considered best for analyzing complicated work flows requiring many decisions. The IBM flowchart template, Form X20—8020, is usually the source of symbols. The template contains both program and system symbols; the system symbols are usually reserved for flow charting computer systems. The symbols are usable for both manual and machine systems. Fig 7-5 illustrates a simple decision flow chart.

Fig. 7-5. Decision Flow Chart (Teacher Request for Specific Book)

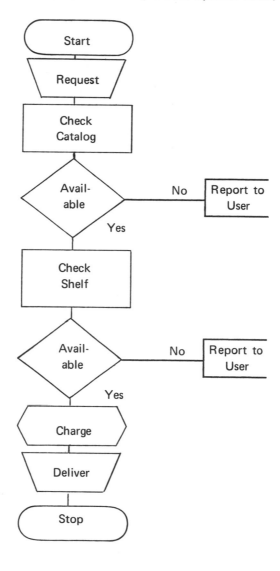

In developing the flow chart, flow or progression may be vertical, top to bottom; or horizontal, left to right. All charts developed should follow the same procedure. The main flow, referred to as the trunk, consists of processes and decisions that are expected to occur. Usually, "yes" decisions follow the main trunk. Exceptions, as noted by "no" decisions, are represented by branch flows, which set up a deviant pattern. Symbols used are connected by directional lines, and arrows represent an exit or entry from one symbol to another in a direction that deviates from the flow direction. Start and stop points are clearly defined. Several consecutive pages may be used for related segments of the flow chart to avoid crowding and to clarify the total picture. A general recommendation is to keep information, product, and personnel chartings separate. The type of charting that will best suit the purpose should be chosen as soon as possible.

The application of flow charting to such LMC processes as the technical services area can do much to streamline procedures, can aid in the training of personnel, and can generally clarify service patterns.

Evaluation

When we wish to evaluate something or someone our intent is "to examine and judge concerning the worth, quality, significance, amount, degree or condition of"[8] whatever is to be evaluated. In order to do this, some norm or standard must be applied against which to gauge the subject for evaluation. However, as soon as the term "standard" is mentioned, there appears to be some confusion of meanings. Hence, it becomes necessary to supply another definition. A standard is "something established by authority, custom, or general consent as a model or example to be followed—a definite level or degree of quality that is adequate and proper for a specific purpose."[9] There are many types of standards, including accreditation and personnel standards. Of particular interest to the media professional are diagnostic standards (represented by the Task Analysis Survey[10] conducted by the American Association of School Librarians) and projective standards (best represented by *Media Programs: District and School*[11]).

Diagnostic or benchmark standards are based on a model of conditions existing in LMC's that have programs of superior quality. School LMC's participating in the Task Analysis Survey had to meet stated criteria of excellence for inclusion in the study. These standards become practical to use because they represent conditions as they exist. One major problem of diagnostic standards is that they frequently fall short of what we believe should be the pattern of conditions in a given situation. They do not satisfy one's desire for optimum conditions.

Projective standards are directed to conditions as they ought to be. They are guidelines for the development of programing. Because projective standards cannot be easily realized, however, they become controversial. The typical administrative reaction to the national school media standards has been simply to challenge the credibility of the recommendations. Nevertheless, standards do meet many of our needs, serving as a basis for comparison with existing conditions and goals for long- or short-range planning for educational improvement.

The LMC standards that are available are part of a larger field of educational standards and the overall question of standardization in education. Both quantitative and qualitative factors are usually considered in any educational standard, though it is not necessarily imperative that the standards include both factors.

Quantitative standards provide numerical measurements and detailed requirements for programing services. Standards stated in numerical terms and applied to a given situation make measurement, evaluation, and, where applicable, enforcement relatively easy. However, if quantitative standards are used as the only criterion, there is no way to judge the results of the quantitative inputs against an educational output. They require continuous monitoring and evaluation.

Qualitative standards, on the other hand, represent an attempt to express in functional terms the same ideal requirements as quantitative standards, encouraging a level of service that is adequate for each school in terms of its own needs. Because they are not expressed in exact quantitative amounts, they are difficult to measure or to enforce. Obviously, standards that reflect some coordination of quantitative and qualitative factors are to be desired.

Many external devices can be used in evaluating the school media system. Using projective national standards and/or diagnostic standards as a basis for comparison is a common method. Regional, state, and local standards, where available, are additional tools. Some schools or school districts use consultants, whether paid or voluntary, as another means of determining the worth or quality of the media system. The professional consultant, besides using various standards available for comparison, usually brings several years of experience to the task of evaluation.

If a systems approach has been employed, then needs have been ascertained, objectives determined, programs implemented, and continous monitoring for feedback on performance has been instituted. Program concepts and objectives may be adapted from various external sources, although terminal objectives and performance criteria have been created for the specific school situation.

There is a special need to evaluate the library media system, since philosophically and operationally media personnel devote themselves to a particular vehicle for educational improvement. The evaluation is needed, therefore, to prove out the system. This is more important now than at any other time, because taxpayers and educators, worried about the cost factor in education, want to achieve the maximum benefit at the lowest cost. Any alternative approach that can guarantee a reasonable degree of success will be considered very carefully. The lower the cost factor, the greater the possibility that the approach will be implemented. The LMC is only one way of achieving educational goals.

Thus, the LMC's value to a sound educational program is not necessarily known and appreciated, particularly if a dollar factor is involved. An adequately funded LMC is not an insignificant budget item. Costing out a comprehensive LMC program and comparing its cost with that of other programs provides an idea of how many program priorities are established. A fair estimate of cost may be arrived at by computing the following: staff costs, media inventory costs, furnishings and equipment costs, and the square foot cost of space occupied. For a more complete picture, the cost of custodial service, electricity, heat, and telephone can be prorated and added to the previous total. Also, all funds available for the present fiscal year should be added.

Another way of evaluating the LMC is to dismiss the concept of the LMC as a separate entity. As in a planning-programing-budgeting system, cost and responsibility for optimum use of the LMC are assigned to the various school departments and/or teachers or programs. This procedure precludes the evaluation of the LMC by the school teaching staff when the question is raised about the ability of the LMC to meet their needs. Evaluation is directed to programs and hinges on teacher and student use of the LMC. The intent here is not to avoid evaluation but rather to assign responsibility for use of the LMC where it belongs. The investment in an LMC system is made because of the judgment that the system will improve teaching and learning. If this is not the case, evaluation of the curriculum and instructional methodology usually reveals the reasons for the lack of improvement.

The entire school media system should be subjected to continuous evaluation in relation to the school program. The head of the LMC should assume primary responsibility for coordinating all facets of evaluation, though it is expected that the total media staff, school administration, teachers, and students will also be involved. There are tools which can be used as guides to general media system evaluation, such as *Evaluative Criteria,* [12] designed for the evaluation of elementary, middle, and senior high schools. Usually these criteria have media system review components so that the school can gauge media services in relation to programs of the total school. The evaluation pattern of these tools usually consists of approximately a year's self-evaluation by the school staff, followed by a visit from a consultant team to review and evaluate.

Of principal significance to evaluation today is the development of program objectives for the varied components of foundation, support, and primary elements of the media system.

Data Collection and Report Writing

Work does expand to fill the amount of time available. This statement applies particularly well to data collection, report writing, and the dozens of tasks which, when lumped together, can well take all of the time that should be devoted to program development. A good rule to follow is to collect data only when required, such as for standard reports to central administrative headquarters and for annual state reports.

Collecting circulation statistics merely to indicate that circulation was up or down by two percent can be a waste of time, unless some definite use of the statistics is intended. If, however, a pilot project on the use of paperbacks is underway, with a special appropriation of $2,000 for purchase of paperbacks, then it would seem logical to provide a statistical analysis of use as well as a narrative report of the experiment.

The annual report can be an effective informational piece as well as a major public relations document. The report should do essentially three things: 1) report concisely and informatively on the significant happenings during the past year; 2) provide recommendations for program improvement; and 3) provide a forecast of expectations for the following year. Clearly, this report should be used in conjunction with the annual budget request. If the budget includes the PPB system or some modification of it, program objectives are stated. The annual report highlights significant achievement in terms of meeting the stated objectives. Recommendations for improvement develop naturally as a need for new program inputs is seen. The forecast of expectations deals with anticipated new or additional outputs or, conversely, with a decrease in existing levels of performance.

Public Relations and Publicity

Public relations consists of the total LMC image projected to its public—i.e., the community, the school staff, and the students. Publicity is the method used to inform the LMC's public about what is being done, how it is being done, and the degree of success that is achieved.

The media staff is principally responsible for the public relations program of the LMC. It should be realized, however, that anyone who comes in contact with the LMC may develop an attitude (favorable or unfavorable) toward the program. An effective public relations program is constructed from a careful analysis of media system elements and an evaluation of the needs of its public. Some of the steps taken to ensure success are as follows:

1. Students, teachers, and administrators are involved in the preview, evaluation, and selection of media as well as the establishment of policy and procedures guidelines that set the pattern of service for the school and the environment for the LMC.

2. Students are involved in special programs emanating from the LMC. They receive, as needed, guidance in research, reading, and the design and production of media. Service and facilities are available to accommodate special interest groups.

3. Teachers are satisfied that the LMC is meeting the media and service needs of their students. Teachers have assistance as needed, through structured in-service programs or individual consultation on curriculum planning and implementation, and through the design or modification of media for instructional purposes. Their requirements for professional media and information are satisfied.

4. School administrators and the central administrative staff receive reports as needed, are provided with both planning and operational assistance as new programs are developed and implemented, and receive on a continuing basis professional information of interest to them and to the total school staff.

5. For other agencies encompassed by the system, such as public libraries, regional educational centers, and so on, there is a planned exchange of information and there are clearly defined levels of cooperation which can be advertised. Where applicable, the writing of projects for the development of federal or state funded programs is carried out cooperatively.

6. The general public or community is kept informed of school activities and the special contributions of the LMC to the success of these programs through commercial news media, through publicity hand-outs carried home by students, and indirectly by children, who provide visible evidence of program assistance.

7. The Board of Education, representing the attitudes and opinions of the public, receives news releases that pertain to the school LMC, and LMC bulletins, issued on a regular basis; reports and special displays of media and equipment are provided as needed.

TECHNICAL SERVICES

The area of technical services is an important support element. It is sometimes poorly understood by users because procedures are not clear to them.

The user of the LMC wants media ordered, processed, and placed in his hand the following day, if not sooner. His position is readily understandable. Most people want to avoid the lengthy delay between the placement of an order and the announcement that the material is ready for use. The technical services office is designed to handle this program element expeditiously and without a great deal of fanfare.

The technical services area includes acquisitions, preparation and organization of media, circulation/distribution, and maintenance of media and equipment.

Acquisitions

Media professionals should be familiar with the budgeting and ordering procedures for their school districts. Full knowledge of these important procedures is a must if one is to do an effective job in acquisitions and indeed in any area of technical services.

The following information is needed for carrying out the acquisitions function efficiently:

1. What is the school district fiscal year? Though more and more communities are adopting the uniform fiscal year, July 1–June 30, many districts follow a different fiscal year.

2. What is the purchasing year allowed under district regulations? In some districts operated on a uniform fiscal year, orders can be sent to vendors before school closes sometime in June, with billing from vendors requested for some time after the new budget year. Most school districts allow purchasing for eight to nine months but have a fixed deadline for placement of final orders.

3. The acquisitions department needs to be able to place orders throughout the budget year. Unfortunately, in some districts bidding and other procedures allow orders to be placed only once. Others may limit the placement of orders to only two or three times. Such a procedure handicaps the LMC program. One should always be able to

place special orders for new media that will just fit a particular instructional or recreational need, that will solve a particular teacher's or student's need, or that suit a newly implemented instructional program. Procedures that limit the number of orders should be changed, through use of a strategy developed cooperatively with school administrators, business office officials, and others.

4.   Most school districts have "standard" requisition and purchase order forms. Some districts require that all orders be typed on requisition forms in the LMC, and the business office personnel then transfer that information to purchase order forms. Other districts allow the direct typing of purchase order forms by LMC personnel, to expedite the process. Still other districts allow orders to be placed on multiple copy order forms, and the business office merely generates a purchase order form to provide an encumbrance for the amount of the order. One must become familiar with the forms employed and the procedures for their use.

It is desirable to place orders as expeditiously as possible. In any budget year, the bulk of the orders should be placed as soon as funds are released by school business officials. Sixty to seventy-five percent of funds should be expended initially, with the remainder held for new media and special order requirements. The two reasons for this procedure are: 1) the fact that media are needed provides ample justification for immediate ordering; and 2) funds must be available during the year for new media and to meet special program needs that develop.

If the process of selecting media is an orderly, on-going activity, the LMC staff will have available at all times a fairly comprehensive "considerations" file of media already evaluated by various selection teams. This stage of readiness is vital if the business at hand is to be conducted efficiently. A typical budget request for a certain number of dollars per pupil for media can be modified to state that a certain number of dollars is needed to purchase the attached list of media required in the instructional program of the school.

Two important problems that relate to the technical services program of cataloging, preparation, and organization of media must be considered. The first problem concerns the establishment of policy and procedures for handling audiovisual media forms. The second problem involves decision-making about who is to handle the task of cataloging, preparing, and organizing media for the school or district.

Cataloging and Processing Media

Standard operating procedures for cataloging printed resources have combined the use of the Dewey Decimal Classification[13] and Sears.[14] Elementary school LMC's and schools with modest collections and a modest potential for growth have usually used the abridged version of Dewey, while secondary schools have used the unabridged version.

Audiovisual media have presented a major problem for those involved in the cataloging and processing of these resources. Audiovisual specialists, who may have controlled these collections in the past, generally used an accession system, assigning a number to each item purchased. Symbols (such as FS for filmstrips) were often used with the accession number. During the early days of the audiovisual field, resources were housed in a central facility called an Audiovisual Center or Instructional Materials Center, and were distributed as needed. The user usually had access only to a prepared list or book catalog, which was arranged alphabetically by title and subject. He requested an item, using the proper procedure; the item was retrieved, distributed to him, and later collected. This was a typical closed-stack operation.

Library media specialists, on the other hand, have tended to use a subject classification scheme, which groups media on the same subject. There is also a trend among these specialists to store all media forms on the same subject in the same location. If access to open shelves is allowed, there appears to be some advantage to the user to find all media on the same subject housed together. If different media forms are housed in separate locations, there is still an advantage to the user in having a single class number to unlock the collections.

Several guides have been produced that deal with the audiovisual media problem, including *Standards for Cataloging Nonprint Materials*.[15] and *Non-Book Materials: The Organization of Integrated Collections*.[16] These guides have been officially endorsed by national media organizations. *Standards for Cataloging Nonprint Materials* was produced under the aegis of the Association for Educational Communications and Technology. *Non-Book Materials*, though a publication of the Canadian Library Association, received the endorsement of the American Library Association.

In the cataloging of audiovisual media, two points are obvious: 1) a nationally recognized and endorsed system should be used, and 2) basic decisions on processes should be made on a district, regional, or other network basis rather than at the individual school level. In this way, students and teachers find some continuity articulated through the grades.

Centralized or Commercial Cataloging and Processing

Media should arrive at the individual school LMC in processed form. There are only two ways of ensuring that the material will be pre-processed: the centralized processing service or commercial processing.

Recognizing that the task of cataloging and processing should be removed from the individual school LMC, the library media specialist should raise some questions: What will centralized processing cost? What are the alternatives?

A case study of one school district of approximately 30,000 students, which has employed centralized processing since the early 1940s is used as an example here. A processing center of about 5,000 square feet is staffed by three professionals and eleven support personnel to catalog and process all media for 50 schools. In a recent year the center cataloged and processed 56,810 items, including books, filmstrips, disc and tape recordings, slides, maps, and pictures.

What is the cost of this operation? Fig. 7-6 provides some estimated costs for the staffing of this center. The salaries cited are probable salary ranges for professional and support staff. Actual dollar amounts may vary considerably. Assuming a minimum salary for the three professionals involved, cost would be $27,000, whereas if we assume a maximum salary (which is the level that they will all reach some day, if they enjoy their work) of $16,000 each for the three professionals, then the cost would be $48,000. Using these figures provides an average cost for three professionals of $37,000. For support personnel, there is an average cost of $60,500 for eleven support personnel. Total staffing costs would range from a minimum of $71,000 to a maximum of $125,000, with the average being $98,000.

Fig. 7-6. Staff Costs for One Processing Center

	Minimum	Maximum	Average
3 professionals @ $9,000 to $16,000	$27,000	$ 48,000	$37,500
11 support staff @ $4,000 to $7,000	44,000	77,000	60,500
Staffing Costs	$71,000	$125,000	$98,000

Pursuing data gathering a bit further, it is necessary to ask whether these 56,810 items processed represent the maximum load for the staff? Will personnel costs go up if additional funds become available for media and the number of items received is doubled? A crucial question might be, how much is this costing per item? This figure is computed by dividing average staffing costs by the number of items processed, to arrive at $1.73 per item. This figure is not entirely correct, of course, because the staff provides other services, such as maintaining a union catalog and preparing bibliographies in special subject areas.

Not mentioned to this point is the fact that, wherever possible, kits are purchased at $0.39 each. Extrapolating that figure to cover the preparation costs if kits were not available, it is necessary to multiply $0.39 by 56,810 items, showing an additional cost of $22,156 and bringing the per item cost to $2.12. There are also other costs which are commonly overlooked or simply absorbed: cost of 5,000 square feet of floor space, equipment costs, electricity and fuel costs, and maintenance cost.

Assuming that a catalog of commercially processed media is available, one may note a price of $0.79 per item for standard processing. Quickly computing the cost ($0.79 times 56,810 items), one finds a gross processing cost of $44,880 when the job is done by a commercial firm and $120,156 when it is accomplished within the district. Someone is left with the task of justifying an expenditure of $76,276 per year above commercial costs for cataloging and processing, plus other costs not computed.

What does the commercial vendor offer? Commercial cataloging and processing houses are usually regular book jobbers that carry large inventories. They are automated to a considerable extent and can handle expeditiously a large volume of business. Some of the specific services offered by one vendor[17] are wide choices, pre-selected collections, cataloging, processing, and free quotations. Over 65,000 titles, pre-school through young adult, are available in cataloged and processed form. Titles included in the vendor's catalog have been pre-selected for quality, since they are recommended in "standard" library selection tools such as the *Elementary School Library Collection*,[18] *Junior High School Library Catalog*,[19] *Senior High School Library Catalog*,[20] and other reputable sources. In addition to the choice of items in the catalog, complete collections—often called opening day collections—for elementary, junior, and senior high schools are also available.

Does commercial cataloging provide a problem-free system? Unfortunately, there is no such thing. Even when dealing with a reputable vendor, one encounters the same problems that would be found in dealing with a school district centralized processing center. One general problem, for example, is that there are sometimes long delays before an order is filled. A solution to this is to specify a cancellation date (such as 90 to 120 days). If unfilled orders are cancelled, then the buyer can expend LMC funds within the fiscal year, either by direct purchase from other sources or by electing to purchase other items. Another problem is that commercial vendors often recommend that the LMC over-order by 20 to 30 percent. Because of the general difficulty in supplying titles, approximately 20 percent (and in some cases 30 percent) of the books ordered will not be available for some reason. Two options are: to over-order by providing the vendor with the original order plus a supplementary list of books also needed, or to place only the basic order but to plan on a shorter cancellation date, so as to free funds for direct purchase.

At the present time, school LMC's need cataloged and processed audiovisual media, but no commercial vendor is providing such material adequately. The closest attempt is that catalog cards are supplied with the purchase of audiovisual media. The centralized processing center previously discussed did provide cataloging and processing for some 9,400 audiovisual media items which, in all probability, could not be purchased in commercially processed form.

In order to justify its existence, centralized processing should operate at a higher level of efficiency and should handle a much larger volume of media. Regional or other networks are one possible alternative to high cost district service and poor performance on the part of commercial vendors.

District and regional cooperatives might find it useful to organize central processing services for audiovisual media until the commercial field "catches up." The service would then be phased out.

Circulation/Distribution

All media forms and equipment eventually end up as part of the organized resources of the LMC, being processed to the point of storage. The circulation/distribution procedure begins when the media must be retrieved for use (see Fig. 7-7).

Fig. 7-7. Media Cycle

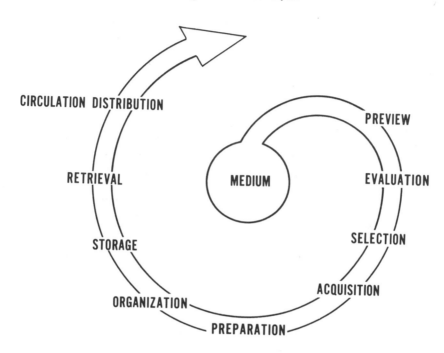

The term "circulation/distribution" describes the two functions that are coordinated at a single LMC work station. In the past, these functions were separate and distinct where separate library and audiovisual services were provided for a school. In a school library, circulation generally implied active participation by a patron:

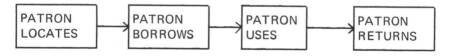

On the other hand, distribution as an audiovisual concept implied an active service function by staff:

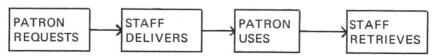

LMC staff-patron interaction relative to circulation/distribution, whether in person or by phone, takes place at the service desk. Equipment for distribution to teaching stations need not be housed in this area; however, a work order for distribution would be initiated from this work station. The booking of films is coordinated in the same way. Unless the LMC is very large, the circulation/distribution service desk becomes the information center through which all patron requests are initiated.

Circulating Media

All media forms circulate from the service desk. Circulation procedures should be kept simple and all media forms should be allowed to circulate outside the school as needed on an overnight basis. Fines should not be levied for overdue items, though patrons should pay for lost or damaged media forms and equipment.

The school LMC can use mechanical or automated charging systems. It appears that for some years to come, the manual system will continue to be used. For most schools, a manual self-charging system that uses date-due cards is more desirable than slips that must be pasted in books or somehow affixed to the media form (see Fig. 7-8). These are available from library supply houses. This process eliminates the need to stamp each item to be borrowed. Cards are pre-stamped prior to the day's business and the borrower merely takes one, or is handed one, for each item borrowed. Book cards, or cards for other media borrowed, need not be dated immediately but can be handled during slack periods or at the end of the day.

One large problem faced by media personnel is how to handle loan transactions for individual filmstrips or other media forms that cannot accommodate the usual book pocket. Several methods are available:

1. A lined sheet of paper is kept for each media form, on which the borrower lists items to be taken. As items are returned, names are scratched from the list. Date due cards may be used.

2. Cards prepared for each media form are kept at the service desk in trays. When a patron borrows a particular item, the card file is scanned, the card pulled for the patron's signature, and the card filed along with other items circulated. When the media form is returned, the transaction card is returned to the file. Date due cards may be used.

3. A reasonable alternative, which can be used at any school level, is simply to have blank cards available for the patron to complete when he wishes to borrow an item for which no standard "bookcard" is available (Fig. 7-9). The borrower supplies the following information: media symbol, title of item, his name, and location. Though the method does present some problems, such as the legibility of patrons' handwriting or the inability of very young children to handle the situation adequately, it does work well. It solves the clerical problem of typing cards to prepare a file, searching the file for the transaction card when a patron wishes to borrow, and re-filing cards when the item has been discharged. When used in combination with "date due" cards, the system is adaptable to most situations.

Fig. 7-8. Date Due Card   Fig. 7-9. Transaction Card

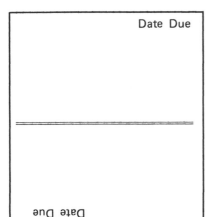

Mechanical, electrically operated charging systems are available from major library supply houses. They are simple to install and operate and can handle charging and discharging, reserves, overdues, renewals, and circulation statistics. They are frequently recommended when the volume of transactions approaches 300 a day. Many public libraries that have far fewer than 300 transactions a day use the system because the method features a borrower's card. Although there is usually no need for a student card for LMC borrowing privileges, student I.D.'s are common in secondary schools for admission to sports events and so on. Where there is a possibility for double duty, this process may be employed.

An automated circulation control system is also possible for many schools. If a school district has a computer available—and most districts of any size today will have access to one or are part of a regional system that has one—many systems can be automated. In the individual school, the major problem is usually securing guaranteed access to a computer on a continuing basis.

The automated system can handle both charges and returns, entirely omitting the slipping process. Usually a daily status report on items borrowed is produced, so the media specialist knows daily what items are out, who has them, and when they are due back. Overdue notices are also usually generated by the computer process.

Distribution of Equipment

There are probably as many methods of handling equipment distribution in a school as there are school districts. In any case no one system will be suitable for all because of the many variables found from school to school, such as physical lay-out of the building and the amount of equipment available. Flexible and efficient procedures are needed for an effective pattern of distribution.

The delivery of equipment to teaching stations should be cut to a minimum. If the supply of equipment is adequate and security is regulated, equipment should be deployed to fixed locations throughout the school. Many of the newer schools being built provide for decentralized storage of equipment. Patterns range from departmental storage at the secondary level to first-, second-, and third-floor storage space in multi-level buildings, to cluster storage, where an equipment storage closet is expected to serve four to six classrooms. A pattern of assigning equipment to various grade levels in elementary schools, where rooms are close to each other, has also been used. Any of these patterns will reduce distribution from a central storage area. Of course, if equipment storage is decentralized, a reserve equipment pool must be maintained for emergency breakdowns or for conflicts in use.

Although decentralization offers definite relief for the LMC in terms of delivery, and puts equipment close to the people who will use it, it is certainly not without problems. The questions of inventory, maintenance, and repair plague the LMC staff. Unless teachers are willing to cooperate, the usual operational check of equipment after use becomes impossible. The concept of optimum utilization of equipment is abandoned, since assigning equipment permanently to a teaching station guarantees only that the assignment has been made and that the potential for use is probably greater than if the device were not there. Certain devices may not be used at all; others may receive minimal use. There is also the problem of possession; once equipment is assigned, should a department be asked to relinquish a device?

Regardless of the size of the media staff, including willing students, it is desirable to reduce delivery service and equipment operator service to a minimum. It is essential to have an in-service training program to show teachers how to operate standard equipment. As an alternative solution, the teacher could designate a student, or students, from each class to learn the fundamentals of projection and general equipment operation. The alternative presented is highly recommended for three reasons: the teacher's time is spent preparing students for learning experiences rather than readying equipment, student operators are a part of the group and feel an obligation to do a good job, and the media staff is relieved of the pressure to get student operators to various teaching stations, where they remain for educationally unproductive periods of time ranging from 15 to 50 minutes. Since the training of very young children is not possible, teachers in the primary grades must learn to operate the equipment. At this level, however, paraprofessionals are being used as teacher aides; if paraprofessionals are available, they are the logical people to train. Projectionists or equipment specialists should be provided for fixed location operations, such as in auditoriums, multi-media lecture halls, and automated learning laboratories.

The reservation and scheduling of equipment should be handled at the service desk. A reservation sheet should be available so that teachers can sign for equipment; if possible, they should also be able to request equipment reservations by phone. In most schools, a day's notice is usually adequate for reservation, depending on the availability of equipment. It is suggested that one reservation sheet be used for each day and that enough sheets be available at one time to book equipment for a period of at least a month. Unless the equipment inventory is extremely modest, a visible file or record of equipment on hand should be available for rapid scanning. Forms are available from commercial supply houses. While some equipment booking procedures are better than others, no one method is perfect in every situation. Fig. 7-10 shows two alternatives. Pattern A, which provides for the reservation of equipment by day and period in clearly marked spaces, may be used where adequate space can be allowed for the anticipated number of reservations or if the availability of equipment limits the number possible. This form is used by the media clerk at the end of the day to schedule deliveries by simply adding equipment identification numbers, the names of students who will deliver the device, and any comments relative to the assignment. Pattern B is unstructured and allows for variations of space on the page required to book equipment as needed. It probably is also better suited for schools operating on flexible rather than fixed time schedules. At the end of the day or period of use, all equipment used should be collected, checked to verify readiness for use, and organized for distribution the following day.

Fig. 7-10. Generalized Equipment Distribution Forms (A—B)

Form A

Period	Teacher	Rm.	Equipment	Equip. No.	Student Aide	Comments
1	Thomas	4	16mm proj.	MP3	John	
2						
3						
4						

Form B

Time Needed	Teacher	Rm.	Equipment	Equip. No.	Student Aide	Comments

Maintenance of Media and Equipment

The effectiveness of the LMC program may be seriously impaired if media and equipment are not kept in good condition. The media system that has dog-eared books, dirty and scratched records, and projectors with blown-out lamps is doomed to failure. Beyond the maintenance performed in the individual school, there is usually a need for in-depth support at the district level or through contractual service plans with commercial firms.

Maintaining printed media is similar to maintaining audiovisual media at the individual school level. For printed media, cleaning and mending are regularly carried out with dispatch using various supplies readily available from commercial library supply houses. Beyond the mending of torn pages and frayed bindings, printed media are regularly sent out to a commercial firm for re-binding. On request, the techniques of book mending and repair will usually be taught to a group of interested people by a sales representative of these same commercial supply houses. Printed media are ordinarily given a casual inspection at the service desk or during an annual inventory.

As pointed out, some of the maintenance tasks required for audiovisual media can be equated with those performed on printed media. In the main these tasks revolve around cleaning processes for the various audiovisual forms and the splicing of damaged 8mm and 16mm films or audio tapes. Supplies to accomplish these tasks are available today from commercial library supply houses as well as from distributors of audiovisual equipment and supplies. Beyond this simple maintenance, it becomes a matter of replacement of the medium or, in the case of 16mm films, the replacement of footage. Inspection of most audiovisual forms is tedious and time consuming. In most LMC's no effort is made to inspect audiovisual forms, except those that can be scanned quickly or 16mm film, which can be machine-inspected automatically. It is more common to rely on either written or verbal reports from users on the condition of media used. This procedure is acceptable as long as every effort is made to have reports filed, and as long as action is taken to remove worn or defective items from circulation and to provide the maintenance required, to replace the item, or to remove it totally from the active rolls.

In most school districts, maintenance and repair of equipment is shared with a district center or a commercial firm. The degree of sophistication of equipment (such as the presence or absence of television, language laboratories, and multi-media large-group instructional areas) generally determines the availability of qualified equipment technicians in the school or district.

Equipment should receive an operational maintenance check after each use. This can sometimes be omitted, if each user fills out a simple check form about the condition of the equipment before dispatching it to another user. A maintenance and repair file must be kept as part of the inventory file, and inspection and cleaning should be carried out and duly noted at regularly scheduled intervals. The file should also contain a record of lamp changes, minor adjustments, repairs, and annual service checks.

The inexperienced professional or clerk has access to published maintenance and repair information as well as operating instruction guides provided with the purchase of equipment. Also, service manuals obtained directly from manufacturers can be used to keep abreast of specific equipment maintenance and repair requirements.

When qualified equipment technicians are employed for the school or district, they ordinarily perform both annual servicing and equipment repairs as needed. If the technician performs a multi-purpose function (including graphics, media processing, and equipment maintenance), then adjustments will have to be made in the individual's schedule. These are decisions that must be made at the local level.

SUMMARY

♦ The support elements of the media system contain two complex operational components—management and technical services.

♦ Management has been defined as "the operational direction and leadership exercised for optimum operation of the school library media program. It includes the identification, acquisition, organization, administration, supervision and evaluation of the use of funds, personnel, resources and facilities to support a program for utilization of recorded knowledge."

♦ Technical services include the acquisition, organization and preparation, circulation/distribution and maintenance of media and equipment. The concept of technical services may be expanded to embrace the total cycle beginning with preview, evaluation, and selection of media.

LITERATURE AND FIELD INVESTIGATIONS

1. What background information is needed for effective design of the support elements for a school LMC? Discuss the implications of such information.

2. Discuss the relationship between support and foundation elements of the school media system.

3. Investigate various management styles that can be used in working with the media staff.

4. Compare the management structure of the school LMC to those employed in academic and public libraries. Discuss similarities and differences.

5. Design charting systems for the training of media personnel and various services of the LMC.

6. In a selected school district, cost out a system for technical services—centralized or commercial. Provide a rationale for the selection of one system.

7.   In a selected school district, cost out a system for the maintenance and repair of equipment—contracted or local basis. Provide a rationale for the selection of one system.

8.   Evaluate various elements of the LMC program in a selected school.

NOTES

[1] American Association of School Librarians, *School Library Manpower Project (Phase I—Final Report)*. (Chicago: American Library Association, 1970), p. 48.

[2] Peter Drucker, *The Effective Executive* (New York: Harper and Row, 1967), pp. 23-24.

[3] *Webster's Third New International Dictionary* (Springfield, Mass.: G. & C. Merriam Co., 1971), p. 2322; see also Edythe Moore, "System Analysis: An Overview," *Special Libraries*, February 1967, pp. 87-90.

[4] Henry Lehman, "The Systems Approach to Education," *Audiovisual Instruction*, February 1968, p. 145.

[5] Robert Mager, *Preparing Instructional Objectives* (Palo Alto, Calif.: Fearon, 1967), p. 3.

[6] James Liesener, "The Development of a Planning Process for Media Programs," *School Media Quarterly* 1:278-287 (Summer 1973).

[7] Richard Dougherty, and Fred Heinritz, *The Scientific Management of Libraries* (Metuchen, N.J.: Scarecrow Press, 1966).

[8] *Webster's Third New International Dictionary* p. 786.

[9] *Ibid*. p. 2223.

[10] American Association of School Librarians, *School Library Personnel Task Analysis Survey* (Chicago: American Library Association, 1969).

[11] American Association of School Librarians and Association for Educational Communications and Technology, *Media Programs: District and School* (Chicago and Washington, D.C.: American Library Association and Association for Educational Communications and Technology, 1975).

[12] National Study of Secondary School Evaluation, *Evaluative Criteria for the Evaluation of Secondary Schools* (Washington, D.C.: National Study of Secondary School Evaluation, 1969); National Study of School Evaluation, *Junior High School/Middle School Evaluative Criteria: A Guide for School Improvement* (Arlington, Va.: National Study of School Evaluation, 1970); National Study of School Evaluation, *Elementary School Evaluative Criteria: Guide for School Improvement* (Arlington, Va.: National Study of School Evaluation, 1973).

[13] Melvil Dewey, *Dewey Decimal Classification and Relative Index*, 10th abridged ed. (Lake Placid Club, N.Y.: Forest Press, 1971).

[14] Barbara Westby, ed. *Sears List of Subject Headings*, 10th ed. (New York: H. W. Wilson Co., 1972).

[15] Association for Educational Communications and Technology, *Standards for Cataloging Nonprint Materials* (Washington, D.C.: Association for Educational Communications and Technology, 1976).

[16] Jean R. Weihs, Shirley Lewis, and Janet MacDonald, *Non-Books Materials: The Organization of Integrated Collections* (Ottawa: Canadian Library Association, 1973).

[17] *Books for School Libraries* (Williamsport, Pa.: Bro-Dart, Inc., 1976). Vendor's catalog.

[18] Mary Gaver, *The Elementary School Library Collection: A Guide to Books and Other Media*, 9th ed. (Newark, N.J.: Bro-Dart Foundation, 1974).

[19] *Junior High School Library Catalog*, 3rd ed. (New York: H. W. Wilson Co., 1975).

[20] *Senior High School Library Catalog*, 10th ed. (New York: H. W. Wilson Co., 1975).

REFERENCES

Allen, Kenneth, and Loren Allen. *Administration of the Learning Resources Center in the Community College*. Hamden, Conn.: Shoe String Press, 1973.

American Association of School Librarians. *School Library Manpower Project (Phase I—Final Report)*. Chicago: American Library Association, 1970.

American Association of School Librarians. *School Library Personnel Task Analysis Survey*. Chicago: American Library Association, 1969.

American Association of School Librarians and Department of Audiovisual Instruction. *Standards for School Media Programs*. Chicago: American Library Association and National Education Association, 1969.

Association for Educational Communications and Technology. *Standards for Cataloging Nonprint Materials*. Washington, D.C.: Association for Educational Communications and Technology, 1976.

Brown, James, Kenneth Norberg, and Sara Srygley. *Administering Educational Media: Instructional Technology and Library Science*. New York: McGraw-Hill, 1972.

DeGennaro, Richard. "Library Automation: Changing Patterns and New Directions," *Library Journal* 101:175-183 (January 1, 1976).

Dewey, Melvil. *Dewey Decimal Classification and Relative Index*. 10th abridged ed. Lake Placid Club, N.Y.: Forest Press, 1971.

Dougherty, Richard, and Fred Heinritz. *Scientific Management of Libraries*. Metuchen, N.J.: Scarecrow Press, 1966.

Drucker, Peter. *The Effective Executive*. New York: Harper and Row, 1967.

Hart, Thomas. "Centralized Processing: Gain or Bane?" *School Media Quarterly* 3:210-214 (Spring 1975).

Hicks, Warren, and Alma Tillin. *Developing Multi-Media Libraries*. New York: R. R. Bowker, 1972.

Lehman, Henry. "The Systems Approach to Education," *Audiovisual Instruction* 13:144-48 (February 1968).

Liesener, James. *A Systematic Process for Planning Media Programs.* Chicago: American Library Association, 1976.

Liesener, James. "The Development of a Planning Process for Media Programs," *School Media Quarterly* 1:278-287 (Summer 1973).

Liesener, James. *Planning Instruments for School Library/Media Programs*. College Park, Md.: School of Library and Information Services, University of Maryland, 1974.

Liesener, James, and Karen Levitan. *A Process for Planning School Media Programs: Defining Service Outputs, Determining Resources and Operational Requirements, and Estimating Program Costs.* Final report of project funded by the Maryland State Department of Education, Division of Library Development and Services. College Park, Md.: School of Library and Information Services, University of Maryland, 1972.

Lyle, Guy. *Administration of the College Library*. New York: H. W. Wilson Co., 1974.

Mahar, Mary H. "Evaluation of Media Services to Children and Young People in Schools," *Library Trends* 22:377-386 (January 1974).

National Study of School Evaluation. *Elementary School Evaluative Criteria: Guide for School Improvement*. Arlington, Va.: National Study of School Evaluation, 1973.

National Study of School Evaluation. *Junior High School/Middle School Evaluative Criteria: A Guide for School Improvement*. Arlington, Va.: National Study of School Evaluation, 1970.

National Study of Secondary School Evaluation. *Evaluative Criteria for the Evaluation of Secondary Schools.* Washington, D.C.: National Study of Secondary School Evaluation, 1969.

Rogers, Rutherford, and David Weber. *University Library Administration*. New York: H. W. Wilson Co., 1971.

Rose, Lois, and Winifred Duncan. "LC's National Standard for Cataloging Children's Materials," *School Library Journal* 22:20-23 (January 1976).

Spitzer, Dean. "Educational Media and the Delphi: Looking Toward the Future," *Audiovisual Instruction* 20:5-8 (December 1975).

Veit, Fritz. *The Community College Library*. Westport, Conn.: Greenwood Press, 1975.

Weihs, Jean R., Shirley Lewis, and Janet MacDonald. *Non-Book Materials: The Organization of Integrated Collections.* Ottawa: Canadian Library Association, 1973.

Westby, Barbara, ed. *Sears List of Subject Headings.* 10th ed. New York: H. W. Wilson Co., 1972.

Willard, D. Dean. "Seven Realities of Library Administration," *Library Journal* 101: 311-317 (January 15, 1976).

8

PRIMARY ELEMENTS OF THE LMC PROGRAM

OBJECTIVES

Describe the primary elements of a school LMC program.

Design various primary elements for an LMC program in a selected school.

This chapter deals with the most critical factors in the LMC program, the primary elements of the system. The primary elements are visible. They make a difference in the way teachers teach and the way students learn, and they focus on the instructional components of the educational program.

Primary elements constitute a system in and of themselves. They represent a group of interrelated and interlocking services. Although other media personnel have a role to play here, this is primarily the domain of the library media specialist. The primary elements are:

1. **Planning and implementing curriculum.** This thrusts the media professional into the educational scheme when new learning requirements are being developed and sustains the relationship through the practical day-to-day instructional program.

2. **Instruction and in-service.** This element provides a two-fold approach to improving learning capabilities, through an instructional program (for students) and in-service programs on the utilization of the media system (for teachers).

3. **Design and production.** Provides a continuing opportunity for both creative and practical message production by teachers and students under the guidance of the media staff.

4. **Guidance and consultant services.** This is a two-fold approach to a continuing personalized, individualized relationship with students and teachers. The guidance aspect (for students) relates to their individual instructional and personal needs, whereas the consultant aspect (for teachers) relates to their teaching needs and professional improvement.

These elements represent operational functions that must be performed on a continuing and effective basis if program accountability is to be achieved. As previously noted, occupational definition in school libraries has been obscured by an "everything for everyone" philosophy. The idea that one person can do all things completely and competently cannot be sustained. Attempting to extend the services of a program beyond the physical capabilities of the individual and the operational potential for program continuation can produce only negative results.

PLANNING AND IMPLEMENTING CURRICULUM

This element deals with the media staff's interaction with administrators and teachers at a school or district level in four areas: instructional content, methodology of teaching, programing activities for students, and the gathering of media and technology required to meet the needs of students and teachers. Beginning with the research and development phase of curriculum, it continues and intensifies on a day-to-day basis in the implementation phase.

Curriculum involvement of media personnel used to be an "after-the-fact" proposition, asking the teachers "How can I help you?" This approach is not valid in today's LMC. The immediate task of the school library media specialist is to find out about the instructional program, either through research or through direct interaction with school and district instructional personnel who know the area. After learning about existing program objectives, the content dealt with in subject areas, the methodology employed, the media used in instruction, and the activities programed for students, the library media specialist then has the basis for a professional judgment about what the media system can do to improve teaching and learning.

How and where can the media professional become involved in this most important aspect of education? The answer is not difficult to find. The media professional staff must be assigned the specific task of research and referral, based on data available in the field. As information specialists, they must review on a continuing basis the literature of all fields related to the education of children. This group must be the best informed of the school and district professional staff. It follows that they should channel this information to teachers, administrators and others. This means more than circulating professional journals as they arrive. It means more than the selective dissemination of information (where the task is to cull the literature for information related to areas of interest to selected teachers and either duplicate the information found or forward a bibliography to them). It means more than publishing a monthly "contents" publication, which will provide teachers with copies of the tables of contents of journals received in the LMC. The optimum situation will find the media professional literally carrying the word to teachers and administrators, reviewing for teachers and administrators the concepts or evidence offered in the literature, recommending visitations where they would be helpful, planning and coordinating pilot projects where desirable, and in general functioning as a catalyst in educational improvement. A library media specialist can do these things. As a subject specialist as well, which a media professional is or should be, more intensified action research can be initiated in the specific area of expertise of the individual media professional. This can be the most valuable activity for the media professional because this is where educational improvement begins. Professional media staff assignments should cover areas of educational concern, and media staff meetings should be devoted in part to reports on potential activities for the media staff in this direction.

Curriculum Planning

The media professional should be involved in two aspects of curriculum planning: general curriculum development and the specific planning of LMC functions. In curriculum work, educators should draw on the knowledge of subject disciplines, the work of psychologists, sociologists, psychiatrists, and others, endeavoring to make scientific research data available.

Many schools and school districts develop curriculum through the "scissors and paste" method, borrowing from other districts that which appears to be most applicable to their own situations. The heavy reliance of school districts on the work of textbook publishers who provide a packaged, articulated program in all areas—social studies, science, reading, music, spelling, and so on—clearly indicates the need for competent media professionals who can add a new and refreshing approach to teaching and learning.

A typical definition of the school curriculum is that "the curriculum is all of the learning activites; planned, organized and carried out under the auspices of the school." In theory, at least, it develops out of the philosophy of a particular social group for the educational experiences of their young. As we know it in the schools, the curriculum is a plan for group action. This is seen in the organization of schools and the methodology generally used in teaching.

In our schools, children study subject matter; by definition, this is what we know about a subject. Because of the "knowledge explosion" of the latter half of the twentieth century, information is doubling every eight to ten years; thus, the task of selecting subject matter for study presents a major problem to the educator. Generally accepted criteria for selection leave much to be desired, as do procedures for the selection of content. Among the criteria used are the following:

1. To what extent is the specific subject matter required in a field of knowledge? Are prerequisites needed by individuals who are to study in a particular field?

2. To what extent has the specific subject matter in a field of knowledge been selected consistently through the years as representative of the field?

3. To what extent can the individual use the subject matter in a practical way to achieve success?

4. To what extent will the subject matter be considered interesting to the learner?

5. To what extent will the subject matter contribute to meeting society's goals for its children?

These criteria or others equally scientific are applied consistently by individuals and curriculum groups to their fields of interest. The procedures used in selecting subject matter relate directly to the criteria available. In other words, the criteria may be applied to subject matter selection in one or more of the following ways: the best judgment of the individual curriculum worker, consensus of a group of experts, direct experimentation in the field, or an analysis of what people in a given field of work do, in order to determine the subject matter needed to perpetuate or improve activities in the field. There is little scientific evidence that any subject matter content at any level is absolutely essential to the education of children.

The three I's (individualization, independent study, and inquiry) relate to methodology rather than subject matter. Each organizing structure, regardless of its relative success in the school, is directed toward accomplishing these goals. Whether the school provides homogeneous or heterogeneous grouping of students, whether there are formal groups or a "nongraded" program, whether teaching is by teams or by individual teachers, the objectives of individualization, independent study, and inquiry are present. The three I's can be accomplished regardless of the internal organization of the school.

Individualized instruction refers to a program that is tailored to the individual, with recognition of his differences, interests, needs, and mode of thinking and learning. This goal corresponds to a principal aim of education: "developing the unique personality of the individual within the framework of our democratic society." Three methods have been used to provide individualization in the schools: variations of rate of progress; a relationship between content and purpose; and curriculum organization. Rate of progress means that individuals may progress at their own rate of speed through the program. While the process may be effective to a degree, in the main all students do the same thing in the same way. The content and purpose approach implies a relationship between these elements. When purpose is considered the main focus, content can be varied to meet the needs of individuals, since the method of reaching the goal is optional. Curriculum organization is invariably thought to be designed to facilitate individual development, whether the internal organization calls for self-contained elementary school classrooms, team teaching, or nongraded practices.

Independent study is considered to be one of the most important elements in individualizing instruction. In independent study the student works in a free atmosphere on a project of his own choosing or one selected cooperatively with a teacher. Through this process, the student can explore and expand his special interests, can refine his work-study habits and skills and can thus become a more self-directed learner. Teacher guidance is an essential for most students, and adequate facilities and extensive media collections are also essential. Independent study should be an integral part of the educational experience of all students.

The third ingredient in the three I's approach is inquiry, which means seeking information or knowledge by questioning. Though associated primarily with the study of science and the scientific method in the schools, inquiry should be considered an integral part of any program. There is no one specific way to carry on a program of inquiry; it may be deductively or inductively approached. However it is developed, procedures require a focusing of student attention on a meaningful problem, student freedom to move around to gather data, and quantities of media. The three I's are interrelated aspects of an educational program designed for an LMC approach.

Planning Curriculum Functions

In addition to the research and catalyst functions already enumerated, media professionals should be assigned to work with all curriculum development committees in the school and district. Whether the program calls for a totally new input, such as environmental studies, or a revision of an outmoded social studies program, the expertise of the media professional is essential if the program is to be educationally sound. This professional's credentials should not merely equal but should surpass those of his teaching associate—to the degree that the media professional has competency in research, bibliography, design and production, organization, and utilization techniques.

If the media professional's educational background is in the subject area under consideration, he should be a full participant in subject matter selection. Content and concept selection will be influenced to a degree by the availability of media. Theoretically, at least, curriculum planners usually focus on objectives and content first; only later do they come to terms with media. The thinking is that they should not be tied to what is available today in the way of resources. In large measure, this line of thinking is very reasonable. With the design and production capabilities of many school districts and the ability of the commercial market to respond to educational needs, this pattern can succeed.

Beyond content selection, the media professional, even without specialized knowledge of subject matter, can and should be a principal contributor to curriculum improvement. Three related areas are considered: media, instructional methodology, and the programing of student activities or experiences.

Media, the printed and audiovisual resources to be employed in the teaching-learning process, fall quite readily into a principal area of expertise of the media professional. The role of the media professional is not merely to develop a bibliography to be used later by teachers and students. The function is to coordinate the search of the curriculum team for media that will satisfy subject matter requirements and also the selection criteria established for the school and district. Subject matter needs and criteria for selection are viewed in the light of knowledge about students who will be the recipients of and participants in the program. A review of media selection aids, an analysis of media currently available in the school, assistance in the direct preview and evaluation of media, an explanation of the LMC's financial potential to provide media, and guidance in designating and producing media—these are basic contributions that the media professional can make.

The library media specialist must be able to guide curriculum workers toward the exploration of methodologies that genuinely focus on the three I's: individualization, independent study, and inquiry. The trend today is to use the term "teaching strategies" instead of the equivalent term "instructional methodology." The teacher in the modern educational program is a planner and director of instruction, rather than a lecturer. In this role, the teacher must balance all factors related to instruction and individual students if he is to be effective. Knowledge of students will include abilities, experiential background, and interpersonal relationships. This diagnostic appraisal cannot be totally accommodated in the curriculum planning stages. Knowledge of the curriculum will include subject matter competency, awareness of media resources, and alternative prescriptive approaches. The options that the media professional can offer by making teachers aware include media as an alternative to lecturing and texts; LMC and other media system facilities as an alternative to a strict classroom orientation; cooperative teaching endeavors using LMC personnel; and methods of structuring individual, small group, and whole class activities.

Programing student learning activities is a part of a total teaching strategy. This must be based on a knowledge of individual differences. In the implementation phase of the curriculum, teachers will recognize clearly the implications of students' "learning styles." Riessman has concluded that each individual develops a unique preferred style:

> Everyone has a distinct style of learning, as individual as his personality. These styles may be categorized principally as visual (reading), aural (listening), or physical (doing things), although any one person may use more than one.[1]

The media professional's contribution is in formulating activities that are best implemented through individualization, inquiry, and independent study as they relate to media utilization. The media professional spells out the LMC's potential for individual, small group, and class activities and recommends student options and media to be used in the activities chosen.

Students have demonstrated the capacity to work effectively either as full partners or as partial contributors in curriculum development. Their contributions in content selection, methodology, media selection, and activities can usually be relied on as honest. When they participate, as learners, in the process of curriculum development, students can provide immediate feedback on the potential success or failure of a program.

Curriculum Implementation Functions

If the media professional is involved in curriculum planning and works effectively in that capacity, the functions of implementation fall into place in the on-going instructional program of the school. Schools that develop instructional methodologies geared to the extensive use of media rather than a traditional textbook orientation rely heavily on the media system. If the media professional has not been involved in curriculum development or has not been highly effective in that capacity, the problems that arise in trying to relate to teachers and students become enormous.

A group of interrelated functions deals with the readiness and ability of media professionals to meet with individual teachers or groups on a continuing basis to coordinate media services with the needs of instruction. If the media and services of the LMC are to benefit the instructional program and students, then there must be meetings with departments (at the secondary level) and grade level teachers (in the elementary schools). The purpose of the meetings is to guarantee the availability of media when and where needed and to select those media forms best suited to the capabilities of students; to guarantee the availability of space and media personnel when and where needed; to structure tentative activities for individual students, small groups, and entire classes, which will provide for optimum use of and benefit from the media system; to assess teacher needs for background information and teaching tools; and to arrange for teacher and student review of utilization skills and techniques. Meetings of this type are best scheduled to coincide with the initiation of units of study or with areas of transition in a nongraded approach.

The media professional's schedule should be flexible enough to allow attendance at these meetings and also to permit him to meet with teachers on an individual basis in the LMC or other locations. Continuity in meeting with individual teachers about their instructional needs and individual student requirements is vital to the success of the entire school program. Capturing the individual teacher's attention and interest guarantees success in student utilization of the media system. Interaction with teachers must rate high on the list of priorities for media staff time.

Participation in activities outside the confines of the LMC proper is a natural extension of the media system. Whether it is merely to view student projects elsewhere in the building, to attend department meetings, to observe effective instruction in the classroom, or to teach cooperatively with subject specialists on a long- or short-term basis where media expertise is required, freedom to move about is essential for the media professional. Other media staff personnel may also be involved outside the LMC. A media technician may be involved in taping an assembly program, setting up and operating equipment for special projects, and so on. Availability of media personnel for service throughout the building assures teachers that the media system can meet their needs and fosters great interaction of teaching personnel with the media system. The media professional who works alone is, of course, faced with the problem of "minding the store."

The design and production of media are integral parts of the implementation phase of curriculum, though some work can be accomplished during the curriculum planning phase. At least one competent media professional should be available to help teachers and students design media, although the production aspect is the function of technicians. Much of the work consists of modifying the existing media forms to meet the needs of individual students.

One of the media professional's basic functions in relation to planning and implementing the curriculum is a continual evaluation of whether the media system adequately and suitably meets the needs of the instructional program. This evaluation takes place in the context of the objectives developed cooperatively by the media staff and the LMC faculty and student committees.

INSTRUCTION AND IN-SERVICE

This fundamental element concerns the basic need of students and teachers to learn how to better utilize the media system in the teaching and learning process. For some time to come, this need will be an imperative for educators interested in developing self-directed learners who can function on their own in a learning situation. It has been said that "the library (LMC) will function as the teacher of that neglected half of knowledge—'the knowledge of where to find it'— and as the interdisciplinary synthesizer which establishes interrelations among various fields of knowledge."[2]

Instruction and in-service are defined as the formalized program of teaching service. Instruction is the term selected for aspects relating to students. In-service is the term used to denote formalized aspects of teaching teachers to become more effective professionals.

Instruction

The professional media staff should assume responsibility for teaching the skills students need to work independently in the school LMC or other libraries. Most of these skills are directly transferable at any age and, of course, these skills remain one of the few educational benefits that can realistically be said to have "carry over" value into adulthood.

Of course, if one accepts Leonard Freiser's[3] service concept literally, perhaps nothing resembling skills instruction would be a part of the LMC program. His basic thesis is that the principal task of the learner is to manipulate the ideas presented by many authorities rather than to locate the media needed for such manipulation. The media staff function would be to provide everything needed for the student. In essence, Freiser envisions the time when information retrieval would be a totally automated process, and suggests that non-involvement by students in searching would hasten the time. The technological capability to accomplish this goal appears to be at least 20 to 30 years away.

Investigative and research skills are needed by today's student, and each school should provide such instruction. The justification for this position is that by learning how to learn, the individual acquires the skills needed to begin functioning independently in learning. It is interesting to note that the concern for investigative skills extends well beyond the concern of media personnel; it is directly related to basic requirements in reading programs.

Knowledge of students' capabilities and the curriculum are key indicators of what can be accomplished in an instructional program.

Two approaches to skills instruction that are compatible with modern pedagogy are the use of instructional systems and small-group intensive instruction. These approaches can be integrated with instruction in various subject disciplines or can be separated from this relationship. The integrated approach is most desirable.

The Learning Activity Package (L.A.P.) is an example of an instructional system. L.A.P.'s were originally developed as a reaction against an antiquated teacher-directed methodology in curriculum content areas. Advocates of this system visualized a means of establishing a nongraded or continuous progress program in the schools. It was seen as one practical method for solving the problems of individualization. One of the early pioneering school districts to use the L.A.P. structure was the Nova School System, Fort Lauderdale, Florida, which developed an innovative and comprehensive program.

Two basic ideas are fundamental to the L.A.P. approach. The first is that the teacher's role should change from that of lecturer to that of resource person, one who develops and administers a new strategy for teaching. The teacher who uses this sytem for teaching spends his time answering student questions and relating to small groups and individuals instead of lecturing to a large group. The second idea is that the student should not be a passive receiver of information, but should assume a more active and responsible role in learning.

In practice, a school or school district would move from developing curriculum guides for group teaching to preparing student guides for learning. For example, an articulated sequence of L.A.P.'s would be developed in the social studies from the primary grades through the senior high school and beyond. Each would be designed for a unit of approximately three to four weeks' duration for the average student. Each would allow a student to move at his own pace through both a common core of experiences and an in-depth sequence keyed to exploratory experiences.

The L.A.P. approach is offered as a reasonable alternative to traditional library skills teaching. It is one systematic way to teach essential media skills effectively and efficiently. Using the L.A.P. removes the library media specialist from a formal teaching schedule and at the same time ensures that each student will have the opportunity to learn these skills independently.

Many alternative methods of application are possible using the L.A.P. structure. If scheduled class periods are required by administrative fiat, they can be offered as a structured sequence and still provide a refreshing alternative to group-paced instruction. At any grade level, when the need arises for a particular skill, L.A.P.'s may be fed into the program for a particular class or group or individual. Perhaps most important, individual users of the media facility can be given a self-instructional program that does not rely on any one teacher or any specific time schedule.

It is possible to develop an articulated sequence of L.A.P.'s covering use of the card catalog, reference tools, and so on, for elementary grades through high school. However, such a sequence is not required. It is entirely possible for a media professional to create one L.A.P. for a single topic (e.g., Readers' Guide), which would be suited to the needs of any senior high student. Similarly, an analysis of school organization and curriculum will provide insight into the what, where, and how of creating basic skills packages in a given area.

The L.A.P. is intended to be a self-directed, self-pacing instrument. Not a workbook, it is rather a program of objectives and activities that direct the learner to experiences through which he can become proficient in a given area of study. The structure is prescribed and the format is reasonably consistent, although the writer has considerable latitude in building in alternatives. A typical outline would include the elements shown at the top of page 191.

The **primary idea** for the package is specifically the subject or title of the package. Keyed to the primary idea is the **rationale**, which is a brief statement telling the student why he should learn about this primary idea or subject.

It should be possible to break the primary idea or subject down into three or four ideas or concepts. These become the **secondary ideas** for the L.A.P. and represent the basic learning areas required of students. Each part of the package containing secondary ideas is called a segment. Each segment is structured in precisely the same manner. The statement of the secondary idea is followed by three or four **behavioral objectives**. Behavioral objectives tell the student what he

Primary idea
    Rationale
        Secondary idea I
           Behavioral objectives
      Pre-test
      Activities
        Multi-mode
          —content
          —activities
          —media
      Student self-assessment
      Teacher evaluation
[This same pattern is then repeated for other secondary ideas.]
Self-assessment for entire package
Teacher evaluation for entire package
In-depth activities

must do to demonstrate what he has learned, under what conditions he must perform the learning task, and to what extent he must perform. Mager's *Preparing Instructional Objectives* is an invaluable guidance tool for preparing objectives.

The **pre-test** is usually an optional item for the student. If he can pass the pre-test, he has demonstrated adequately his competency and may omit the section. If it is known that the L.A.P. material will be totally new to students, the development of a pre-test is unnecessary.

The **activities** built into the package provide a common core of understandings for all learners and enable them to fulfill the stated objectives. For each secondary idea or segment, the learner selects from many alternatives and works on activities of his choice. However, it is possible for the writer to specify completion of certain activities. Student options may include reading, writing, listening, viewing, conferences, group work, and other activities. The writer, in planning these activities, must accommodate varying student interests and abilities and must vary the mode, content, activities, and media employed. Media inputs may be both commercially available materials and teacher-produced materials. The most common teacher-produced materials are tapes, slides, transparencies, and worksheets of various types designed to be used in combination.

A **self-assessment** is a self-test that the student administers and corrects himself. The purpose of the self-assessment is to help the student decide whether he has successfully completed enough activities to pass a teacher evaluation. Usually a student-teacher conference is scheduled after the self-assessment to discuss progress and to recycle the student if he has not been successful. Checkpoints for student-teacher conferences may also be built into the various segments if it seems desirable for the student to meet with his teacher.

The **teacher evaluation** must be closely related to the stated behavioral objectives and self-assessment. It should have no surprise elements built into it.

In-depth activities may comprise some 50 percent of student work in L.A.P.'s prepared in specific curriculum content areas. Designed as activities for exploration and discovery, these cover the broad spectrum of student interests and abilities related to the subject. More than any other area of the package, these may be individualized activities.

Some of the principal benefits of this approach to skills teaching are:

1. It is geared to a media approach to learning. The media orientation and unique individualized and independent style are suited to a library media center approach.

2. The student functions as an individual and has both a broad selection of alternative experiences and a variety of media to suit his personal learning style.

3. The media professional need no longer make formal presentations on a continuing basis. While students are working independently, the media specialist can work with other students and teachers as required.

4. For the school administrator who views an LMC program as 99 percent skills teaching, this approach ensures that students will learn media skills on an individual and independent basis.

5. The media professional becomes skilled at developing individualized learning programs for students.

6. The media professional may apply this knowledge and experience as a consultant to teachers in the content areas, whether in the development of L.A.P.'s or merely in the structuring of individualized and independent programing.

An alternative to using an instructional system is scheduling small groups (5 to 10 students) for directed learning experience with the media professional. Because of the size of the group, each student receives a fair share of individual attention, and teaching and learning are accomplished efficiently and effectively. At the elementary school level, where reading is a formalized program in the classroom and the usual three groups are formed, one group at a time can be scheduled for work in the LMC. When project work in social studies or science formalizes a group structure, the same pattern can be used for small group instruction in the LMC. The secondary school pattern permits similar experiences. In a high school that has 40- to 50-minute class periods, small groups can be released for skills work while group discussions are held in the classroom, while group projects are being developed, or at any time when the entire class is not required to focus on a teacher's lecture. A flexible school schedule enhances the possibilities for individualized or small group work in the LMC.

In-Service

In-service is to the teacher what instruction is to the student. In a broad sense it is any activity in which a professional participates that allows him to improve himself on the job. The purpose is to:

—extend the individual's knowledge and learning in general

—keep abreast of new knowledge

—keep current in a rapidly expanding society

—provide him with results of research on learning and on the learning process

—prepare him for new fields and new responsibilities.[4]

Fundamentally, in-service programing is as important to educational improvement as are planning and implementing curriculum. Indeed, in-service is tied into the structuring of curriculum development programs. However, for too many years both curriculum development and in-service have been considered merely as activities that supplemented the actual teaching job. Even today, research and development funds are virtually non-existent in most school districts.

In-service activities may be formal or informal. Formal aspects include attending college for extension course work, sabbatical leave for study, travel, teacher exchanges, participation in research and curriculum revision, and school and school district workshops. Informal types include an array of potentially valuable experiences, among them attending professional association conferences and faculty and departmental meetings in schools and school districts. Although all too frequently faculty and department meetings are devoted to administrative detail, the possibilities for professionally beneficial experiences are very broad. Some areas suitable for exploration include reviewing the school program of studies, articulation of the program through the grades, reviewing procedures for individualization, evaluation of student performance, policy and procedures for day-to-day operations, and demonstrations of potentially successful teaching-learning experiences.

More than anyone else in the school or district, the media professional has the opportunity and responsibility to participate in all types of in-service programing. The media professional can act as a catalyst to improve instructional practices in all content areas through the use of media, to publicize the benefits to students and teachers of using the LMC, and to contribute new information about on-going research in the content areas. If media personnel fail to assume responsibility for involvement, the result will be an instructional program severely limited by a lack of information about the programing potential of the media system. It is only realistic to assume that in-service work will be initiated, carried on, and concluded with the resources available to the participants. The media professional's primary role is to make others aware of the LMC's potential for accommodating varied teaching methods, diversified course content, varied student activities, and the range and depth of media available to meet the needs of students in an individualized program. Beyond this lies the media professional's capacity to fulfill competently the LMC's promise of educational improvement.

Media personnel must develop in-service roles that allow them to initiate and conduct in-service programs at one time, and at another time to participate in and work to improve in-service initiated by others. In-service programs may be confined to the individual school or oriented toward district-wide improvement.

Formal LMC In-Service

The formal in-service approach provides some advantages when a total school or district need is known. The structure is highly visible, and a mutual commitment to the program is shared by initiators and participants. Many avenues are available for initiating in-service work for teachers, designed to increase their knowledge of and competency in using the media system in their teaching. Some workshop activities can be accomplished in less than a day's work, while others could take up to several weeks of full-time work by the participants.

It is recognized that teachers generally lack basic knowledge about audiovisual equipment, general ways to use audiovisual media, and use of printed media. Short term, structured in-service workshops for teachers may have to encompass very basic information and practice in the following areas:

1. Orientation programs geared to the service potential of the media system; these programs are essentially informational in nature

2. How to operate various devices needed for media use, such as projectors, tape recorders, and so on

3. How to evaluate and select media

4. How to design and produce media

5. How to use standard library tools, such as the card catalog and the various indexes available

6. Overview of the LMC instructional program in media investigative skills

Media-oriented in-service programs of a more comprehensive or specialized nature can be structured for longer periods of time, since they require deeper teacher involvement. The programs can be developed for individual departments or grade levels, with participation limited to those working in the area. Other participatory in-service programs can include the entire school staff in general activities designed to improve teaching and learning; in such programs, groups of teachers may relate general concepts, information, and expertise to their own areas. The following types of programs cover general concepts of the LMC:

1. The preview, evaluation, and selection of media related to curriculum planning and implementation

2. Independent study potential of the LMC for various content areas

3. Remediation potential of the LMC for students having difficulty in the content areas

4. Developing resource and/or teaching units in various content areas using the LMC as a base of operations

5. Developing individualized student learning packets in various content areas using the LMC as a base of operations

6. Initiating cooperative reading guidance programs in the school using the LMC as a base of operations and involving teachers, reading specialists, and media personnel

On occasion, in-service work initiated by media professionals has a two-fold function. For example, one function may be to teach teachers how to use television effectively in their work; another function may be to enable the teacher to contribute significantly to the resources of the school as a contributor to the videotape collection. This exchange of information for talent is extended also to dial access programing and to in-service work in media design and production. The in-service objective is structured to produce two vital outcomes: greater teacher competency and needed teacher inputs into the media system. This is a valuable consideration in total in-service programing and is an effort toward maximizing the potential of the situation.

In some schools, media personnel trying to initiate in-service work directly related to the media system experience a great deal of difficulty. This may be because it has never been done before, or because teachers and administrators may be hostile to such recommendations or suggestions. Also, media professionals may not have the interest or desire to spark such a program without direction from administration. The school administration should, of course, be informed and should support any in-service program that promises to benefit the teaching-learning process in the school. Without administrative support and, more importantly, without the interest and support of the teaching staff, such in-service work is impossible.

Some school districts pay in-service participants for their time, others provide credits toward future salary increments, and still others merely allow release time for in-service work. Various combinations of these approaches are found. There are also school districts that make no provision at all for in-service work on a continuing basis. In such a case, it takes an extraordinary amount of tact and diplomacy to generate interest in formal in-service work.

Pay, course credit, and release time from teaching are inducements to participate in in-service work. Interest, the acknowledged need for new skills and knowledge, and an excitement about new ideas are refreshingly different motivating forces. It would be desirable to have all or many of these forces at work in the school. If media professionals are members of the principal's advisory council, steps can be initiated through the council to bring about desired in-service programing. This is particularly effective if the council represents the teaching staff in general and if it is recognized for its leadership function and as a vehicle for the initiation of programs designed to improve education in the school. Another school agency that may have considerable influence is the LMC advisory committee, which should be representative of the faculty and subject disciplines in the school. If the advisory committee is to play more than a nominal role in determining the program functions of the LMC, its members can provide a sounding board for in-service and other ideas and can initiate programing.

A vital consideration in the strategy to improve teacher competency is the method chosen for devising the in-service program and for the actual carrying out of the program. The most beneficial results are obtained when members of the teaching staff are involved in structuring and carrying out the program.

Media Personnel as Participants. Certainly not all in-service programs in a school or district are initiated by media personnel. They do, however, have a responsibility to contribute their expertise to all school and district-wide programs.

Few in-service programs can operate effectively without the skills of media personnel. Invariably, participants in the program need to know about design and production, about the availability of the media required to implement programing, and about media utilization.

In any project designed to improve curriculum development, teachers should meet with media personnel for the following reasons:

1.   To review the availability of media related to the various projects

2.   To preview and select new media to be included in the projects

3.   To obtain assistance in planning, designing and producing media to be included in the package

4.   To structure student activities that require the extensive use of media beyond the textbook

5.   To structure activities requiring independent and small-group use of the LMC

6.   To determine what media skills students will need in order to function independently in the LMC and to integrate the teaching of needed skills into the teacher-prepared package

The media professional must be well aware that conjecture should not be the basis for determining in-service needs for a school or district. The problem must be clearly defined, the alternatives available for problem solving must be studied, and those most in need of help must be involved in the solution of their problems.

DESIGN AND PRODUCTION

Design and production is a rapidly expanding element of the comprehensive school LMC. The element divides into separate but related operations, which are usually carried on in the media production area of the LMC.

The services offered in design and production, as well as the size of the facility and staff allocated for service, vary from school to school. Much depends on the pattern of services emanating from the district media center. One cannot prescribe for a given school because of the number of factors involved. However, every school needs to have a minimal production capability, regardless of the district service pattern.

Design

Design is based on a knowledge of subject matter, of research procedures, and of a systems approach to the design of instructional systems. The function of the design process is to translate this knowledge and a knowledge of learners into specifications for instructional system components (I.S.C.'s). Instructional system components are "all of the resources which can be designed, utilized, and combined in a systematic manner with the intent of bringing about learning.[5]

Fundamentally, design analyzes an instructional situation to determine what idea or message must be conveyed, what material or medium would best convey the message, what device if any is required for the utilization of the medium, what technique or method is best suited to get the message to the learner, and in what setting or physical environment this is best achieved. In order to accomplish the objectives established, it may be necessary to combine several media, use one new medium, or modify an existing form in varied ways. The design generally ends with the writing of specifications for the component required to accomplish the task.

The design function is usually the task of the media professional, working with the teacher who initiated the request. The results of the consultation may be the creation of a new medium or the modification of an existing form (see Fig. 8-1). Usually a teacher initiates a request and states the instructional problem and objectives. He may or may not check back to discuss the work in progress, but he will receive the product when it is completed.

Production

Production is considered a corollary of design. The production worker takes the product of the design phase and translates it into one or several different instructional system componenets, as required. Usually, the school production worker is a technician.

The term "production" has several concepts or levels of service. One level, briefly described above, is the translation of the design function. An average school should have a minimal production capability. This capability fulfills the most common teacher requirements: the production of transparencies, audio reel-to-reel and/or cassette tapes, 2" x 2" slides, videotapes, and varied graphic media. The teacher should have the option of submitting a production request or, if he has the requisite skills, completing the project himself. A second level of production, again incorporating the design function as a necessary input, provides the capability of producing 8mm silent and sound films, filmstrips, and 3¼ by 4-inch Polaroid slides. A third level would allow the design and production of programs for television and dial or random access systems. While levels one and two are usually optional for teachers who pick their own time and projects, the third level represents not only an exceptionally large investment of money but also an educational commitment to technological innovation.

A general teacher service that should be available in every school is the production of disposable media, which means general typing and duplicating services for media needed in instruction. It may also mean typing, duplicating, and stapling a teacher-prepared test or duplicating a page from a magazine article.

What does the design/production function offer students? In the modern school program, which expects students to perform as self-directed individuals, students should have access to design and production facilities so that they can make the most of each learning opportunitv. When possible, they should also be provided with assistance in design and production of media as needed. Although the media staff is usually not expected to extend the same services to an entire student body that they provide for faculty, they should provide access and guidance as needed.

Fig. 8-1. Modifying Media

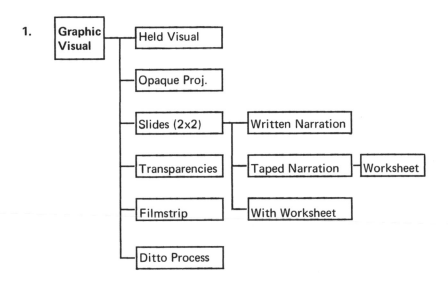

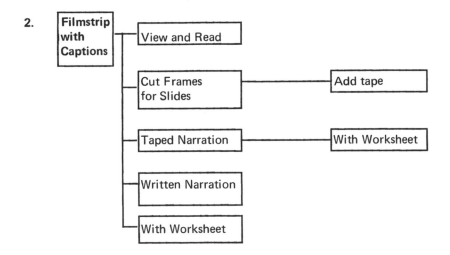

GUIDANCE AND CONSULTANT SERVICES

These are dual, personalized, interactive programs aimed at students and teachers. To provide for differentiated service patterns, guidance is defined as a range of specialized services for students which may vary in intensity with grade levels, orientation of the curriculum, and student needs; consultant services are designed to assist teachers in their instructional work on a continuing basis and to aid in professional improvement.

Guidance for Students

Reference Service. The reference service provided in the school helps the student locate material needed to complete assignments rapidly. Usually, the students required to do research or investigative work are of three types: those who are well-versed in the mechanics of using the LMC, are familiar with the resources available, and are able to function independently; those who have some knowledge of the workings of the LMC but may or may not be familiar with their topics and therefore are semi-independent; and those students who are totally dependent because they have neither learned how to use the LMC nor become aware of the resources available.

The purpose of the service is to provide each student with as much assistance as he needs to complete his work effectively and efficiently. Basically, this means that students are aware that someone in a professional capacity is willing to provide assistance. When the student presents himself and his problem, the professional can help clarify the research needed, and can establish whether or not the student can proceed independently or to what degree he needs assistance. If the card catalog must be searched, for example, the professional assists, providing encouragement and expertise as needed.

The first phase of direct assistance to students is usually complete after the range of resources has been surveyed and selection decided on. Practically speaking, this is where professional assistance usually ends. If staff is available to provide continuity in the reference-research cycle for students, then assistance should go beyond investigation to the evaluation of the information sources selected, the organization of information, and the presentation mode to be used by the student.

Reference assistance to students in an LMC is usually limited to assistance in the investigative or searching phase. Even this limited assistance can save the student much precious time, which can be devoted to other intellectually stimulating activities. Pilot projects are needed in reference service in which the student merely initiates a request for materials on a given subject and the LMC staff does the searching and provides him with a comprehensive collection of resources. Obviously, the principal advantage of this approach lies in the professional's speed and expertise in using the tools of his trade. Resources tapped would include those in the LMC and in other agencies in the media system beyond the individual school. Certainly more comprehensive staffing patterns than are now available would be needed to provide this service on a large scale. However, a pilot program that focused on two or three classes in a school could provide visible evidence of success or lack of success of this sort of reference service.

Some, of course, consider the search to be the most vital and critical factor in the reference scheme. These people prefer to have the student demonstrate his ability to work through the search problem independently because it develops his own reference abilities.

Today's media professional must know students well enough to determine which ones require little assistance and which ones need comprehensive guidance. This interaction also allows the professional to provide feedback to the media staff and teachers about individual students, whether the assignments made are reasonable, and whether the existing media collections can meet the instructional and personal needs of students. As a guide to providing excellent future services, exceptional and difficult search problems and media solutions should be recorded for future reference.

Who can provide this service to students? Requests for location of media in the LMC and the directions for using a particular audiovisual device are tasks that can be accomplished by a media technician who has received training in this area. There is a rather thin line between this function and the professional function. The professional role is to analyze the questions posed by students in order to decide what procedures to follow in solving the problems inherent in the question. Role function, then, depends on which student needs should be met through professional expertise.

The reference service in the school is critical and requires a major focus for development. Student guidance in this area should be personalized and continuing. The student should know what service is available and whom to seek out for assistance; he should feel confident that he will receive help when he needs it.

Reading Services. In an age when instructional technology is making significant strides in education and when the LMC focus is on audiovisual media and technology, reading has become even more important than before. There is little need to explore the general failure of the schools to teach reading effectively. Since James Allen, former U.S. Commissioner of Education, articulated "Right to Read" as a national priority, it has in fact received a national emphasis. The focus on reading has a two-fold purpose: improving the skills required to read, and fostering in students the desire to read. The mere fact that the principal focus of libraries has been reading is no guarantee that what is currently being done is adequate.

Reading is not the responsibility of any one person or group in the school. Those who should be most concerned are teachers, reading personnel, and media professionals. It is recommended that the first step toward improving the school reading program should be to allow these three groups—teachers, reading personnel, and media professionals—to exchange information about their existing roles in the school. A continuing dialogue should focus the attention of this group on the reading needs of students. Program objectives should stress individualized reading, which appears to be the most logical approach. Each professional has something of value to contribute, and the school program of each should maximize his opportunity to contribute. Jeannette Veatch describes the method briefly as "teaching children to read with books of their own choice, usually trade books, through a one-to-one conference with their teacher."[6] The concept is applicable in the primary grades as well as at the upper levels of secondary education. The concept stems, in part, from a generalized reaction against using the textbook, including basal readers, as the prime course content.

The purpose and objectives of the reading program should be clearly stated; alternative program components should be provided for; and there should be adequate data from which to build. The staff should approach the problem not with the attitude that "we can't do anything because of the existing structure," but rather, with the aim of seeing what could be accomplished if there were no constraints. This approach allows consideration of a broad range of alternative means of reaching the program objectives.

The idea of accountability is appropriate here because of the individual contact between the student and professional in an individualized reading program. In short, the professional participants in this reading program can assume a constructive role that is not too far removed from their existing roles.

The school specialist in reading should probably be assigned at least the following responsibilities: coordination of testing, diagnostic work concerning remediation for individual students, participation in selecting media, and sufficient contact with students and professionals to secure adequate feed-back on the reading achievements of individual students and on program continuity. The reading specialist would play a leading role in selecting and coordinating the use of skill-building media.

As the principal coordinator of instructional components, the teacher must develop teaching strategies that will accommodate information inputs from varied sources rather than "pat" answers from a text or basal reader. This use of varied sources is important to the total reading program, and it usually requires that the teacher be more flexible than the other professional participants. Since this is a cooperative program, selection of media becomes an important teacher input. The burden of individual conferences with students rests heavily on the teacher unless either the reading staff or the LMC staff is sufficiently large to take on more of this task.

The media professional should coordinate the selection of media in all areas to accommodate student differences, and should be aware of the reading needs, in all subject areas, of individual students and small groups. This implies being in touch with students as they select media to satisfy instructional assignments, and it also demands a continual assessment of the depth and diversity of the selections made. In large measure, student conferences conducted by teachers and media professionals will overlap. These two professionals must share their views on the progress of individual students and must use the reading specialist's expertise for the collective and individual good of students in the school.

Although the media professional often is assigned or assumes the responsibility for storytelling and picture book hours, book fairs, assembly programs, literary clubs, and other activities designed to stimulate an interest in reading, these should be considered secondary. If adequate staff is available and if the project (such as a book fair or assembly) is a cooperative endeavor, such activities can be held. But tying the media professional in the elementary school to weekly storytelling or picture book hours for all grades is to misuse his time. In other words, a "good" recreational sound filmstrip does not require the presence of a professional at all.

If the traditional library programs are judged to be of value, many of them can be redesigned so that other media staff can assume them or modified for implementation by the media professional. For example, if it is decided to present a continuing program of literature for children, using the best audiovisual media available, then the media professional should select the media to be used, but non-professional personnel can carry out the activity itself. Storytelling can be treated as a special "happening"; students can sign up for this event. Scheduling of this type of activity would be at the convenience of the media professional. Attendance would be based on motivation rather than force. A different attitude prevails, for both students and the professional, when attendance is optional. Indeed, as long as the media professional is responsible for the selection of media to be used, the choice of the actual storyteller should be based on performance in this specialized area—it may be a well-qualified storytelling volunteer or a technician. Booktalks may be taped by media professionals—or students, for that matter—to be used in the classroom or independently in the LMC. The professional needs to stand before the group only on special occasions. In the elementary school, this redesigning of functions and optimum use of personnel can save 12 to 20 or more hours each week of the media professional's time, which can be redirected to the reading program of the school.

Not as much time can be saved at the secondary level because these functions are not usually required. However, the number of hours the media professional spends counting study hall passes and supervising what amounts to a large study hall should be re-evaluated. Of course, if the LMC is little more than a study hall, then the issue goes much deeper than the question of who should supervise. Here the instructional program of the school should be re-examined, including the question of why students have little or no exposure to media and activities in the LMC.

The reading program of the school is not an isolated subject, to be treated independently of other learning experiences. It is rather a total experience for students. It requires close cooperation among the professionals in the school, to ensure that each student is recognized as an individual and also that the teaching-learning process involves an extensive use of media suitable to the individual's need. The media professional must be acutely aware of the basic relationship that exists between reading service and reference assistance, both of which must provide individualized attention.

Communications. Various schemes can be used to give students information about the LMC, the school, and activities in the world outside. Although this aspect of the LMC may seem less important than other program elements, few are unaware of the importance of a good public relations program.

This is usually another good opportunity to involve students in the program of the LMC. The many profitable activities for involvement go well beyond the club organized to shelve books and deliver overdue notices. The need to inform students about policies, procedures, and services of the LMC can be met through a handbook for students and teachers or through a periodic bulletin to students. If students are willing and capable, a student information series can disseminate information by radio, television, tapes, or direct student contact in the classroom. The same array of media can be used to inform students of school programs, activities outside of the school, and various LMC-sponsored activities. Given the opportunity and a degree of responsibility, student response to this type of experience is generally very high. Students who have an opportunity to select media for the LMC and to advertise and recommend their selections provide the LMC with a vital force in the area of public relations. Students can also be actively engaged in teaching others the practical use of audiovisual hardware. Two major qualifications regarding the use of students in the LMC program must be observed: 1) students should not be involved in LMC activities when they are scheduled for educational pursuits elsewhere in the school, and 2) the LMC service must provide a learning experience that is transferable into any leadership or group membership experience. Note again that this excludes relying on student help for pasting, mending, and shelving. The media professional must determine the amount of supervision and guidance required by the LMC student workers and must supervise the activities on a continuing basis. If adequate professional guidance cannot be provided, activities of this nature should be deferred.

Recreational Program Services. Recreational programs in the school are generally termed extracurricular. In the ranking of special guidance service, this aspect of LMC service would receive the lowest priority. It should be recognized, however, that if an adequate staff is available, services beyond the typical individual and group service should be provided. Every individual or group is entitled to reference and reading services, production services, and instructional services.

These beyond-the-ordinary services extend to providing professional staff as sponsors and coordinators of extracurricular activities and providing space for activities. Also included are the initiation of projects for special interest groups in the LMC, and design and production services required by these groups in carrying out their programs.

Consultant Services for Teachers

Consultative is the term applied here to the specialized activities and services provided by the professional media staff to assist teachers in their work. In large measure the media professional's work in developing and implementing curriculum, in designing and producing media, and in in-service work fit squarely into this category. Additionally, the media professional's guidance services to students are directed toward helping teachers do a more effective job.

Reference Service. Closely related to the media professional's responsibility for curriculum development and implementation is the reference consultant service to teachers. The service has broad ramifications and can be fully implemented only when adequate media staff is available. When a teacher initiates a request for assistance about media or information, immediate action should be taken to bring to bear on the request whatever help is needed. Placing books on reserve for student use is an old practice. It should be continued and expanded to accommodate full service, including researching a topic and providing all media available—magazines, pamphlets, pictures, films, filmstrips, and so on. A consultative dialogue ascertains the number of students to be involved, which students will have problems in dealing with the subject, space arrangements necessary to accommodate users, types of activities to be programed, and the need for instructional and production services.

Many teachers merely want help in locating and selecting media for use with a class, group, or individual student. They want to be actively involved in locating and evaluating media before actual selection. Professional assistance in using bibliographic tools, equipment, and media should be available immediately, or arrangements should be made to provide assistance at the earliest opportunity.

The development of instructional systems is another principal consultative function of the media professional staff. Unlike the usual library exploratory or inquiry process, the instructional system is rooted in behavioral objectives and is a step-by-step sequential learning process for the student or students. Each medium employed in the system is evaluated for informational inputs and specific direction is provided for use. The system is controlled by purpose and performance based on predetermined objectives.

Communications. An information service program can provide assistance to the teaching staff. The program should be limited to information related to instruction in the school. Information generally needed includes policy and procedures for operation of the LMC; new services, equipment, and media; special activities of the LMC; reviews of new media; and national, state, and local events, whether TV or radio broadcasts or special programs of the local museum or art gallery.

The information program designed for students can include some information needed by faculty. A joint student-teacher handbook on media policy and procedures is an example. The same medium used to inform students about special activities of the school and events outside may also be employed for teacher information. It is also desirable to provide each teacher with a looseleaf notebook, appropriately labeled "LMC" into which may be filed bibliographies and bulletins from the LMC.

If the LMC is to become a center of inquiry and independent study, a high priority should be placed on feedback to teachers about the student performance. A guidance department in the school would also benefit from this information. Information that can be educationally productive for teacher and student is needed. For example, if a highly developed reading guidance program has been developed, feedback through faculty interaction is a necessity. The progress of students in an individualized, independent program must be carefully assessed and evaluated. Independent investigative or research work carried on by students requires two LMC responses: first, direct assistance to the student as needed; and second, feedback to the teacher on problems encountered by students and on their general progress.

Dealing with teachers is facilitated if the media professional has developed a means of working successfully with teachers on a continuing basis—through membership on the principal's advisory council, through an LMC committee of teachers representative of the school, through a media selection committee structure, and through a reading guidance structure.

Professional Services. Although it is difficult to differentiate between communications and professional services, it is nonetheless clear that the need to provide service to teachers in their professional growth has generally been overlooked.

This component, closely related to in-service work, entails developing professional resources to broaden the teacher's general background in education and in subject areas. The media collection may be very extensive or highly selective, depending on the philosophy of the district. The principal responsibility of the media staff is to route information about trends, innovative programs in subject areas, and general methodology to those who need this information—whether or not it is solicited.

A lower priority may be assigned to this aspect of service when staff is not adequate, but, together with in-service, it provides the force needed to help the teacher help himself. Teacher requests for assistance should be initiated through ordinary channels and the same service should be forthcoming as described under reference service. Many school districts may balk at this type of service on the grounds that teachers will be requesting help about assignments to be completed for professional degrees. However, the quality of teaching will improve when school districts begin to recognize that they have a role to play in teacher education as well as in the teacher's usual student-oriented role.

SUMMARY

+ The primary elements of the media system involve direct relationships between the media system and students, teachers, and the curriculum. Principal areas of concern are planning and implementing curriculum, instruction and in-service, design and production, and guidance and consultant services.

+ Planning and implementing curriculum directs the library media specialist to involvement in curriculum work, from the initiation of new learning programs through the day-to-day implementation phases required in the school.

+ Instruction and in-service provides a straightforward program of instruction in media skills for students and an in-service component for teachers that demonstrates the use of media in instruction.

+ Design and production deals with the creation of and/or modification of media by students and teachers. The design aspect leads to the preparation of specifications for instructional system components, and production refers to the translation of specifications into various media forms.

+ Guidance and consultant services provide a dual service focus: guidance directed to students, consultant services directed to teachers. The major interest of the media professional is to work with students and teachers on a direct personal basis for the improvement of education.

LITERATURE AND FIELD INVESTIGATIONS

1. What background information is needed to design effectively the primary elements of a school LMC program?

2. Compare the primary elements of a typical school media system to those in academic and public libraries. Discuss similarities and differences.

3. Investigate the meaning of independent study, individualization, and inquiry in education. Discuss the implications for the school media system.

4. Examine curriculum guides for various schools and programs. Discuss the implications for the LMC program.

5. Investigate various instructional strategies currently employed in schools. Discuss the implications for the LMC program.

6. Discuss the design/production capabilities of the school LMC as described in the literature.

7. Design one or more of the following: an instructional system for teaching library skills, an in-service program for teachers, a reading guidance program, a reference-information service.

NOTES

[1] Frank Riessman, "Styles of Learning," *NEA Journal*, March 1966, p. 15.

[2] Ralph Ellsworth, *The School Library* (New York: Center for Applied Research in Education, 1965), p. v.

[3] Leonard Freiser, "Toronto's Education Centre Library," *Saturday Review* XLVIII:76-79 (April 17, 1965).

[4] Robert Purdy, and Arnold Finch, "Getting the Most Out of In-Service Education," in *Teacher's Encyclopedia* (Englewood Cliffs, N.J.: Prentice-Hall, 1966), p. 907.

[5] Kenneth Silber, "What Field Are We In, Anyhow?," *Audiovisual Instruction*, May 1970, p. 22.

[6] Jeannette Veatch, "Let's Put the Joy Back in Reading," *School Library Journal*, May 1970, p. 29.

REFERENCES

Ellsworth, Ralph. *The School Library*. New York: Center for Applied Research in Education, 1965.

Erickson, Carleton. *Administering Instructional Media Programs*. New York: Macmillan, 1968.

Fast, Elizabeth. "In-Service Staff Development as a Logical Part of Performance Evaluation," *School Media Quarterly* 3:35-41 (Fall 1974).

Freiser, Leonard. "Toronto's Education Centre Library," *Saturday Review* XLVIII:76-79 (April 17, 1965).

Gasche, Robert. "Yes, They Can Make Slides, Use a Dry Mount Press, and More," *Audiovisual Instruction* 21:60-61 (March 1976).

Gaver, Mary. *Services of Secondary School Media Centers*. Chicago: American Library Association, 1971.

Hannigan, Jane. "The Short-Term Institute: A Vehicle for Continuing Education," *School Media Quarterly* 1:193-197 (Spring 1973).

Jones, Richard. "Learning Activity Packages: An Approach to Individualized Instruction," *Journal of Secondary Education* 43:178-183 (April 1968).

Levitan, Karen. "The School Library as an Instructional Information System," *School Media Quarterly* 3:194-203 (Spring 1975).

Lewis, Phillip. "Media at the Crossroads: Where Should AV Go," *The Journal: Technological Horizons in Education* 2:12-15 (October 1975).

Mager, Robert. *Preparing Instructional Objectives*. Palo Alto, Calif.: Fearon, 1967.

Polette, Nancy. *Developing Methods of Inquiry: A Source Book for Elementary Media Personnel*. Metuchen, N.J.: Scarecrow Press, 1973.

Postlethwait, S. N., *et al*. *The Audio-Tutorial Approach to Learning*. Minneapolis: Burgess Publishing, 1969.

Purdy, Robert, and Arnold Finch. "Getting the Most Out of In-Service Education," in *Teacher's Encyclopedia*. Englewood Cliffs, N.J.: Prentice-Hall, 1966.

Riessman, Frank. "Styles of Learning," *NEA Journal* 55:15-17 (March 1966).

Silber, Kenneth. "What Field Are We In, Anyhow?" *Audiovisual Instruction* 15:21-24 (May 1970).

Talbert, Ray. "A Learning Activity Package, What is It?" *Educational Screen and Audiovisual Guide* 47:20-21 (January 1968).

Thiagarajan, Sivasailam. "Learner Verification and Revision: What, Who, When and How?" *Audiovisual Instruction* 21:18-19 (January 1976).

Veatch, Jeannette. "Let's Put the Joy Back in Reading," *School Library Journal* 16:29-31 (May 1970).

APPENDIX A*

POSITION TITLE   School Library Media Specialist

REPORTS TO   Head of the School Library Media Center

SUPERVISES   Clerk
(may include)   Technician
                        Student Assistant
                        School Library Media Aide

The occupational definition for the school library media specialist appears as the first professional level position since it spells out those basic duties, responsibilities, knowledges, and abilities basic to all other professional positions within a fully staffed school library media center.

The occupational definition as stated should be carefully related to each situation, and its application should be judged on what has to be done in any given program. For instance, it is quite possible that a program may require two media specialists, whose joint talents will meet the prescribed definition.

It is recognized that there may be a need for positions requiring additional knowledge and/or experience in a particular area of specialization such as those identified [below].

The recommendations adopted by the Advisory Committee of the School Library Manpower Project state that completion of a five-year program will be necessary to meet the qualifications of a fully prepared school library media specialist as set forth in this occupational definition.

NATURE AND SCOPE OF POSITION

The school library media specialist represents the first level of professional responsibility on the school library media center staff. This role includes expertise in the broad range of both print and nonprint materials and related equipment. It incorporates the evaluation, selection, classification, scheduling, and utilization of print and nonprint materials; the evaluation, selection, scheduling, and utilization of related equipment to provide the basis for long-range program change and development.

The incumbent participates as a specialist in instructional media, applying the knowledge of media categories to the development and implementation of curriculum. In addition, the school library media specialist fills an active teaching role in the instructional program of the school through instruction in the effective use of media and equipment.

*From *Occupational Definitions for School Library Media Personnel*. Chicago, American Library Association, 1971. Reprinted by permission of the ALA.

MAJOR DUTIES

The school library media specialist applies expertise in selection of all materials, both print and nonprint. This includes the evaluation, selection, and acquisition of materials in terms of the criteria established to meet the needs of the instructional program and the variation of pupil, faculty, and community characteristics and interests. The incumbent relates the utilization of materials and equipment to learning situations to serve effectively various instructional and organizational patterns encompassing subject area and grade level instructional needs. The incumbent provides supplementary resources through local production of materials and use of community resources.

The school library media specialist participates in the development and implementation of policies and procedures for the organization of the physical facilities, materials, and equipment to assure optimum accessibility. This includes the organization of circulation procedures and schedules. The incumbent may be responsible for the organization of materials when this service is not performed at the district level.

The school library media specialist serves as a full participating member of curriculum committees and study groups at grade, subject, or department levels. As such, he applies knowledge of both educational principles and media technology to enrich the instructional program. One of the primary responsibilities of the school library media specialist is to know and support the educational goals of the school and community. The incumbent has the awareness of teacher goals and classroom activities necessary to expedite services in the school library media center. Since this liaison function provides the incumbent with information for long-range planning and program proposals to meet the needs of the school, the school library media specialist analyzes and evaluates the present program and makes recommendations to substantiate projected programs.

The school library media specialist provides reading, listening, and viewing guidance for students and teachers and instills an appreciation for the knowledge acquired through the utilization of a variety of media. He instructs and encourages students and teachers, both individually and in groups, to use materials, equipment, and production techniques effectively and contributes to the in-service education programs for teachers. The incumbent answers inquiries and assists students and teachers to locate resources valuable to their educational needs and to the growth of their personal interests and abilities.

The school library media specialist supervises supporting staff as assigned. The incumbent designates duties and trains subordinate staff members, following the established criteria for instructional, technical, and clerical positions. This supervision includes the diagnosis of the strengths and weaknesses of the staff and the assignment of tasks according to the strengths, while providing opportunities to improve the weaknesses.

Using the knowledge of instructional goals requirements, the incumbent participates in the development of procedures and the recommendation of policies. These procedures and policies must provide an acceptable program for evaluation, correction, and improvement which permits the flexibility necessary to meet the objectives and instructional methods of the school.

The school library media specialist informs the faculty and administration of materials, equipment, innovations, research, and current developments in the field of instructional technology. The incumbent participates in implementing an appropriate public relations program designed to communicate the philosophy and goals of the school library media center to the students, faculty, administration, and community.

The school library media specialist has the expertise as stated above. Through the attainment of additional knowledge and/or experience, he may elect to pursue a particular field of specialization, such as:

Subject area and/or grade level: an expertise in a particular subject discipline and/or grade level and a depth of knowledge in materials appropriate to the educational objectives of the subject discipline and/or grade level.

Organization of materials: an additional expertise in the organization of media, including the classification of print and nonprint materials.

Media production and design: additional expertise in such areas as message design, production, photography, and graphic arts.

Media technology: additional expertise in such areas as reading and language laboratories, programed instruction, dial access, computer technology, random access, electronics, radio and educational television, and communication systems.

KNOWLEDGES

The school library media specialist must have knowledge of:

content of a broad range of print and nonprint materials

evaluation selection criteria for print and nonprint materials

organization of school library media collections

print and nonprint materials related to literature for children and adolescents

reference materials

reading, listening, and viewing skills to assure proper guidance for the utilization of print and nonprint materials

evaluation, selection, and utilization of equipment

administration of school library media programs

theory and function of school library media programs

instructional methods and techniques

curriculum development

learning theory

student growth and development

human behavior

communication techniques

production techniques.

ABILITIES

The school library media specialist must have the ability to:

interpret content of print and nonprint materials

determine and apply suitable criteria for the evaluation and selection of materials and equipment

involve faculty and students in the evaluation of materials

organize materials and equipment

communicate knowledge of materials and equipment and their appropriate use

apply administrative principles within a structural framework

implement established policy

apply the results of institutional experience to the future development of educational goals

contribute effectively to curriculum development

analyze, evaluate, and apply basic research data

establish rapport with students and faculty

plan cooperatively programs involving many variables

work cooperatively and effectively with the head of the school library media center, other school library media center staff, and teachers

teach students how to use materials and equipment critically and independently

assume a leadership role.

APPENDIX B

SCHOOL LIBRARY BILL OF RIGHTS
for School Library Media Center Programs

Approved by American Association of School Librarians Board of Directors,
Atlantic City, 1969

The American Association of School Librarians reaffirms its belief in the Library Bill of Rights of the American Library Association. Media personnel are concerned with generating understanding of American freedoms through the development of informed and responsible citizens. To this end the American Association of School Librarians asserts that the responsibility of the school library media center is:

To provide a comprehensive collection of instructional materials selected in compliance with basic written selection principles, and to provide maximum accessibility to these materials.

To provide materials that will support the curriculum, taking into consideration the individual's needs, and the varied interests, abilities, socioeconomic backgrounds, and maturity levels of the students served.

To provide materials for teachers and students that will encourage growth in knowledge, and that will develop literary, cultural and aesthetic appreciation, and ethical standards.

To provide materials which reflect the ideas and beliefs of religious, social, political, historical, and ethnic groups and their contribution to the American and world heritage and culture, thereby enabling students to develop an intellectual integrity in forming judgments.

To provide a written statement, approved by the local Boards of Education, of the procedures for meeting the challenge of censorship of materials in school library media centers.

To provide qualified professional personnel to serve teachers and students.

APPENDIX C*

Citizen's Request for
Reconsideration of a Work

Hardcover_____

Author_____ Paperback_____

Title_____

Publisher (if known)_____

Request initiated by_____

Telephone_____ Address_____

City_____ Zip code_____

Complainant represents

    _____himself

    _____(name organization)_____

    _____(identify other group)_____

1. To what in the work do you object? Please be specific; cite pages._____

_____

2. What of value is there in this work?_____

_____

3. What do you feel might be the result of reading this work?_____

_____

4. For what age group would you recommend this work?_____

5. Did you read the entire work?_____ What pages or sections?_____

_____

6. Are you aware of the judgment of this work by critics?_____

_____

7. Are you aware of the teacher's purpose in using this work?_____

_____

8. What do you believe is the theme or purpose of this work?_____

_____

---

*From *The Students' Right to Read*. The National Council of Teachers of English, 1972. Reprinted by permission of the NCTE.

9. What would you prefer the school do about this work?_____

_____Do not assign or recommend it to my child.

_____Withdraw it from all students.

_____Send it back to the English department for reevaluation.

10. In its place, what work of equal value would you recommend that would convey as valuable a picture and perspective of a society or a set of values?_____

_____

_____

(Signature of Complainant)

INDEX